D1327771

Spoken Word Production and its Breakdown in Aphasia

Lyndsey Nickels

*Department of Psychology, Birkbeck College,
University of London
and
Department of Psychology,
Macquarie University, Sydney*

Psychology Press
a member of the Taylor & Francis group

Copyright © 1997 by Psychology Press, Ltd.,
a member of the Taylor & Francis Group
  All rights reserved. No part of this book may be reproduced in any form,
  by photostat, microform, retrieval system, or any other means without the
  prior written permission of the publisher.

Psychology Press Ltd., Publishers
27 Church Road
Hove
East Sussex, BN3 2FA
UK

British Library Cataloguing in Publication Data

A catalogue record for this book is available from the British Library

  ISBN 0-86377-466-0
  ISSN 1368-3284

Cover design by Joyce Chester
Printed and bound by T. J. International Ltd.

LLA

616.8552
NIC

N

10223817

WITHDRAWN

...ning and Information Services

This book is due for return on or before the last date shown below.

WITHDRAWN

5 may

-9. DEC. 1998

-1. NOV. 1999

15. DEC. 1999

11 OCT 2001

18 JAN 2002

17 MAY

-4 OCT 2002

20 NOV 2002

10 JAN 2003

27 MAR 2003

-9 MAY 2003

12 NOV 2003

25 MAR 2004

8 NOV 2004

02 JUN 2005

20 JAN 2006

19 JAN 2007

25 JAN 2008

-9 DEC 2009

02 FEB 2010

Don Gresswell Ltd., London, N.21   Cat. No. 1207

DG 02242/71

Contents

Acknowledgements

Thanks are due to all those friends and colleagues who have inspired, cajoled, bullied, corrected, and supported me during my career; may they continue to do so. David Howard and Wendy Best achieved the unenviable task of reading the first draft of this book and made many useful suggestions for changes and corrections, thanks are due to them. Two anonymous referees also gave invaluable feedback on the manuscript and assisted in its improvement. Finally, and most importantly, I should like to thank all those people with aphasia that I have had the pleasure to meet over the last 15 years; it is they that have provided my motivation and my support (and incidentally my data). They are so much more than "research subjects"—thanks for all the laughs along the way.

Preface

When I set out to write this book I rather grandly stated the aim of the enterprise was "to provide a critical review of the present (cognitive neuropsychological) literature in the area of spoken word production deficits in aphasia in the context of current models of spoken word production (at the level of the single word)". I would still hope that the resulting volume does go someway toward achieving this aim and that the reader will accept it as a first step in that direction.

The book is written from my perspective as a cognitive neuropsychologist. My primary motivating force is the observation of the profound communication impairments (aphasia) that can occur as a result of brain damage. For many people with aphasia the cause of most concern is the inability to speak—or at least to say what they want to. "I often had the impression that I had the letter, syllable, or word within my power but through a tempestuous cleavage another element would come and take its place and this would give my speech a quality often incomprehensible and fantastic" (quoted in Critchley, 1970, p.60).

These problems in producing speech are many and varied in form and severity. Some aphasic people will say "chair" for "table", others "cable", and still others "dable" or even "mitterwob". These differences beg the question "why?". Cognitive neuropsychology aims to be able to explain why these differing symptoms occur by relating the aphasic person's impaired and unimpaired abilities to the patterns predicted when models of normal language production are damaged. However, as will become apparent, these models are often unable to account for the patterns of abilities and disabilities shown by the aphasic person. Thus, cognitive neuropsychology in turn serves to evaluate the adequacy of the theoretical models.

OVERVIEW

This book is in two Parts, which are rather different in both style and content. Both assume that the reader has some familiarity with the linguistic and psychological terminology relevant to spoken word production. Within each Part the chapters take a common format—they begin with an overview that outlines the structure of the chapter and the headings under which each topic will be addressed; then follows the body of the chapter; and finally a summary, which tries to clarify the main conclusions to be drawn on that topic and the major issues that still need to be addressed.

Part 1 provides a detailed discussion of the development and structure of current models of language production using data from normal subjects. It is these models that should form the basis of our study of aphasic word-production disorders and it is therefore most important that their processing mechanisms and assumptions are clearly understood. The organisation and content of this Part owes much to Levelt's (1989) comprehensive review of the area in *Speaking*; readers are referred to this book for further details. For a very accessible discussion of many of the same issues (although with different conclusions in some cases), readers should consider Aitchison's (1994) book *Words in the mind*. I have tried to include both detailed discussion of some of the most important issues or influential models in this area and brief mention of a wide range of other work in the area. The latter should be taken primarily as "pointers" to further sources of information for those readers with a particular interest in a given area.

Part 2 focuses on the studies of aphasic naming disorders and discusses these disorders in terms of the models described in Part 1. For readers unfamiliar with this area, an introduction to the topic may be helpful; see, for example, Chapter 6 in Ellis and Young (1988), and also Ellis (1985). The three chapters in Part 2 differ in their approach: Chapter 4, which focuses on semantic errors, clearly examines the predictions of different models and compares this with the data. In contrast, Chapters 5 and 6 focus more on the nature of the different symptoms that have been observed, relating these to models as far as possible. This latter approach reflects the problem with the literature in this field: Different authors use slightly different models with different predicted performance under lesioned conditions. This model is then used to account for the data of the particular patient under scrutiny. However, it is rare for authors to determine whether their preferred model can also account for other patients in the literature, or if other models could also account for their data. The result is a proliferation of models with little attempt to draw the data together. Thus, we have different models (and deficits within models) used to describe similar data, and different data described by similar levels of deficit within a model (see Chapter 5 for the extreme case).

What would seem preferable is an approach where models independently derived from psycholinguistic studies are evaluated in terms of the patient data and adapted accordingly (the approach taken in Chapter 3), with authors considering a number of models with respect to their explicative power. Cognitive neuropsychologists should exploit the current advances in psycholinguistic models and apply them to their theoretical interpretations of patient data.

EXCLUSIONS

In order to keep this book to a manageable size, I have been extremely rigorous in restricting the focus to producing single words and the breakdown in this process. In my discussion of both the control and the patient studies, I have restricted myself primarily to data concerning word production and excluded studies using word reading or repetition as far as possible.

There are many other topics that could plausibly have been included within the scope of the book including: sentence processing, production of connected speech and the consequent disorders of these processes; theories of semantics and the nature of semantic representations; visual processing and visual agnosia, optic aphasia; disorders of short-term memory. Some readers will no doubt disagree with where the boundaries are drawn—suffice to say they had to be drawn somewhere.

Finally, I had originally intended to include a chapter on rehabilitation of naming disorders; this is now not the case—I had (over)reached my publisher's word limit already. Additionally, Wendy Best and I had recently finished a review paper on this topic (Nickels & Best, 1996a) and I felt there would be little I could usefully add. However, it is clear that the ultimate aim of research into the nature of spoken word-production disorders should be to further enable us to provide effective therapy for those disorders.

PART ONE

Models of spoken word production

Introduction

When we speak we have the problem of "putting our ideas into words". Models have been developed that aim to explain what is necessarily involved in this process, from the initial conceptualisation of an idea to be expressed to the final articulation of the word, or combination of words, that expresses that idea. The level of conceptualisation of an idea will not be addressed here but rather the emphasis shall be on putting that idea into words. In fact, as has already been made clear, this book explicitly avoids discussion of more than production of a single word at a time. However, as will become evident, even with these restrictions the field is complex and fraught with theoretical conflict!

Thus we begin, in Chapter 1, with the nature of the representation of words in the mental lexicon. This leads on to a discussion of how these representations are retrieved and the problems that are associated with ensuring the correct lexical item is selected. A number of different models are outlined in the course of the chapter, with a primary division being drawn between those models that propose discrete nonoverlapping stages of processing (e.g. Levelt, 1989; Morton, 1970) and those that propose a continuous flow of activation from one level of processing to another (e.g. Dell, 1986).

The phonological information that is retrieved from the stored lexical representation cannot be articulated directly, and in Chapters 2 and 3 we discuss the processes that convert this information into a form that can be used by the articulators for speech. In Chapter 2 we begin with two "slot-and-filler" models, which describe the procedures by which the segments of a word are inserted into a syllabic frame. The motivation for this mechanism comes from speech error data (both naturally occurring and elicited slips of the tongue) and these are discussed in detail as this is a key concept for the field. Chapter 3 continues by examining further models and integrating this stage of word production with models of lexical retrieval. The chapter concludes with a discussion of theories of motor programming and possible mechanisms for speech monitoring.

CHAPTER ONE

Lexical representation and access

OVERVIEW

Although most authors would agree that a store of knowledge about lexical items is required, there is less agreement regarding the nature, organisation, and mechanism for retrieval of representations. This chapter aims to review some of the literature addressing the issue of lexical access, the first stage in the production of a word.

The chapter begins with a discussion of what size of units are stored in the lexicon (WORDS OR MORPHEMES?). Does it contain an entry for every word we know or are the words broken down into their component parts, which may then be combined as we use them?

This leads on to a discussion of how these stored entries are retrieved (LEXEMES AND LEMMAS). One of the main issues here is whether there is a one- or two-stage process in lexical retrieval. We discuss in some detail an influential experiment, which argues for two stages in lexical retrieval (KEMPEN AND HUIJBERS), and then contrast this with a no less influential model, which incorporates only a single stage of retrieval (MORTON'S LOGOGEN MODEL).

Discussion of the logogen model leads us to a problem that is common to many models of word production (whether they incorporate one or two stages of lexical retrieval)—that of convergence on the right word. In particular, we outline Levelt's detailed analysis of how to avoid selecting the superordinate for production when aiming for a particular exemplar of that category (e.g. to say "dog" rather than "animal") (THE HYPERNYM PROBLEM). Although we will not discuss different semantic theories in detail, we briefly describe some semantic theories that may overcome the hypernym problem (NONDECOMPOSITIONAL THEORIES). As their title suggests, these do not break down concepts into sets of semantic features or primitives but rather represent the concept described by the word as an indivisible unit.

The chapter then moves on to examine the extensive role that speech errors have played in the development of theories of word production (SPEECH ERRORS AS EVIDENCE). In "TIP-OF-THE-TONGUE" STATES words that we are certain are within our vocabulary seem temporarily unavailable. The (partial) information that people can recall about these words has been widely investigated. We review the literature from this area in some detail and examine the theoretical conclusions that have been reached. In particular, it seems likely that there are two stages of lexical retrieval (one semantic and one phonological) and that there is also a stage at which partial phonological information is available. The logogen model cannot explain these findings, and therefore in the next section we look in more detail at models that incorporate both these stages (TWO STAGES OF LEXICAL RETRIEVAL). The first model we discuss (BUTTERWORTH'S SEMANTIC LEXICON MODEL), is similar to the logogen model except that it incorporates an explicit level of lexical-semantic processing (the semantic lexicon). This model also claims to be able to account for the partial (phonological) information that is often available to speakers when in a tip-of-the-tongue state.

However, having two distinct levels of lexical representation does not necessarily mean that these representations have to be accessed strictly sequentially. We next examine a class of models that incorporate both lexical-semantic and phonological representations but do not require processing to be complete at one level before the next level is activated (INTERACTIVE ACTIVATION: LEVELS BUT NOT STAGES). In these models, as soon as there is activation at the first, semantic, level it will be "passed on" to the second, phonological, level. The activation then cycles between the two levels until the point is reached at which the most highly activated item is selected for word production. Recently there has been a great deal of interest in determining how activation is occurring in the production system, to distinguish between the different theories— whether it is in sequential and nonoverlapping stages or continuously flowing through the model. We study in some detail the experimental evidence that has been used to address this issue (THE TIME COURSE OF LEXICAL ACCESS: PAUSES; UTTERANCE INITIATION TIMES; LEXICAL DECISION LATENCY) and the responses of the proponents of different architectures to the challenges these data present (GLOBAL MODULARITY WITH LOCAL INTERACTION).

One issue that is rarely made explicit in the psycholinguistic literature but becomes of great importance when investigating acquired language disorders is whether the same phonological lexicon is used for both comprehension and production (ONE LEXICON OR TWO?). This is a fiercely debated topic and we briefly review some of the experimental evidence.

The ease (speed and accuracy) of word retrieval can be affected by a number of factors associated with words. The final section of this chapter summarises the literature regarding the effects of five of these and discusses the possible loci of their effects within models of spoken word production (VARIABLES AFFECTING LEXICAL ACCESS: IMAGEABILITY AND CONCRETENESS; FREQUENCY AND FAMILIARITY; AGE OF ACQUISITION).

The relationship between the sound of a word and its meaning is largely arbitrary. This relationship has to be learned (stored) for each word so that it may be retrieved for use at a later date. This store, the "mental lexicon", is the mediator between conceptualisation and preparation for articulation (phonological encoding) and consists of at least four different types of knowledge about lexical items. First, there is a specification of the item's meaning, that is, a specification of the conceptual conditions that must be fulfilled for the item to be selected. Second, details of syntactic properties including word class (noun, verb, etc.) and requirements for syntactic arguments (subcategorisation rules) are given. Third, each item has a morphological specification, and fourth, a specification of phonological form. The latter includes details of syllable and accent (stress) structure, and the composition in terms of phonological segments (e.g. phonemes). There may also be additional properties associated with each item including those aspects that refer to pragmatic or stylistic variables.

WORDS OR MORPHEMES?

How are the words we know stored in the lexicon? Are they stored as complete indivisible units or as parts (morphemes; stems and affixes) that can be combined. For instance, is "disagreement" one entry or three (dis-; agree; -ment)?

The "Full Listing Hypothesis" states that every word form the speaker knows is explicitly listed in the lexicon, so "disagreement", "disagreements" and "disagreeing" will all be separately listed. This contrasts with the approach traditionally preferred by many linguists, whereby regularities in lexical representation are stated by rules, with only those items not accounted for by rule being listed in the lexicon (see Butterworth, 1983, for a review of this debate).

The Full Listing Hypothesis seems implausible when languages such as Turkish and Finnish are considered. In these agglutinative languages, words consist of strings of morphemes, that is, a root plus affixes that add to the meaning of a word, e.g. in Turkish (Hankamer, 1989) "indirilemiyebilecekler", meaning "[they] will be able to resist being brought down", with the root "in" (descend). Hankamer (1989) has calculated that a single Turkish noun can appear in more than 4 million different forms, although most of these forms will never be used by an individual Turkish speaker. Rather than suggest that each form is stored in the lexicon, it is more likely that the Turkish speaker has stored representations of all stems and affixes and a set of procedures or rules to produce new words as output depending on the conceptual input. Hankamer suggests that an account incorporating elements from both theoretical extremes seems the most promising. Thus, in addition to the listing of stems and affixes and the productive use of rules to generate new word forms, some (frequently used) morphologically complex forms are listed.

In contrast to Turkish, English has relatively little spontaneous generation of "new" words, with most inflected and derived forms being those used before. However, this does not mean that the English speaker cannot produce new words (or understand them), merely that it is rare to do so. For example, "unreformattable" is a perfectly possible word but not one that most speakers will have uttered (or heard) before.

What then of inflections (e.g. -s; -ing; -ed, etc.) and derivations (un-; -ment) in English? Do they differ in the way they are stored? Garrett (1980) argues for lexical representation of stems alone, with affixes being added by other processes after access of the stem. In contrast, Butterworth (1983) claims that the evidence for this theory is inconclusive and by no means decisive in rejecting the Full Listing Hypothesis. Butterworth notes, however, that supporters of the Full Listing Hypothesis are not forced to deny that speakers have knowledge of affixing rules but merely that they are not routinely used. Other authors have variants of these theories of the nature of lexical storage. For example, Aitchison (1994) concludes that inflectional suffixes (-s; -ing, etc.) are added as needed with stems alone stored but that derivational forms (un-; -ment, etc.) are stored as whole-word units. Stemberger and MacWhinney (1986) also suggest that high frequency inflected forms are stored whereas low frequency forms are computed on-line. Marslen-Wilson, Tyler, Waksler, and Older (1994) draw a distinction (at least for comprehension) between the representation of semantically opaque derived forms (where the meaning cannot be determined from the component parts, e.g. release, department), which are stored as undecomposed wholes, and semantically transparent derived forms (where their meaning *can* be determined from the stem and affixes, e.g. happiness, rebuild), which are stored in a decomposed form as stems and affixes.

LEXEMES AND LEMMAS

Assuming that (at least for English) most word forms are stored in the mental lexicon, while remaining neutral as to whether inflected and derived forms are fully listed or constructed by rule, how are these word forms retrieved? In particular, is all the stored information retrieved simultaneously or is retrieval broken down into two or more stages?

Kempen and Huijbers

Kempen and Huijbers (1983) introduced terminology distinguishing two parts of a lexical entry that are considered to be independent. Thus, the lemma is the part of a lexical entry that refers to syntactic (grammatical) and semantic (meaning) properties, relevant for grammatical encoding (sentence planning) and utterance planning. This contrasts with the lexeme, which consists of the morphological and phonological properties of an entry essential for phonological encoding (assembling the sounds of a word for production) but largely irrelevant for grammatical encoding. Each lemma maps on to its corresponding lexeme, that is it "points" to where in the store of lexemes (the phonological lexicon or form lexicon) the morpho-phonological information for that item is stored.

Kempen and Huijbers (1983) argue for this distinction on the basis of the results of a number of experiments that measured the length of time it took subjects to describe a picture after seeing it. Dutch subjects were required to describe pictures of actions in terms of either a single word (subject noun, e.g. girl; verb, e.g. kick), sequences of words (noun + verb, e.g. girl-kick; verb + noun, e.g. kick-girl) or sentences (subject + verb, e.g. the girl kicks; or verb + subject, which is a possible construction in Dutch). In their first experiment they found that subjects were faster to describe the pictures using a subject noun alone (S) than using a verb alone (V) or SV and VS sentences, whose averages were close together.

To account for these data, Kempen and Huijbers propose that the naming processes for actor (the person doing the action, who in these sentences is the subject) and action start simultaneously and proceed largely in parallel. "Lexicalisation" (retrieval of word information corresponding to a concept) is postponed until the "to-be-expressed"

concept has been fully identified. In other words, in the SV condition the actor's name is retrieved only when both the actor and action have been recognised. (Identification of an action takes longer than identification of an actor as evidenced by the latencies in the S condition being faster than latencies in the V condition.) However, data from a second experiment necessitated the addition of the "double look-up hypothesis" to the model. Thus, initially an "abstract" (nonphonological) lexical item is retrieved. Only when this abstract lexical item (lemma) corresponding to both actor and action has been retrieved will the phonological form (lexeme) be retrieved for the first item to be produced, followed by that for the second.

In this second experiment, Kempen and Huijbers studied the extent to which practice effects found over successive trial blocks were disrupted by the introduction of a new set of verbs for the same actions. Thus, half-way through the experiment subjects were instructed to change the verb they were using for a particular action. For example, if they had been using the verb "meppen" (slap) they would be required to change to describing the same action using "slaan" (beat). They proposed that if the slower speed of SV responses compared to S responses is caused by lexical processing of the verb (i.e. finding the appropriate lemma to correspond to the picture), then introducing a new verb will slow the responses even more (by eliminating the effects of practice on retrieval of the lemma). On the other hand, if some form of pre-lexical processing of the action (attention or identification) is causing the delay for SV compared to S (Lindsley, 1976), then shifting towards new action names should not disrupt performance (except, perhaps, for some deterioration due to temporary factors such as distraction and loss of concentration). Thus, if lexical processing was implicated in the latency for SV and VS responses, then a substantial disruption of performance was predicted for both SV and VS reaction times following the transition to new verbs (with longer delay for VS). The results of the experiment upheld these predictions. Kempen and Huijbers conclude that the delay in producing an SV sentence (compared to an S alone) is due to the need to wait until the lemma for the verb has been retrieved in addition to the lemma for the S. Only when both lemmas have been retrieved can the phonological form for the S be retrieved.

However, acknowledging that there is a logical division into lemma and morpho-phonological form (lexeme) does not mean that these are necessarily retrieved independently or successively. A number of models propose a single level of access (e.g. Forster, 1976; Morton, 1970, 1979), whereas other authors have developed models with two levels and/or stages of representation and access (e.g. Butterworth, 1989; Dell, 1986,

1989; Garrett, 1980; Levelt, 1989; Levelt et al., 1991a; Roelofs, 1992; Saffran, 1982).

Morton's logogen model

In Morton's (1970, 1979) Logogen Theory, lexical items are represented as logogens. A logogen is a counting device that is incremented whenever there is an input of an attribute that matches one of those attributes specified within the defining set for that logogen. Thus, in speech production the logogens accumulate information from the cognitive system. The cognitive system is a store of conceptual-semantic information. It sends this conceptual-semantic information regarding the concept to be expressed to the output logogen system (labelled "Phonological Output Lexicon" in Fig. 1.1). Each logogen has a

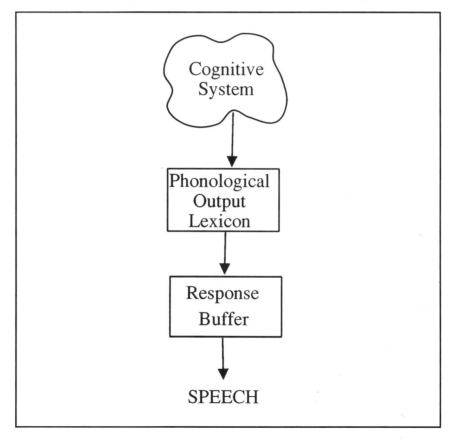

FIG. 1.1. The proposed stages of spoken word production: Morton's logogen model (adapted from Patterson & Shewell, 1987).

threshold, and when the count of accumulated evidence exceeds the threshold the logogen "fires", making the appropriate response available (i.e. when sufficient semantic information has reached the logogens to uniquely specify one item). The accumulation of conceptual-semantic information leads to the firing of a specific logogen, which sends a phonological code to the Response Buffer, leading to a vocal response. This phonological code is the morpho-phonological form information for that particular lexical item. There is no point during the production of a spoken word when lexically specified semantic information is accessed without phonological form information.

THE HYPERNYM PROBLEM

One of the attractions of logogen theory is that it is a parallel accessing device. All logogens are simultaneously active in accumulating conceptual-semantic information. However, it is not necessarily a trivial matter to ensure that the correct logogen will fire. In particular, what Levelt (1989) refers to as the "hypernym problem" cannot be solved by the logogen model in its present form, nor, Levelt claims, by most decompositional theories of lexical access, which assume that a word is retrieved on the basis of a combination of conceptual-semantic "features".

For example, if the speaker intends to express the concept DOG, then all the conceptual conditions will be met for the logogen/lemma "dog". However, the meaning of "dog" entails the meaning of its hypernym, "animal". Why, then, doesn't the speaker say "animal" rather than "dog"? Perhaps the frequency (how often a word is used) of the word has a role in this process. Certainly, if frequency were taken into account, "dog" has a higher frequency than "animal" (147 compared to 129, Francis & Kucera, 1982). In the logogen model, words of higher frequencies will have logogens with lower thresholds. Thus, "dog" will have a lower threshold than "animal", and will need less activation to bring it to threshold and fire than "animal". However, the frequency account is not sufficient as not all hypernyms are lower in frequency than their hyponym. For example, "collie" has a frequency of 2, whereas its hypernym "dog" has a frequency of 147; similarly "thing", although a hypernym of "animal", is higher in frequency (702 compared to 129).

In an attempt to solve the problem of why we do not produce a hypernym (superordinate) term instead of the specific word intended, Levelt (1989) proposes three principles. These, he claims, will guarantee correct convergence on a single item if incorporated in a processing model.

1. The uniqueness principle: No two lexical items have the same core meaning.   A lemma's core meaning or conceptual core condition is a privileged, "most salient" meaning component. The "negation test" procedure suggested by Miller (1969) can be used to determine a lemma's core. Subjects are asked to complete sentences such as "They do not ski, but they ..." (Levelt, 1989). Subjects seem to apply "minimal negation", preserving most of the meaning of "ski" under negation. The most frequent response was "skate", which also denotes some form of human locomotion over a frozen surface, involving some instrument attached to the feet. It is primarily the character of the instrument that differs, and this represents the core meaning of "ski". This principle assumes there are no true synonyms, each member of a possible pair of synonyms responding differently to the negation test. Without empirical evidence this is difficult to disprove, but intuitively there are some pairs that might cause concern in their response to the negation test (e.g. start–begin).

2. The core principle: A lexical item is retrieved only if its core condition is satisfied by the concept to be expressed.   Levelt   admits that this principle is not particularly strong but suggests that it is a first step towards solving the hypernym problem. Thus, as a word and its hypernym will never have the same core meaning, the word will not be produced when the hypernym is required. However, because the meaning of the word will entail the core meaning of the hypernym it still will not prevent the hypernym from being retrieved instead of the required word. He uses the example of "ski", which has as a hypernym "glide". Applying the negation test to "glide" yields verbs like "stick", where there is no smooth continuity in the notion. The core of "glide" would appear to be the feature of smooth continuity, which is different to that of "ski" described earlier. Thus, if the speaker intends to express the concept GLIDE, the core principle guarantees that no subordinate term will be used. However, if "ski" is the required word, the core condition of "glide" will also be satisfied. Thus, an additional principle is needed to prevent retrieval of the hypernym.

3. The principle of specificity: Of all the items whose core conditions are satisfied by the concept, the most specific one is retrieved.   This principle will prevent the retrieval of "glide" when you wish to express the concept SKI, as "ski" is the more specific word, thus solving the hypernym problem.

Levelt (1989) therefore considers each lexical item to be a testing device for the realisation of its own core condition. This is one way in which logogens might be thought to work. In addition, "Implementation of the principle of specificity will guarantee correct convergence" (Levelt, 1989, p.214). Unfortunately, Levelt is not explicit on the crucial issue of how this principle might be implemented. Inhibitory links from words to their hypernyms might be one possible solution.

Nondecompositional theories

Another possibility for overcoming the hypernym problem is to employ a different type of semantic theory—a nondecompositional theory. As stated at the outset, it is beyond the scope of this book to delve too deeply into the nature of semantic representation. However, these types of theories (e.g. Collins & Loftus, 1975; Fodor, Garrett, Walker, & Parkes, 1980; Roelofs, 1992) assume that an abstract (conceptual) representation of a word maps directly onto that word. Thus, rather than words being retrieved on the basis of a combination of features (or other "primitive" concepts) as they are in decompositional theories, a single abstract representation is used to access a word. The properties of this representation are stored in semantic memory in terms of the relationships of that concept to others, e.g. by "is a" or "has a" links between concepts (Collins & Loftus, 1975). Roelofs (1992) gives the example of the lemma "father", which in decompositional theories would be retrieved on the basis of features such as MALE, PARENT. However, in nondecompositional theories MALE and PARENT would be specified in semantic memory, and to retrieve the lemma "father" a single abstract representation of the concept is used—FATHER. Thus, in his spreading-activation theory of conceptually driven lemma retrieval, Roelofs solves the hypernym problem by assuming that conceptual component nodes are linked to lemma nodes only via nondecomposed concept representations, as in the example given.

Rosch, Mervis, Gray, Johnson, and Boyes-Braem (1976) argue for a basic level of categorisation. Basic objects are the categories "at the level for which the cue validity is maximised. Categories at higher levels of abstraction have lower cue validity than the basic because they have fewer attributes in common; categories subordinate to the basic have lower cue validity than the basic because they share most attributes with contrasting subordinate categories" (Rosch et al., 1976, p.428). For example, apple, orange, potato, and cabbage are basic-level concepts with perceptually distinct exemplars across the categories and perceptually salient features shared within a category. At higher levels in the hierarchy different exemplars of a category such as fruit or vegetable do not share many salient perceptual features. At lower levels different categories share too many perceptual features for discrimination to be easy (e.g. Granny Smith vs. Golden Delicious apples). Rosch et al. argue that the basic level is the most useful level of classification, the first learned and most easily named. This then argues for the direct entry into the hierarchy at the basic level, as defined by perceptual characteristics of objects. The hypernym problem does not arise for Rosch et al., in fact, the reverse is more of a problem—why should anyone ever say "fruit" for "apple"?

SPEECH ERRORS AS EVIDENCE

Speech errors or "slips of the tongue" are by no means infrequent occurrences in everyday speech and they have been extensively exploited for the insights they can provide into the organisation of speech production. Speech errors are not found to be simply random deviations in processing but are systematic with some errors that do not occur.

Fromkin (1971) demonstrated that the units that change and move in speech errors correspond well to the entities proposed by linguists for the statement of formal grammars (features, morphemes, phonemes, etc.). She suggested that these error units reflect the planning units for speech production. Other investigators have similarly used speech error data as support for a theoretical position (e.g. Dell, 1986, 1989; Garrett, 1975, 1980; Shattuck-Hufnagel, 1979, 1987; Stemberger, 1985).

Speech error data has been used by a number of authors to argue for two levels of representation in lexical access for speech production, in contrast to the single level of representation of logogen theory (e.g. Butterworth, 1989; Dell, 1986, 1989; Fromkin, 1971; Garrett, 1980). The argument for two levels of lexical representation, one organised semantically (by meaning) and the other phonologically (by sound), is based on the apparent independence of errors where the target is substituted by a semantically similar word as opposed to a phonologically similar word. Examples are (Fromkin, 1971, cited in Butterworth, 1989):

(i) Semantically related: I like to – hate to get up in the morning
                            the oral – written part of the exam

(ii) Phonologically related: bottle (target: bottom) of page five
                            while the present – pressure indicates

Within the single level of lexical representation advocated by the logogen model it is by no means easy to explain the occurrence of these two types of error. Semantic errors can be accounted for easily: As the lexicon (comprising output logogens) accumulates semantic information from the cognitive system, a range of semantically related items will be activated at one time and random noise within the system (e.g. temporary lowering of a threshold due to recent firing of a logogen) may result in a nontarget semantically related logogen firing.

In the logogen model a low frequency target with a high frequency semantically related neighbour is more likely to result in an error. This is because higher frequency items have lower thresholds, and therefore the semantically related neighbour will need little additional activation (or little further lowering of the threshold) to be selected before the target has reached threshold. Thus this model predicts that incorrect responses will tend to be more frequent than the target words. Levelt (1989) analysed the word substitutions listed by Fromkin (1973a). He found there were 23 cases where the substitution was clearly an associate of the target word. Of these, 17 errors were higher in frequency than their targets, with only 6 lower in frequency (significant at 0.02 level). However, Levelt (1983) found no effect of frequency on the occurrence of colour-naming errors in a task requiring description of visual patterns (see also Martin, Weisberg, & Saffran, 1989).

Although semantically related errors can be explained, it is difficult to explain the occurrence of phonologically related real words (e.g. "cap" for "cat") as errors from a lexical level of representation within logogen theory. This is because the logogens accumulate *semantic* information and any noise or other processing error will therefore result in a semantically related error. Once the phonological form is successfully retrieved, errors may occur in the subsequent phonological encoding processes (the processes by which the phonological form is transformed into an articulatory code). These are random phoneme errors that will result in errors that are predominantly not real words (with occasional words occurring by chance). However, a pre-articulatory editor that is more successful in detecting nonwords than combinations of errors resulting in real words (Motley, Camden, & Baars, 1982) could be used to explain the data. Thus, when attempting to produce a word, a phoneme substitution error occurs, which may result in a word or a nonword at random (e.g. "cas" "cav" "cap" "can" for "cat"). The speech-monitoring mechanism is better at noticing those errors that are nonwords than real words. This results in more real words being produced than would be expected by chance (but without them being the result of a lexical level error). This "lexicality effect" in speech errors will be discussed in more detail when considering models of phonological encoding (Chapter 2).

"TIP-OF-THE-TONGUE" STATES

Models with a single level of representation and "all or none" retrieval of lexical items, such as the logogen model, also have difficulty in accounting for additional data from normal subjects regarding "tip-of-the-tongue" (TOT) states. The experience of having a word "on the tip of your tongue" is familiar to most of us: We are sure that we know the word we are trying to retrieve—what it means and maybe even an idea of what it sounds like (how long it is, other similar sounding words)—but yet fail to be able to recall the word.

Brown and McNeill (1966) were the first to study experimentally the type and extent of information subjects had available in TOT states. They induced these TOT states by reading definitions of uncommon English words to subjects and asking them to supply the appropriate words. For example, when the target word was "sextant", subjects heard the definition "a navigational instrument used in measuring angular distances, especially the altitude of sun, moon, and stars at sea". Subjects who did not recall the target word immediately but felt they knew the word provided data of two kinds while they searched for the target. They gave an indication of how many syllables they thought the word contained and the identity of the first letter, and also any words that came to mind in the attempt to access the target. These words were classified into those that were similar in sound (e.g. secant, sextet, sexton) or similar in meaning (e.g. astrolabe, compass, dividers, protractors). Brown and McNeill concluded that in the TOT state subjects have knowledge of some letters the word contained (particularly the initial letter), the number of syllables, and the location of the primary stress. The nearer subjects were to successful recall, the more accurate the information they possessed.

Koriat and Lieblich (1974) argue that the claims made by Brown and McNeill regarding the extent of partial knowledge of targets in the TOT state need modification. They suggest that the TOT state, as defined by Brown and McNeill, could be divided into a number of substates that varied in degree of knowledge. In addition they suggest that a distinction should be drawn between knowledge based on the population of potential targets and that based on information regarding the specific target in question. Thus, their subjects demonstrated correct detection of partial information even when they declared they had no knowledge of the target. Koriat and Lieblich suggest that when in this "don't know" state, subjects utilise information regarding correlations between semantic and phonological forms of words; for example, it is likely that the first name of a person unknown to the subject would have fewer syllables than an unknown drug name. Koriat and Lieblich do not, however, claim that this can account for all the partial information available in TOT states, merely that there may be information available that does not rely on knowledge of the specific target.

Widlof (1983, cited in Ellis, Miller, & Sin, 1983) encouraged subjects to vocalise during the induced TOT state, in contrast to the written responses required in the majority of studies. This method resulted in a number of nonword responses that were phonologically related to the target (in addition to phonologically and semantically related real words). For example, on hearing the definition "word blindness; difficulty in learning to read or spell" one subject produced "fleksi, pleksi, pleksia, dyslexia". Brown and McNeill also note the occurrence of errors of this type in their corpus. These attempts to produce the target seem to be based on partial information about the word's pronunciation.

A.S. Brown (1991) summarised the TOT literature and observed that the following consistent findings emerge:

1. The TOT phenomenon appears to be a nearly universal experience. Most subjects report such memory blocks whether in anecdotal reflection, diary studies, or laboratory investigations.

2. A variety of stimulus materials can elicit TOT states. Although definitional cues are the most widely used, TOT states have also been found to occur with faces, simple line drawings, nonsense syllable pairs, and odours.

3. TOT states are reported to occur in daily life about once a week and to increase with age. In the lab, TOT states appear to occur on about 10% to 20% of all attempts to retrieve very low frequency targets.

4. Most naturally occurring TOT states are triggered by names of personal acquaintances, followed by names of famous persons and objects.

5. Words related to the target come to mind on between 40% and 70% of TOT states. Both orthographically and semantically related words are thought of but with a predominance of orthographically related words. (Most studies involve written recall and tend therefore to classify responses as orthographically rather than phonologically related.)

6. Subjects in a TOT state correctly guess the first letter of the target on about 50% of occasions (above chance).

7. The last letter of the target word also seems available, as evidenced by direct letter guesses and inferences from phonologically related responses, although this may partly be a

reflection of morphological regularities in the language. Knowledge about other letters in the target is limited.

8. Information on a target's syllabic structure is available in a TOT state as inferred by subjects correctly guessing the number of syllables 50% to 80% of the time (although subjects not in a TOT state correctly guess the number of syllables on about 38% of occasions).

9. Around half of all TOT states are resolved within a minute of the blocking experience.

Brown (1991) divides the hypotheses regarding the cause of TOT states into two broad classes—"blocking" and "incomplete activation". The blocking hypothesis suggests that similar sounding words (which may be erroneously retrieved in the search for the target) obstruct the retrieval of the target, resulting in a TOT state. Brown points out that a major flaw with this interpretation is the substantial proportion of TOT states in which no related words are reported. The incomplete activation hypothesis argues that a TOT state occurs when the target is less activated than related words or fails to reach a criterion level of activation (threshold).

Jones (1989; Jones & Langford, 1987) designed a series of experiments to test these two competing hypotheses. These studies modified the procedure used by Brown and McNeill (1966) by accompanying each definition with a different type of word prime: phonologically related, semantically related, both semantically and phonologically related, and unrelated to the target. For example, the subject would be presented with the definition "medieval forerunner of chemistry" and the (phonologically related) prime "axial" for the target "alchemy". As TOT states were more common when prime and target were phonologically related (or phonologically and semantically related) than when they were semantically related or unrelated, Jones (1989) concluded that the results were consistent with the blocking hypothesis.

However, there are a number of problems with these studies. In particular, the different prime conditions were not balanced across targets—each prime co-occurred with a different set of target words and therefore the effects of the target-prime relationship cannot be separated from the different susceptibility of a particular target set to TOT states (Brown, 1991; Meyer & Bock,1992). Meyer and Bock (1992) used the same prime-target pairings as Jones (1989) and found the same result—phonologically related primes led to the highest proportion of TOT states. However, crucially, this condition also led to the fewest correct responses. Thus, they suggest that the set of stimuli paired with the phonologically related cues were particularly difficult, a result borne out by a *post-hoc* analysis of the retrieval of these words when no cue was given (Experiment 2).

Meyer and Bock (1992) carried out two further experiments following Jones' basic procedure but presenting each target's stimulus definition in every condition to avoid problems from differences in difficulty among the stimuli contributing to any effects found. These experiments found that targets were correctly retrieved substantially more often when their definitions were followed by phonologically or semantically related words than by unrelated words (in contrast to Jones' results, where phonologically related word primes resulted in more TOT states). They argue that these results are more consistent with the partial activation than the blocking hypothesis, as there was no evidence that the provision of semantically or phonologically related information reduced the accessibility of the target words, as the blocking hypothesis would predict. The accounts of TOT responses discussed later all favour the incomplete activation hypothesis, as suggested by Meyer and Bock's results.

When considering responses produced in the TOT state, although the logogen model can easily explain the occurrence of semantically related words, it is difficult to conceive of how phonologically related words might be produced (just as with speech error data). Furthermore, the occurrence of partial knowledge regarding the phonological form of the word (as occurs in the TOT state) seems incompatible with a threshold model. In this model either the logogen reaches threshold and the complete form becomes available or it remains below threshold and no information can be retrieved; there is no point at which partial phonological information is retrieved.

Brown and McNeill (1966) appear to advocate a single stage of retrieval, just as in logogen theory, using an analogy with a key-sort system. Cards are punched for some set of semantic features, and an input of a set of semantic features will retrieve a collection of entries that have those features. Each card contains details of the phonological form of the entry. Like the logogen model, this system has no difficulty in accounting for the retrieval of words that are semantically related to the target; however, Brown and McNeill seem unable to produce an explanation in terms of this system that adequately accounts for the partial knowledge of phonological form. Their discussion is mainly in terms of differing degrees of degradation of the representations, ranging from incomplete to complete but faint entries. In the course of their discussion they appear to advocate another means of access for entries by means of features of the phonological form "The features that are first recalled operate ... to retrieve a set of SS [sounds similar] words. Whenever an SS word ... includes middle letters that are matched to the faintly entered section of the target then those faintly entered letters become accessible" (p.335). Thus, Brown and McNeill seem obliged to use a two-stage model of access in order to account for retrieval of phonologically related (SS) words and the fact that subjects in a TOT state sometimes eventually recall the target word. However, this still necessitates that the representations are in some way degraded or difficult to read. If this were the case, then one might expect consistency in the items that produced TOT states, with these items never being produced correctly immediately. Inconsistency in which items induced TOT states in a particular subject over a number of trials would be good evidence that representations were not degraded.

Brown and McNeill's hypothesis entails a systematic approach to the target as with each attempt more phonological information becomes accessible. If it is assumed that responses made during a TOT state are "windows" on the search process, then each successive attempt would be expected to show increasing similarity to the target. Kohn et al. (1987) found that of those TOT states where more than one incorrect response was provided (23% of total) less than 1% showed any systematic phonological progression towards the target (e.g. "n-, neo, nepotism", p.251). They interpret this as evidence against a linear approach hypothesis such as that proposed by Brown and McNeill (1966). They suggest that instead "the observed responses in such sequences may provide a window on a multichannel search process ... and that occasionally brings either a semantically or a phonologically motivated association close enough to threshold to be uttered" (p.260).

TWO STAGES OF LEXICAL RETRIEVAL

Other authors have developed models that can explain more easily the availability of partial phonological information in TOT states, usually incorporating the two levels of lexical representation described earlier (Kempen & Huijbers, 1983; Levelt, 1989).

Butterworth's semantic lexicon model

For instance, Butterworth (1989) develops a model that incorporates these two levels of lexical representation as a "semantic lexicon" (SL) and "phonological lexicon" (PL). Lexical access in speech production is considered to occur in two temporally distinct stages. First, the speaker accesses the semantic lexicon, which is a transcoding device that takes as input a semantic code and delivers as output a phonological address. Second, this address is taken as input to the phonological output lexicon, which is another transcoding device delivering the phonological form as output. The output of each stage may be held in a buffer prior to accessing the next stage. Access is strictly a top-down procedure, with no information flowing back to higher levels apart from the results of checking procedures (although in comprehension information can flow from the semantic lexicon to the cognitive system, hence the two-way arrows in Fig. 1.2).

Butterworth conceives the semantic lexicon as consisting of pairs of feature sets associating a set of "semantic" properties with a set of "phonological" properties. Semantic properties are seen as semantic features that constitute the semantic search criterion for a word in the semantic lexicon. The phonological properties denote characteristics such as number of syllables, stress assignment, onset phoneme, vowel, and coda. A set of phonological properties represents an address for a

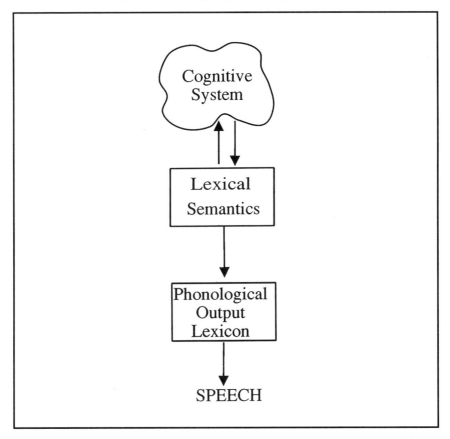

FIG. 1.2. The proposed stages of spoken word production: Butterworth's semantic lexicon model (Butterworth, 1989).

word in the phonological output lexicon. Within the phonological output lexicon there are pairs of addresses (as output from the semantic lexicon) and strings of phonemes forming words. Similar addresses will access similar sounding words, incomplete addresses may be consistent with several words.

Butterworth's model gives a straightforward explanation of the occurrence and independence of semantically related and phonologically related errors in spontaneous speech. Semantically related words may arise either because of an error in the semantic search criterion (due to a random error in the semantic system, e.g. caused by interference from other ideas/stimuli etc.) or due to a failure to match a correctly generated semantic search criterion with the correct semantic lexicon representation. Either type of error could result in semantically related words being produced that would be phonologically unrelated to the target. However, an error in the semantic search criterion might also result in an unrelated error. Phonologically related errors, in contrast, would occur when there is a failure to match a correctly retrieved phonological address with the corresponding address in the phonological output lexicon and a near neighbour is activated instead of the target.

Butterworth argues that knowledge of partial information regarding targets when subjects are in TOT states can also be explained by this model. Thus, having accessed the phonological address from the semantic lexicon, the speaker is unable to retrieve the item at that address in the phonological output lexicon. The speaker at that point may produce no response, alternatively he or she can use the address itself to provide information about the target. Addresses bear a systematic relationship to their contents, with similar addresses pointing to similar sounding words. The speaker therefore could retrieve a neighbour, producing a word similar in phonological form to the target. Alternatively, the information in the address itself may be exploited, deducing from this perhaps the syllable structure and onset of the word. This information could then be either explicitly stated or perhaps incorporated into "guesses" at the word, resulting in phonologically related responses (words and nonwords).

This intuitively appealing account does, however, need expansion to become entirely convincing. For example, it is not specified why, or how, within a normal system the phonological form of a word might not be retrievable from its address at the phonological output lexicon. Butterworth appears to be assuming that this is a transient problem and that a word might be successfully retrieved on one occasion but not on another. Similarly, there is little detail on the precise mechanism by which a specific address for an item in the phonological output lexicon could be used to access instead an item with a similar address. It would seem to imply that, rather than a simple one-to-one mapping of an address with an item in the phonological output lexicon, features of an address can activate all items with corresponding features (for example, all one-syllable words, or all words with the onset /st-/). In much the same way as entries in the semantic lexicon (and output logogens) accumulate semantic information, perhaps the entries in the phonological output lexicon accumulate information from the phonological address. Finally, although Butterworth is explicit that there is temporal separation of the two stages of access, he does not specify the nature of access itself. It would seem most likely that some kind of threshold is incorporated in the semantic lexicon and phonological output lexicon, but it might also be possible that there is some degree of accumulation of partial information in the buffer prior to the next stage of processing.

Another, similar, account is provided by Burke, MacKay, Worthley, and Wade (1991) who also suggest that the retrieval deficit in TOT states is in the linkage between a phonological word system and a semantic word system. They argue that connections between lexical semantic and phonological nodes become weakened due to infrequent use, nonrecent use, and ageing, causing a reduction in the transmission of activation. In most retrievals the semantic representation of the word allows direct and immediate access to the phonological representation, enabling vocalisation. However, this weakening of connections results in the phonological entry being merely primed but not fully activated, instilling a certainty of knowing in the absence of production ability.

INTERACTIVE ACTIVATION:
LEVELS BUT NOT STAGES

Not all models that incorporate two levels of representation have two stages of access, and it is important to maintain the distinction. Both Dell (1986, 1989) and Stemberger (1985) have developed connectionist models in which there are two levels that are similar to the levels of lemma and phonological form (or Butterworth's semantic lexicon and phonological output lexicon). However, the mechanism by which an item is accessed (in these models) involves the bidirectional flow of information between levels—that is, interactive activation (see also Roelofs, 1992).

Connectionist models involve networks of simple units (also called nodes) joined by connections and organised into levels. Each unit has a level of activation that can spread along the connections to activate other units. The spread of activation is modified by "weights" on the connections—positive weights will lead to activation of the unit receiving the activation, negative weights will lead to a damping down or inhibition of activation. The larger the weights the larger the effect on the unit receiving the activation. Individual units may vary in the level of activation that they start out with (before any activation is added from external sources or from the spread of activation within the model). Interactive activation models are one type of connectionist architecture where there are connections in both directions between levels—activation is both fed forward and back through the network. These models do not learn but are "hard-wired", with the experimenter setting the weights on the connections.

Dell and Stemberger's interactive activation models both have units at a lexical level, where one unit corresponds to a word (similar to the lemma level), and at a phoneme level, where one unit corresponds to a phoneme (and the pattern of activation across a set of phonemes is equivalent to the phonological representation of a word). Dell's model also has a number of intervening levels of units (although he omits these from simulations in later versions of the model such as Dell, 1989).

The models do, however, differ in the nature of the connections between the units and levels. Stemberger (1985) (see Fig. 1.3) proposes weighted links between levels, with weights varying on different connections ; inhibitory links within levels—so that when one unit is active it will attempt to "damp down" the activation of the other

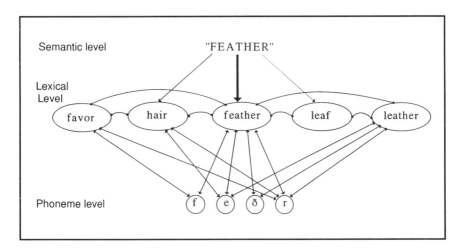

FIG. 1.3. Stemberger's interactive activation model (adapted from Stemberger, 1985). An arrow denotes an activating link and a dot an inhibitory link. The thicker the line, the greater the activation. Some of the inhibitory links have been omitted for clarity.

(competing) units at that level; and resting levels of activation, which vary with frequency—units corresponding to high frequency items will start out with more activation than those for low frequency items, even before any activation is added to the network. In contrast, Dell (1986, 1989) has no variable weights, nor inhibitory links within levels; every connection is excitatory, bidirectional and has the same strength (Fig. 1.4). In order to keep the network stable (in the absence of inhibitory links), activation of the units decays (decreases) passively over time, with the decay rate being greater than the spreading rate. Like Stemberger, Dell assumes a variation in resting level of activation for word nodes according to frequency.

In both these models an activated unit (node) will send some proportion of its activation to every other unit it is connected to. Highly activated nodes will have large effects on other nodes, whereas less activated nodes will have smaller effects, thus differences in activation at one level will be reflected at other levels. Activation feeds back to higher levels of the system; for example, activated phoneme nodes will spread activation to all the words that ever access those particular phonemes, leading to partial activation of nontarget words. Several levels of the language system are being processed at a given moment and are interacting. There can be no sense for these models in which there are two stages of access as processes at both levels are linked in time.

Both of these interactive activation models account for semantic and conceptual errors in a similar way to noninteractive models. Conceptual/semantic information activates all words (all units corresponding to those words) that ever represent that information. By summing the activation from large parts of the semantic structure a unit for a word will reach a sufficient level of activation (across the network as a whole) to be produced. If a nontarget word is higher in activation than the target it will be selected for production. Errors arise due to noise in the system, which Stemberger (1985) suggests comes from three sources:

1. Random variation in the resting level of activation of units (nodes), with errors occurring at the extremes of this variation.
2. Variation in frequency; errors on high frequency targets are less common.
3. Systematic spread of activation to nontarget units from semantic units or feedback.

Dell (1986) also discusses "external" sources of error such as environmental factors (e.g. distraction by other auditory/visual stimuli etc.), nervousness, tiredness, or brain damage. He also notes the

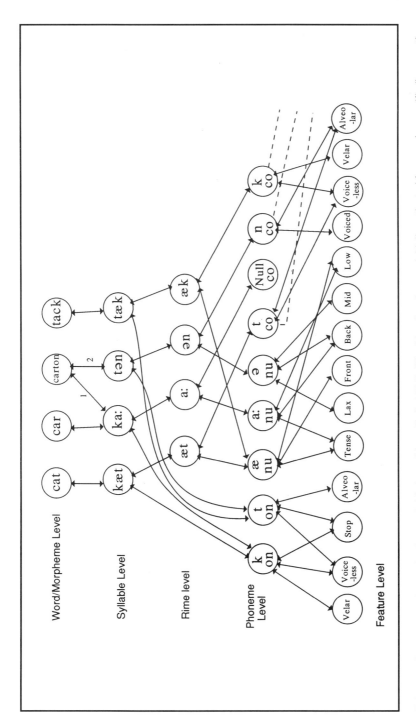

FIG. 1.4. Dell's interactive activation model (adapted from Dell, 1986). Word level nodes are initially activated from an (unspecified) semantic representation. At the phoneme level, on: onset, nu: nucleus, co: coda.

27

difficulty in predicting and/or modelling the effects of these variables. For example, "does tiredness slow down everything or does it make everything more noisy?" (p.318).

As combinations of sources of information (from different levels within the model) are emphasised within interactive activation models, they predict that errors will often show multiple relations with the target. Thus, semantically related errors should often also show a phonological relationship to the target (for example, saying "shirt" for "skirt" is an error that is both semantically and phonologically related to the target). A number of authors (e.g. Dell & Reich, 1981) have argued that in semantic word substitution errors, the errors are phonologically related to the target to a greater degree than would be expected by chance. This data is less easily explained by models where semantically related and phonologically related errors are produced by independent mechanisms that cannot interact to produce an error (i.e. those models that advocate two stages in lexical access). In order to account for the occurrence of errors that are both phonologically and semantically related to the target, Butterworth (1981) argues for a checking mechanism that filters out items dissimilar in sound to the target. This checking mechanism operates by running the selection of each word twice and comparing the outputs from the semantic lexicon. If the outputs are similar (in their phonological addresses) then output continues, if not then selection starts again. Thus, this checking mechanism will be more likely to detect those semantic errors that are phonologically quite different to the target. The resulting errors will therefore be phonologically related to the target, despite having originated at the semantic level with no phonological influence on their initial chance of occurrence.

Levelt (1992) cites a personal communication with Garrett, who suggests that many mixed errors may be "environmentals" (intrusions of words that happen to be in the speaker's span of attention), and perhaps once these are excluded the occurrence of mixed errors may not exceed the level expected by chance. Levelt gives as an example the Martin et al. (1989) study, which examined the speech errors made when subjects described visual patterns of coloured pictures linked by lines. Levelt argues that the response set in the experiments (the colour and object names) contained a highly apparent subset of items that were not only semantically related but also phonologically related (e.g. peacock, parrot, pigeon, penguin; shirt, shawl, shoes, shell). It was these items that the subjects tended to confuse. Levelt suggests that this probably has nothing to do with the fact that these items were phonologically related—any other marked relation among the items may have produced the same result.

Although superficially the models appear very different, in fact other than the degree of interaction between levels there is little to distinguish the interactive activation models of Dell (1986, 1989) and Stemberger (1985), and those of Butterworth (1989) and Levelt (1989), which similarly involve two-stage lexical access. The nature of the representation of the phonological form differs, with Stemberger and Dell employing distributed representations across phoneme nodes as opposed to strings of phonemes, which Butterworth implies are stored (and retrieved) as a unit that may contain different types of information within it, e.g. stress, syllable structure, segments (see Chapters 2 and 3 for further discussion). However, there is no apparent reason why the addresses from the semantic lexicon could not activate a string of phonemes within a set of phoneme nodes as opposed to accessing them as a unit. Thus, the key issue is whether there are two, temporally distinct, stages of lexical access, as Butterworth and Levelt would claim, or no such distinction, as in interactive accounts.

THE TIME COURSE OF LEXICAL ACCESS

Pauses

The temporal properties of speech, and in particular pauses, are used by Butterworth (1989) as evidence for temporally distinct stages in speech output. Pauses are not distributed evenly, or randomly, through a speaker's output. There is an alternation between hesitant phases with a high ratio of pauses to speech, and relatively fluent phases when the ratio of pauses to speech is low. Some pauses are assumed to reflect planning in speech production (Butterworth, 1980). Although reducing planning demands (for example, in reading aloud) reduces the proportion of pausing, Butterworth (1989) suggests that it is virtually impossible to talk sense without pausing at least 20% of the time.

A cycle of one hesitant and one fluent phase corresponds to the expression of an "idea" as defined operationally by judges (Butterworth, 1975). The pauses in the hesitant phase are thought to represent "planning phases" for outline planning of the whole idea. In fluent phases ("execution phases"), pauses are almost exclusively for lexical selection or marking major syntactic boundaries (see Butterworth, 1980, for a review of the evidence). Butterworth proposes that in the planning phase all the words for the current "idea" are selected in the semantic lexicon and held in a buffer until the word is to be output. During the planning phase, a word that is to be produced has to be accessed from both the semantic lexicon and the phonological output lexicon. However, during the fluent execution phase the word has already been selected from the semantic lexicon and there is a pause only while the word is retrieved from the phonological output lexicon. This account reflects the fact that lexical pauses were found to be 50% longer in planning phases than in execution phases (0.89sec vs. 0.57sec).

Utterance initiation times

Schriefers, Meyer, and Levelt (1990) used a picture-word interference paradigm to examine the hypothesis that lexical access proceeds in two serially ordered and independent stages. According to the "two-stage" model (e.g. Butterworth, 1989; Garrett, 1980; Levelt, 1989) there should be an early stage of lexical access with exclusively semantic activation and a late stage with exclusively phonological activation—these activation states reflecting lemma selection and morpho-phonological form retrieval, respectively. Interactive activation (IA) models would also seem to predict an early stage of exclusively semantic activation. However, there should then be a stage of both semantic and phonological activation as feedback from morpho-phonological form to lemma maintains the lemma's semantic activation. Whether or not a late stage of exclusively phonological activation occurs would depend on the precise setting of parameters within the IA networks themselves (e.g. decay rate). Because they have different time courses of semantic and phonological activation, the two different types of model (stage or interactive activation) therefore give different predicted results from the picture-word interference task.

The picture-word interference paradigm usually involves the subjects being presented with a line drawing of a common object. Superimposed on each picture appears a printed interfering stimulus (IS), which can be a word. Subjects are required to ignore the IS and name the picture as fast as possible. As phonological rather than orthographic processes were being studied, Schriefers et al. used a slight variation of the paradigm whereby the IS was presented auditorily rather than visually. They used four different types of interfering stimuli—an unrelated word, a semantically related word (category coordinates), phonologically related word (sharing two or more initial phonemes and if possible stress and syllable number) and a repeated word "blanco" (blank). They also used a silent condition when no interfering stimulus was presented. For example, a pictured object DESK ("bureau" in Dutch, the language of the experiment) would be presented with either a semantic IS "stoel" (chair), a phonological IS "buurman" (neighbour), an unrelated IS "muts" (cap), the word "blanco", or silence. The interfering stimuli were presented either 150msec before presentation of the picture (Stimulus-Onset-Asynchrony, SOA = –150msec), or simultaneously with the picture (SOA = 0msec), or 150msec after the onset of the picture

(SOA = +150msec). Different patterns of result were obtained at each SOA (summarised in Table 1.1).

When the interfering stimuli were presented before the presentation of the picture, a semantically related item slowed the speed of naming that picture, but phonologically related distractors had no effect. When the interfering stimuli were presented later (particularly after presentation of the picture) phonologically related items speeded naming, and semantically related items had no effect). Therefore, Schriefers et al. argue that their data provides evidence for an early period of exclusively semantic activation and a late stage of exclusively phonological activation. These data replicate, in part, data from other authors who also found early semantic activation (Glaser & Dungelhoff, 1984; Lupker, 1979). However, Glaser and Dungelhoff also found semantic interference effects with later IS presentation (up to SOA = +100msec). It therefore seems possible that there is an intermediate period when both semantic and phonological activation occur. (Alternatively it may be that the time course of activation for individual items and subjects may differ, causing apparent "overlap" of semantic and phonological activation.) Further experiments are required using smaller time steps to provide more detailed information on the time course of activation.

Schriefers et al. point out that it is not possible to assign the effect of semantically related interfering stimuli unambiguously to the stage of lemma access. It could be argued that this effect arose earlier from interference at the stage of retrieval of semantic information regarding the picture. In a further experiment, they found that the semantic interference effect is only obtained when subjects name a picture but not when they had to decide whether they had seen a picture before or not. Thus, Schriefers et al. argue that this is support for the attribution of the semantic interference effect to the stage of lemma retrieval.

TABLE 1.1
Summary of Schriefers et al. (1990, Experiment 2) results

SOA	RTs	Summary of effect	Implication for activation at that time step
−150	semantic > unrelated, phonological > blanco, silence	semantic interference no phonological effect	semantic activation
0	semantic, unrelated > phonological, blanco, silence	no semantic effect phonological facilitation	phonological activation
+150	unrelated, semantic, blanco > silence > phonological	phonological facilitation	phonological activation

However, it would seem plausible that the recognition task could be performed without recourse to semantic information but merely on the basis of visual features. If this was the case then the lack of a semantic interference effect on this task would be unsurprising.

Lupker and Katz (1981) performed some experiments that are relevant to this issue. They attempted to examine the early processes in picture-naming, using a task where subjects were required to respond to picture presentations by deciding whether they were pictures of dogs or not. They hypothesised that subjects would establish, in working memory, a general set of features that could characterise the visual appearance of a dog. Those features could then be compared with the incoming visual information. They concluded that subjects did appear to be handling the task at a visual level as animal pictures were harder to reject than nonanimal pictures on negative trials. On this task, in contrast to the effects found in naming tasks, superimposed interfering stimuli of either nonwords or unrelated words produced no interference effects. However, IS of the same semantic category (names of other animals) did produce interference on positive (dog) trials. Lupker and Katz argue that the locus of the semantic interference effect is an input process that is common to both the naming task and the identification task. This common process is the evaluation of visual information for either determining the concept represented before naming or determining whether or not the information characterises a dog. The semantic category effect is held to arise because the information from a semantically similar word matches reasonably well with that provided by the picture, suggesting that the word's name may be an appropriate label for the picture. Determining that the label is inappropriate takes extra time, providing extra interference in the same semantic category condition in comparison to when the word and picture are unrelated.

The different conclusions drawn by Lupker and Katz (1981) and Schriefers et al. (1990) regarding the locus of semantic interference effects once again seem to make it unwise to draw strong conclusions on the time course of lexical access in language production on the basis of the current data. The locus of the phonological facilitation effects is also far from certain. Schriefers et al. assume that it operates at the "processing stage during which the word form of a picture name is retrieved" (p.96) but it is conceivable that the effects might operate at the post-lexical level (e.g phonological encoding).

The strongest claims that can be made from these studies is that there appears to be an early stage of semantic activation and a late stage of phonological activation without being able to specify the precise level of this activation within a particular model. There may or may not be an intermediate phase of both semantic and phonological activation. This does not allow for discrimination between the two-stage and interactive activation models. If no period was found when there was both phonological and semantic activation, then two-stage models would appear to be better able to explain the data than interactive activation models. Nevertheless, as Schriefers et al. state, "it might be possible to set the parameters of a network model in such a way that a stage of pure semantic activation and a stage of pure phonological activation result" (p.100). However, whether the models would still be able to account for other phenomena (such as mixed errors) under these conditions is crucial.

Even if an overlap of phonological and semantic activation was found, the two-stage theory need not be rejected. Whether or not this overlap would be predicted would depend on the precise nature of the access mechanisms. Butterworth (1989) would appear to predict no overlap, as the output of the semantic lexicon (lemma retrieval) is the address for the phonological output lexicon. However, if information is transmitted continuously from the semantic to the phonological level in cascade but without feedback (Humphreys, Riddoch, & Quinlan, 1988; McClelland, 1979; Nickels & Howard, 1994; Plaut & Shallice, 1993), an intermediate stage of semantic and phonological activation would be predicted.

Lexical decision latency

Levelt et al. (1991a) used a different paradigm to compare the predictions from the two-stage and interactive activation models. They used an auditory lexical decision task during object-naming. An auditory test probe (a word or nonword for lexical decision) was presented after presentation of the picture but before naming, and the lexical decision response was given manually. Test probes were either identical, semantically related (associates of the target), phonologically related, or unrelated to the target name.

Levelt et al. assumed that semantic activation of the target item would affect the lexical decision latency of a semantically related test probe, whereas phonological activation would affect the decision latency for a phonologically related probe. They argued that by varying the time between presentation of the picture and presentation of the test probe, semantic and phonological activation could be traced over time.

At a short lag (between presentation of the picture and of the stimulus for lexical decision), lexical decision was significantly slowed for the semantic, phonological, and identical conditions relative to unrelated (semantic, phonological, identical > unrelated). At a medium lag, phonological showed significant interference relative to semantic, unrelated, and identical (phonological > semantic, unrelated, identical);

and at a long lag, phonological showed significant interference and identical significant facilitation relative to semantic and unrelated (phonological > semantic, unrelated identical).

Levelt et al. discuss the results in relation to the two-stage, interactive activation, and cascade-type models. (In cascade models activation flows continuously between levels in a feed-forward direction only, with no discontinuity of processing found in stage models, nor feedback as in interactive activation.) All three models predict the early semantic activation and late phonological activation that the data seem to support. However, contrary to the predictions made by Levelt et al. regarding the two-stage model, the data suggest early phonological activation. Similarly, there is no evidence for late semantic activation as might be predicted by the interactive activation models. Cascade-type models appear to fit the data best as they would predict early phonological activation—with this level being activated before processing is complete at the semantic level. Cascade models also predict that late semantic activation will not occur (after the lemma has been selected). However, none of the models appear to be able to explain easily the pattern of early interference and late facilitation for identical probes.

Levelt et al. do, however, propose a mathematical model embodying the two-stage view that they felt was fully compatible with the lexical decision data described earlier. The argument is complex and makes many assumptions regarding how lexical decision is performed. In particular, they appear to be advocating a single lexicon for input and output (although the argument can still hold for models that have separate input and output lexicons provided there are some feedback loops incorporated into the model; Monsell, 1987; see later and Chapter 3). The crucial point is that at some stage in word production partial phonological information becomes available. When this corresponds to a phonologically related item (or the identical probe) it can boost phonological competitors to the lexical decision probe and delay lexical decision latency.

However, this partial information could be from any stage in the naming process and not confined to phonological encoding as Levelt et al. suggest. For example, in Butterworth (1989) such partial information is available on retrieval of the lemma (in the semantic lexicon) as part of the phonological address for that word. Levelt et al. appear not to allow for an intermediate level of representation of the phonological form prior to phonological encoding for articulation, although other authors consider this necessary. Detailed consideration of the nature of phonological encoding is essential to any argument of this kind (see Chapters 2 and 3 for further discussion).

Furthermore, Levelt et al. assume that semantic analysis in the lexical decision "channel" can be affected by the presence of an active semantically related item in the naming "channel". Although most authors would agree that semantic interference effects are found in lexical decision tasks, some would dispute that the "decision" is made at the semantic level. It is possible that the lexical decision task can be performed at the level of the input lexicon without recourse to semantics (Franklin, 1989b), although semantic access may also occur. Many models allow for feedback from the semantic system to the phonological input lexicon (e.g. Patterson & Shewell, 1987) and would predict this to be the source of semantic interference effects. Although the differences between these two explanations are minor, in an investigation of the time course of activation even small changes in the level at which interference is thought to occur, or the type and level of feedback within the model, could make significant differences in the pattern of activation expected.

The predictions that can be made as to the effects on lexical decision of various stages in the naming process are complex at best, especially if considerations such as multiple levels of feedback between processes are taken into account. The picture-word interference task would seem to make clearer predictions and as such be better suited to investigations of the time course of activation in naming.

Global modularity with local interaction

In a reply to the paper by Levelt et al. (1991a), Dell and O'Seaghdha (1991) argue that Dell's (1986, 1989) model can indeed explain these experimental results. They argue that "the scheduling of semantic and phonological activation in the lexical network is strongly influenced by external inputs from modular linguistic rule systems. These signals add greatly to the level of activation of the units receiving them, and thus strongly influence the levels of activation at the different levels of the lexical network. In essence, these signals impose the rule-governed structure of a language at each level by determining when a selected unit is realized at a lower level" (Dell & O'Seaghdha, 1992, p.300). The sequence of these external signals is purely serial and top-down. Thus, external signals are received in sequence by nodes at the semantic, word, phonological, and phonetic/articulatory levels. They illustrate this using a "simplified network", which in fact consists of only one node at each level! In this illustration the time course of activation is largely determined by the external signals, with most of the activation being at the level that has just received the signal. Local interaction does still occur between levels but this is mostly confined to adjacent levels (i.e. there is one-level-up feedback but little or no two-level-up feedback).

It is argued that this interpretation of Dell's (1986) model can account for the effects described earlier and the speech error data. However, in order to be fully convincing the experimental simulations of the speech error data need to be demonstrated with this new version. It is also by no means clear that a scaled-up version of this model (with more than one node at each level) would have the same characteristics. Levelt et al. (1991b) in their reply to Dell and O'Seaghdha (1991) argue that the lexical bias and repeated phoneme effect would indeed disappear as (in the full, 1986, model) they involve nonlocal interaction between the phonemic and morphological (lemma) level.

Other authors have also disputed Levelt et al.'s claim that interactive activation models cannot account for their data. For example, Harley (1993) described a connectionist model that, he argues, can also predict their experimental findings (Fig. 1.5). This connectionist model has

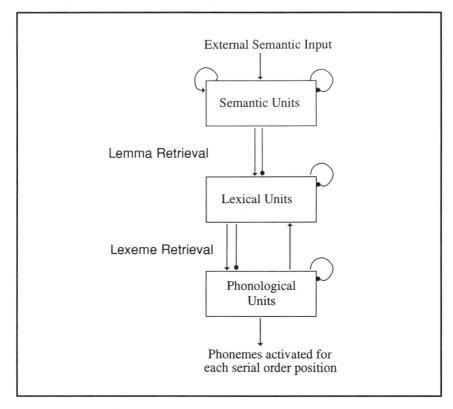

FIG. 1.5. Harley's connectionist model (adapted from Harley, 1993). An arrow denotes an activating link and a dot an inhibitory link. There are within-level inhibitory links at each level, and also within-level excitatory links at the semantic level.

three basic levels of units: semantic feature units, lexical units, and phonological units. Every unit is connected to every other unit but, unlike Dell's (1986) model, connections can be inhibitory as well as excitatory. Additionally, there is inhibitory feedback within levels, and feedback of activation between the phonological and lexical levels (but not between lexical and semantic levels). Harley argues that this model can not only account for Levelt et al.'s findings but also gives rise to "interactive" effects in speech production (i.e. "mixed" errors, which are semantically and phonologically related to their targets, occur more often than would be expected by chance).

Levelt et al. (1991b) conclude by arguing that the full "balancing act" has not been achieved to reconcile Dell's model with both their experimental findings and the speech error data. They do note, however, that "the interaction between Dell's (1986) modelling and our experimentation has been most profitable ... in the emerging recognition that the connectionist models of lexical access ... must incorporate a substantial degree of modularity" (p.617). Of course, if modularity seems necessary in these models, why then should interaction also be incorporated? Although the motivation was clearly to be able to account for the speech error data, Levelt et al. (1991b; Levelt, 1992) argue that it is unsatisfactory for this to be the only reason. However, Dell (1989) suggests that the feedback can also allow the network to serve as a word recognition device, that is, as a common system for input and output of words.

ONE LEXICON OR TWO?

The issue of whether there is a common lexicon for input (comprehension) and output (production) of phonology is far from resolved. In the early versions of the logogen model, Morton (1969) incorporated only a single lexicon (logogen system), which was used for both recognition and production of phonological and orthographic word forms. However, experimental evidence showed that hearing a word does not speed up later recognition of the same word written down (in contrast to recognition of the same word presented auditorily, which would be speeded) nor vice versa (Clarke & Morton, 1983; Winnick & Daniel, 1970). Thus, as the ability to explain this kind of data (from these repetition priming tasks) was a primary motivation for logogens, Morton revised the model to include, instead, four separate lexicons: input and output lexicons for each of orthography and phonology.

This position was criticised initially by Allport and Funnell (1981) arguing that the priming data only motivated a distinction between orthographic and phonological lexicons but not between input and output. This debate has continued with Monsell (1987) summarising the evidence from priming and dual task studies. Monsell argues that some data from repetition priming are more compatible with separate but linked input and output pathways than with the idea of a common phonological lexicon. These include the observation of stronger priming from mouthing than from other phonology generation tasks (Monsell & Banich, cited in Monsell, 1987) and the failure to obtain priming from syllable counting (Gipson, 1984, 1986).

Monsell goes on to review the dual-task experiments of Shallice, McLeod, and Lewis (1985). A common lexicon view would appear to predict that simultaneous generation and identification of different phonological forms should lead to considerable interference between the tasks. Shallice et al.'s study aimed to investigate this prediction. The task involved subjects performing a primary task of reading aloud words that were presented at a rate for each subject just below their personal maximum. While performing this task they also had to monitor an auditory list of words for a semantically defined target (a proper noun among other nouns). The results showed relatively little interference in this dual-task condition (nor did reading errors occur at the point of successful auditory detections). This would seem to be contrary to the predictions of the common lexicon view.

However, Shallice et al. also investigated performance when carrying out pairs of other tasks, which they claim are comparable to those in the first experiment. Both of a pair either required lexical input processing (shadowing plus the auditory semantic monitoring task) or output processing (reading words aloud plus phoneme monitoring). Massive interference was found when performing these pairs of tasks.

Although Monsell does point out some serious problems in interpreting Shallice et al.'s data, e.g. performance was at ceiling in the single-task condition which makes the true size of the dual-task decrement hard to estimate, he claims that a strong argument can nevertheless be founded on the absence of a serious cross-talk in the basic dual-task condition. He argues that in a system with a common lexicon a difficulty like that found in the Stroop task should occur. In the Stroop task, there is massive interference when naming the colour of the ink in which a different colour name is written (e.g. RED written in blue ink). This is interpreted as a difficulty in ensuring that the correct colour-name representation is produced. Monsell suggests that with a common lexicon the same problem of keeping separate two different sources of activation should occur in the dual input-output task paradigm—and argues there is no evidence to suggest it does.

Monsell concludes that there seems to be no evidence favouring a common lexicon model but "several fragments favouring separate pathways" (p.297). Allport (1984) argued that there was no convincing evidence from neuropsychology against the single-lexicon hypothesis; however, Howard and Franklin (1988) suggest that the pattern shown by their patient, MK, was an illustration of just such a dissociation. Neuropsychological data will be discussed in greater detail in subsequent chapters.

VARIABLES AFFECTING LEXICAL ACCESS

The final section of this chapter concerns a number of properties associated with words that have been argued to have an effect on lexical access in normal subjects. This is a large area and by necessity only a brief overview will be attempted here, focusing on those studies that have found effects on spoken word production.

Imageability and concreteness. Imageability and concreteness are rated variables. Imageability is rated by subjects on the basis of how easy it is to create a visual or auditory image of the referent corresponding to the word. Concreteness, in contrast, is rated on the basis of how available the referent of the word is to sensory experience. Although the ratings are on the basis of different instructions, the two measures are highly correlated. Indeed, many authors use the terms interchangeably and choose not to distinguish between these two variables.

Although "imagery" has been discussed in detail with regard to memory (e.g. Pavio, 1971), these variables have been studied relatively little in the context of word production. Marcel and Patterson (1978) studied the effect of these variables on reading accuracy in normal subjects (using pattern-masking to produce errors) and found that imageability but not concreteness affected accuracy. They propose a semantic locus for the effects of this variable, a proposal that is now widely accepted. Morrison, Ellis, and Quinlan (1992) also studied the effects of imageability on word production but failed to find a significant effect on picture-naming speed. However, the range of imageability values used in this study was rather restricted (somewhat inevitably in the context of a picture-naming task).

The nature of any effect is rather less clear; few authors would claim that naming speed or accuracy are affected by the stimulus's capacity to conjour up a mental image. Marcel and Patterson (1978) relate the effects to a division in semantics into "those referring to the sensorimotor sphere and those based on logical and linguistic concepts". This is similar to Pavio's (1971, 1991) dual-coding theory where he argues that concrete or high imageability words are better recalled because they are coded using both a verbal and a nonverbal code. In contrast, Plaut and Shallice (1993) interpret imageability in terms of number of semantic features ("richness" of semantic representations) in their connectionist model of word reading. This is derived from Jones' (1985) parameter "ease of predication". This correlates highly with imageability and refers to normal subjects' estimates of how many "simple factual statements" they could generate for a particular word (i.e. how many sentences of the form "a dog is a type of animal", " a dog often lives in a kennel" they felt they could generate).

Frequency and familiarity.   Frequency is generally used to refer to word frequency as measured by objective counts of written and spoken language. Most studies, even when investigating spoken word production, have used written word frequency counts such as Kuçera and Francis (1967) as the measure of frequency.

A number of authors have proposed that word frequency is an important determinant of the speed and accuracy of lexical access in word production (e.g. Monsell, Doyle, & Haggard, 1989; Riddoch & Humphreys, 1987; see Monsell, 1991, for an extensive review of frequency effects in word reading). Morrison et al. (1992) review the literature regarding frequency effects in picture-naming and note that it is widely accepted that the less frequent a word is "the slower one will be to name a pictorial representation of the object". The classic citation is Oldfield and Wingfield (1965), who found just this pattern (but see later). Effects of frequency are generally accepted to be related to lexical access, but the precise relationship is by no means agreed. Some authors suggest that frequency effects are "in the links" between semantics and phonology (e.g. McCann & Besner, 1987; Vitkovitch & Humphreys, 1991)—higher frequency words having "stronger" links, easier access. Others suggest that frequency effects arise from differences in the resting levels of activation of lexical representations or nodes (e.g. Dell, 1986, 1989) or variation in thresholds (Morton, 1970). Balota and Chumbley (1985) are unusual in claiming that frequency effects are occurring as a result of post-lexical processing. They used a delayed naming task and claim that the frequency effect reflects the increased time necessary to access or implement a motor code for lower frequency items. However, it is possible that the effect could be confounded with a syllable-frequency effect (see later). Additionally, Savage, Bradley, and Forster (1990) failed to replicate Balota and Chumbley's results (see also McRae, Jared, & Seidenberg, 1990).

Gernsbacher (1984) argued that "experiential familiarity" (subjects' ratings of how familiar they were with a word) rather than written word frequency was the relevant variable (in word recognition studies). She suggests that it may be a more comprehensive measure, possibly reflecting word production as well as exposure to spoken and written forms. Additionally, familiarity may be a more accurate measure particularly for low frequency items when the objective counts are less reliable (with some words never appearing in the corpus).

Another measure, frequency of occurrence of syllables, has recently been argued to be an important variable in word production. Levelt and Wheeldon (1994) have found independent effects of syllable frequency even when word frequency is accounted for. They argue that the locus of this effect is in retrieval of syllable plans from a mental syllabary prior to word production (see Chapter 3).

Age of acquisition.   Rated Age of Acquisition (AoA) is a measure where adults estimate the age at which they believe they acquired a word as a child. This measure has been found to correlate highly with measures of the age at which children actually acquire words (Carroll & White, 1973; Morrison, Ellis, & Chappell, in press).

The claim that word-frequency effects are "really" effects of Age of Acquisition (AoA) has been made with respect to a number of tasks with normal subjects; rated AoA has been shown to be a better predictor of performance than word frequency in, for example, picture-naming latencies (Carroll & White, 1973; Lachman, Schaffer, & Hennrikus, 1974) and oral word reading (Brown & Watson, 1987; Gilhooly & Logie, 1981a) but not in auditory or visual word recognition (Gilhooly & Logie, 1981b). This suggests that AoA effects may be primarily characteristic of the word production system (Gilhooly & Watson, 1981).

In a recent paper, Morrison, Ellis, and Quinlan (1992) re-analysed the data from Oldfield and Wingfield (1965), which have been taken as a demonstration that word frequency is a good predictor of naming latency in normal subjects. They argue that Oldfield and Wingfield failed to take into account the possible effects of variables that correlate highly with frequency, such as length, imageability, and age of acquisition, in their analysis of naming latencies. In their re-analysis, Morrison et al. showed that when length and word frequency were held constant in a multiple regression, AoA had a significant effect on object-naming speed (although they did not take into account the possible effects of familiarity on performance), and there was no independent effect of frequency when AoA was held constant. This pattern of results was confirmed in a subsequent naming experiment. However, in a semantic categorisation task, where pictures had to be categorised as man-made/not man-made, no effects of AoA were found. Morrison et al. use this result to argue that the AoA effect resides in the retrieval and/or execution of phonological word forms. One possible difficulty in drawing this conclusion is that retrieval of the correct name of the picture must require use of a much more elaborated semantic description than is needed for the categorisation task; AoA effects might lie in the process of retrieving a semantic representation sufficient to support word retrieval. Additionally, the man-made or not distinction can also be drawn on the basis of visual features in many cases (living things do not usually have straight edges, whereas many man-made objects do).

SUMMARY

This chapter has addressed the nature of lexical representation and lexical access.

We began with a discussion of whether the lexicon stored words or morphemes. This issue seems far from resolved. There are those who would argue for "full listing" of words with derivational but not inflectional affixes, others who would draw the boundaries in terms of frequency or semantic transparency. Indeed, much of the work in this area comes from studies of comprehension (and often using visually presented stimuli) rather than word production, so we also have the problem of whether the modalities (input and output, auditory and written) are strictly comparable. We stayed neutral on this topic and the remainder of the chapter (and indeed the book) can be viewed as referring to the retrieval of morphemically simple words. This is not to say that morphology is unimportant in word production—far from it, it is clearly essential when sentence production is considered. However, there are many issues regarding lexical retrieval in production that can be addressed without commitment to a view on morphological representation and processing.

The main issue regarding lexical representation that recurs through this chapter is whether or not there are one (e.g. logogens, Morton, 1970) or two levels of representation (e.g. lemmas and lexemes, Kempen & Huijbers, 1983; semantic and phonological lexicons, Butterworth, 1989). Both experimental evidence and speech error evidence seem to point to two levels of representation. Models of speech production must be able to account for word substitution errors that are similar to the target in terms of semantics (meaning) or in terms of phonology (sound), and the fact that in tip-of-the-tongue states partial information is often available regarding the sound of the word without the complete phonology being available. Morton's logogen model is unable to account easily for the latter two phenomena. However, Butterworth's adaptation of this model incorporates a stage of lexical-semantic access prior to retrieval of the phonological form that overcomes these problems.

More recently, the debate regarding lexical access has centered on whether there can be said to be independent, sequential stages of access. Thus stage models (e.g. Morton, 1970; Butterworth, 1989) are compared with interactive activation models (e.g. Dell, 1989) that have a continuous flow of activation through the model—lexical items do not have to be selected at the semantic level before activation of the phonological level begins. The time course of lexical access has been investigated recently using a number of complex experimental techniques. Schriefers et al. (1990) used a picture-word interference task and found interference (on naming speed) from a semantically related word presented before the picture, and from a phonologically related word presented after the picture. However, the extent of any overlap in semantic and phonological activation between these points remained unclear. Levelt et al. (1991a) looked at interference to speed of (auditory) lexical decision during naming of a picture. They too argue for early semantic activation and late phonological activation, but also found early phonological activation. In the discussion of this paper we were concerned about the complexity of the task and the difficulty of interpreting the nature of the effects (which crucially depend on quite how lexical decision is hypothesised to occur and the nature of the relationship between input and output processes). Although we fully support any attempt to investigate experimentally the time course of processing, in these experiments there is a danger of the tasks becoming too complex to be able to interpret the results unambiguously. Nevertheless, further experiments are clearly necessary, particularly looking at the effects of manipulating the time at which the interfering word is presented in the picture-word interference task.

The evidence from these two tasks seemed to support a less interactive system than had been proposed by Dell (1986, 1989) as there was little late semantic activation. In response to these data, Dell and O'Seaghdha (1991; see also Harley, 1993) proposed a model that they claimed showed the pattern of activation supported by Levelt et al.'s experiments. This model showed global modularity with local interaction—in other words, the effects of interaction between levels was much less marked than in the original model proposed by Dell, and confined mainly to levels immediately next to each other. However, we noted that this model needed scaling up to be convincing in its claims (currently having only one node at each level of representation) and that it remained to be seen whether it could still produce the "interactive" effects (such as errors with both a phonological and semantic relationship to the target) that it was originally designed to simulate.

Clearly, the debate regarding the precise nature of the architecture of the spoken word production system is far from closed. However, evidence continues to be accumulated and models adapted in the light of this. Further research can fruitfully be applied to looking both at the time course of retrieval and activation and the nature of the information that is available. The most promising route seems to be one that uses converging evidence from increasingly sophisticated experimental techniques, speech error corpora, and also neuropsychological data.

CHAPTER TWO

Phonological encoding: Slots and fillers

OVERVIEW

In Chapter 1 we discussed theories of the mechanisms leading to the retrieval of the phonological form of a word. Subsequently, the phonological form has to be translated into an articulatory programme for controlling the speech musculature. The process by which this occurs is known as phonological encoding.

Almost all models of phonological encoding incorporate some kind of "slot-and-filler" mechanism. There is a separation between the sounds of a word and the position of each sound in that word. These two parts of a word's phonological form have to be combined by inserting the sounds (fillers) into their position in a word frame (their slots). It is this process that represents the source of many speech errors. As this mechanism is so widespread in its use we will discuss the motivation for this approach in some detail (see Garrett, 1976, 1980, 1984, for the same slot-and-filler approach applied to different levels of processing).

Thus, to orient the reader, the chapter begins with a description of the classification system used for speech errors that are phonologically related to their targets (PHONOLOGICAL ERROR CLASSIFICATION). We then move on to a detailed description of the factors that have been found to constrain the occurrence of speech errors and these phonological errors in particular (CONSTRAINTS ON ERROR PRODUCTION). This account follows closely Shattuck-Hufnagel's (1979) paper that motivates the structure of her model. We then describe her model (SUMMARY OF SHATTUCK-HUFNAGEL'S PHONOLOGICAL ENCODING MODEL) and discuss how she proposes that the various error types might arise within it (ERROR GENERATION).

In Shattuck-Hufnagel's original (1979) conception of her scan-copier model, the slots were merely a sequence of phoneme slots with no internal structure. In 1987 she reviews the evidence for a level of structure between that of the word and phoneme (THE ROLE OF THE SYLLABLE). She concludes that there is evidence for word onsets to be distinguished from the remainder of the word. On the basis of this she revises her model to incorporate late insertion of word onsets into the series of slots that make up the word frame (AN AMENDED SCAN-COPIER MODEL). We examine whether this late insertion of word-onset consonants is plausible by describing some experiments by Meyer (1990, 1991; Meyer & Schriefers, 1991) that investigate the TIME COURSE OF PHONOLOGICAL ENCODING WITHIN A WORD.

The second model that we discuss in detail is that of Dell (1986, 1989), which also incorporates the distinction between phonemes and their position in the word but does so in a very different architecture (INTERACTIVE ACTIVATION ACCOUNTS OF PHONOLOGICAL ENCODING). In Chapter 1 we discussed briefly this type of interactive activation model, but here we examine this particular model in greater depth. We describe the phenomena that the model was designed to account for (BUILT-IN FEATURES OF DELL'S MODEL) and then go on to discuss novel predictions that Dell tests experimentally (PREDICTIONS ARISING FROM DELL'S MODEL). The chapter concludes with further discussion of effects that interactive activation models can account for with ease but may be less easy for noninteractive models (such as that of Shattuck-Hufnagel) to account for (STEMBERGER'S (1985) MODEL AND MORE ON LEXICAL BIAS).

PHONOLOGICAL ERROR CLASSIFICATION

In the development of her model, Shattuck-Hufnagel (1979) used the Massachusetts Institute of Technology (MIT)–Cornell University (CU) corpus of 6000 speech errors collected over a period of 6 years. Error patterns in the corpus were found to generally confirm Fromkin's (1971) finding that error segments usually correspond to linguistically motivated units (i.e. words, phonemes, etc.). The errors are divided into five major types, as listed (Shattuck-Hufnagel, 1979 p.299). However, Shattuck-Hufnagel notes that the surface classes of errors may not necessarily correspond to underlying error mechanisms.

1. Substitution: A target segment is replaced by an intrusion segment, which may or may not have an apparent source within the utterance, e.g.
   (a) It's a shallower test – chest, but broad
   (b) Anymay, I think (anyway)
2. Exchange: Two target segments change places in the target sequence, each serving as the other's intrusion segment, e.g.
   (a) emeny (enemy)
   (b) It's past fassing – fast passing by
3. Shift: A target segment disappears from its appropriate location and appears at another location in the target sequence, e.g.
   (a) State-lowned-_and – owned-land (state-owned-land)
   (b) in a b_ack blo – black box
4. Addition: An extra segment is added to the target sequence; this intrusion may or may not have an apparent source within the utterance, e.g.
   (a) either the plublicity would be bad (publicity)
   (b) they bring abrout – about a
5. Omission: A target segment is dropped from the target sequence; there may or may not be a similar sequence elsewhere in the utterance, e.g.
   (a) the d_ug – the drugs
   (b) piano sonata _umber ten (number)

The errors are also categorised along the dimension of direction of influence, that is, the sequential relationship between the target and the presumed source segment. If the candidate source is later in the sentence, the error is classified as anticipatory. If the candidate source is earlier in the sentence, so that the error follows it, then the error is classified as perseveratory. Some additions, omissions and substitutions are anticipatory (e.g. 4(a), above) or perseveratory (e.g. 4(b), above), but others appear to have no source in the utterance (e.g. 1(a) and (b); 5(a) and b). All shifts are either anticipatory or perseveratory, as each must have an identifiable source. Exchanges are not classified as either anticipatory or perseveratory because they involve a component of each direction of influence from source to error.

CONSTRAINTS ON ERROR PRODUCTION

In common with most other authors, Shattuck-Hufnagel assumes that errors occur because of a minor malfunction in normal speech production processes. Thus, constraints on error patterns are a function of both the normal process of sentence production and the nature of possible malfunctions. She discusses four constraints on error patterns that have been established in earlier studies of error data and basically confirmed in the MIT–CU corpus (Shattuck-Hufnagel, 1979, p.302), and notes the implication of each for theoretical accounts of speech production.

1. Error segments may appear several words earlier in an utterance than they belong, e.g. "and the *class* (target: exam) will be an in-class exam".

Implication: The span of sentence processing must be greater than a single word (Lashley, 1951).

In other words, more than one lexical item must be retrieved and held in memory at any one time. It is not the case that words are retrieved one at a time as they are required for insertion into an utterance. Thus, in the example given, "class" must have been available at the point at which "exam" was to be inserted at the beginning of the utterance even though it was not required until much later.

2. Errors often (although not invariably) involve the units and devices of linguistic grammars: phonemes, morphemes, words, and sentence constituents.

Implication: These entities are part of the psychological representation during normal sentence processing for production. Moreover, the moved/changed segments must have been represented independent of their target slots or locations (Fromkin, 1971; Fry, 1959; Garrett, 1975; Shattuck, 1975, cited in Shattuck-Hufnagel, 1979).

However, Shattuck-Hufnagel points out that the difficulty with this constraint lies in determining the strength of the claim that can be made about the equivalence of planning units and linguistic entities. She argues that there is clear error evidence for independent representation of phonemes, morphemes, words, and sentence constituents. She notes that syllables, subsyllabic units (such as onset and rime), and distinctive features seem to participate in errors differently, suggesting they play a different role in the planning process.

Although syllables do move and change as units, in the MIT–CU corpus it was found that other sequences of phonemes move and change in errors far more often. (Only 10% of phoneme sequence errors involved whole syllables.) She gives examples such as "cassy put" (pussy cat) where phoneme sequence errors do not correspond to a syllable (or to subsyllabic units such as onset or rime). As detailed later, Shattuck-Hufnagel (1987) presents evidence claiming to support a level of representation involving word onsets (segments before the vowel) and rimes (the remaining segments, which may be subdivided into nucleus [the vowel] and coda [the segments following the vowel]), but in the original description of the slot-and-filler theory this did not feature.

Similarly, distinctive feature exchanges, although rare (only two in the whole MIT–CU corpus), do occur. Although there are many phoneme substitution errors where the target and intrusion segments differ by only a single feature, Shattuck-Hufnagel argues that these can be accounted for as phoneme errors under a feature-similarity constraint and do not require a mechanism for ordering single features one by one. Shattuck-Hufnagel (1979) suggests that "features and syllables may play a role in defining the slots that planning segments are copied into, in some way that needs further specification" (p.332).

3. A target and its intrusion can be described as single segments at the same level of description: In general, a phoneme substitutes for another phoneme, a word for a word, etc.

Implication: Some aspect of the planning mechanism permits malfunctions that result in substitutions within a level of description but not across levels (Shattuck, 1975). In the MIT–CU corpus 96% of errors can be described as a change in or movement of a linguistically motivated segment (e.g. word, phoneme) in the utterance.

4. A target-intrusion pair almost always shares linguistically relevant characteristics: Phoneme pairs share distinctive features; morphemes share syntactic category; words share phonological, syntactic, and/or semantic characteristics; sentence constituents share syntactic structure, etc.

Implication: These dimensions are part of the psychological representation of utterances during planning for production. The representations used for processing must capture the constraints on which segments interact and which do not (e.g. consonants tend to interact in errors with other consonants but not with vowels).

However, often a target-intrusion pair shares characteristics of many different types, e.g. a phoneme target may share distinctive features as well as word or syllable position and phonetic context with its intrusion and presumed source (e.g. "we'll put your trash bans back" for "… trash cans back", where both phonemes are word initial, preceding the same vowel and both stop consonants); a word target may share phonological as well as syntactic and semantic characteristics with its intrusion (e.g. "calf" for the target "cow"). Shattuck-Hufnagel makes it clear that the shared characteristics need not all be taken account of in the same representation or level of processing in production planning.

The latter two constraints do have a danger of leading to circularity in error analysis. It is often the case that there could be a number of apparent sources of error or that the error could be described as a segment at a number of levels (e.g. a feature or a phoneme movement error). If the principle of segment similarity (combining constraints 3 and 4) is used when in doubt regarding the category of an error, then it is not possible to test the validity of the constraints.

Shattuck-Hufnagel assumes these constraints, with some qualifications as outlined, and derives four more from her further analysis of the MIT–CU corpus.

5. *When a planning segment moves to a new location in an error, that movement is limited to a small set of possible slots or locations, which are predictable on the basis of either other error changes in the sentence or its underlying structure.*

Implication: These "slots" or locations must be predefined in some way during the planning process, independent of the segments they are to contain.

Shattuck-Hufnagel gives two major sources of evidence to support this claim. First, there are constraints on the locations to which segments can be moved in an error. Second, there is evidence for similarity between the "slot" of a target segment and the "slot" of the intrusion source. Exchanges provide the strongest evidence both for representation of segments (e.g. words, phonemes) independent of slots and that slots are represented independent of segments. The probability that a pair of symmetrical independent (no source) substitutions would occur in the same utterance to produce an exchange is very small. She concludes, therefore, that the production process involves a representation that includes the downstream target well before its preceding word is articulated. If two segments A and B exchange so that B appears in the position A should have filled, then a mechanism is required that will maintain the downstream source slot B and ensure that the displaced target segment A appears there.

Source/target slot similarities are said to take three forms in the MIT–CU corpus:

(i) Exchange errors at the phoneme level take place between phonemes that are in comparable syllable positions (207/211 errors). For example, in the error "guinea kig page" (guinea pig cage), the exchanging phonemes both appear in word/syllable initial position.

(ii) When substitutions, additions, and omissions have an apparent source in the utterance, the source usually appears in the same position as the error. For example, for 70% of anticipatory phoneme errors, target and candidate source are in similar syllable positions (although, of course, some of these may have occurred in similar positions by chance). In the error "one, thoo, three" (one, two, three), for instance, the probable source for the error in the onset of "two" is the onset of "three".

(iii)   Anticipatory and perseveratory phoneme shifts move segments into locations that are similar to their target locations (over and above phonotactic limitations).

6. *Anticipatory and perseveratory errors often involve the "double use" of a target segment*, once in its appropriate location and once as an intrusion.

Implication: The planning process must include a step that, when it goes wrong, permits a segment to be used more often than it should be in a given utterance. Shattuck-Hufnagel (1979) proposes a scan-and-copy mechanism that scans the set of planning segments for the appropriate item to copy into each slot in a separately represented "slot framework". The scan-copier mechanism can transfer information into the appropriate slot without destroying it and so can account for the double use of a planning segment in anticipatory errors as well as perseveratory ones.

7. *Errors often appear in utterances that contain sequences of similar segments or repeated instances of a particular unit.*

Implication: The production process must include a mechanism by which similar or repeated sequences facilitate errors.

In order to explain the occurrence of exchanges using a scan-copier mechanism, Shattuck-Hufnagel necessarily adds a monitor to the model (the check-off monitor). The scan-copier mechanism can explain the erroneous copying of segment B into slot A, but is unable to explain why segment B, which is still available (as described earlier) is not also correctly copied into its own slot B, creating an anticipatory error rather than an exchange. Shattuck-Hufnagel proposes that the target segment is marked in some way as already used by the check-off monitor, and only then does it become unavailable to the scan-copier. However, in the case of an exchange, the appropriate segment B is no longer available to the scan-copier, as it is marked as already used. Therefore, the displaced target segment from the earlier slot (segment A) has to be used.

She proposes that mistakes by the scan-copier mechanism will be facilitated by segmental similarities between the targets and similarities between the slots in the two locations. When the scan-copier and check-off device operate properly no errors occur. If both fail to work, then the misselected segment also fails to be marked as used and is available for reselection, resulting in anticipatory/perseveratory errors.

When a repeated segment seems to facilitate an error it is known as a trigger segment. For example, in the error "Well, they're rell (well) rid of her" (Shattuck-Hufnagel, 1979, p.308), the target segment is /w/ in "well rid", the source of the intrusion is presumed to be the /r/ in "rid".

The trigger segment in this error is the /w/ of the first "Well", which is identical to the target, but remains unchanged in the error. Shattuck-Hufnagel (1979) argues that such a segment appears in a surprising number of cases and may play a role in the generation of some errors. The trigger segment is related to Lecours and Lhermitte's (1969) concept of "pair-destroying errors", which they introduced to describe a similar phenomenon in the phoneme substitutions of some aphasic patients.

Many different kinds of partial repetitions of sequences in the target utterance seem to be associated with errors. This suggests that the production mechanism is capable of keeping track of the segments that have appeared and will appear in an utterance. A scan-copier and check-off monitor system, when it misfires, will sometimes result in double use of planning segments, and these must be detected and edited out. The error monitor scans a planned utterance for repetitions and suspiciously similar sequences. Shattuck-Hufnagel argues that this explains (i) why speakers sometimes change correct utterances into errors; (ii) how speakers can claim to know what an unspoken error was going to be—this "in-the-head" detection of errors would be a natural result of an error monitor; (iii) how trigger segments participate in the error process.

8. Errors of all five basic types occur for each error segment observed, although constraints vary from one error or segment type to another.

Implication: The most parsimonious model is the one in which a single underlying mechanism accounts for all error types across all segment types (phonemes, words, etc.). Differences in constraints arise from the fact that the mechanism operates at several different levels of representation with access to different kinds of information. Shattuck-Hufnagel (1979), therefore, proposes that the same malfunction occurs at many different levels in the production process. This malfunction is misselection, among similar available planning segments, of a segment to be copied into a particular slot.

Garrett (1975) points out that the production mechanism is a means of translating ideas into sequences of well-integrated articulatory gestures that occur in a particular order. Because that order is not inherent in the intent to voice a given thought, it must be imposed during the psychological process by which sentences are planned for articulation. That words are probably not retrieved one at a time from the lexicon in the order in which they are spoken is supported by the occurrence of anticipatory errors. It is suggested by both Garrett and Shattuck-Hufnagel that slot-segment representation, scan-copier and monitor mechanisms achieve the correct sequencing for output (at a number of levels, including words into sentences, phonemes into words).

SUMMARY OF SHATTUCK-HUFNAGEL'S
PHONOLOGICAL ENCODING MODEL

Shattuck-Hufnagel derives her model from the inferences suggested by the constraints described earlier. To reiterate its structure, it has three parts:

1. a dual representation, consisting of serially ordered slots and an equal number of independently represented target segments, at least at the word level and at the sound level;
2. a scan-copier that selects the appropriate segment from the set of available planning segments and copies it into each slot;
3. two monitors: a check-off monitor, which marks or deletes segments as they are copied into their target slots, and an error monitor, which detects and deletes or otherwise edits error-like sequences in a planned utterance.

At the level of word ordering, an ordered framework of word slots is generated and a corresponding set of target lexical items is retrieved from the lexicon and stored in a short-term buffer. The scan-copier scans the set of target lexical items in the buffer for the one that belongs to the first of the ordered slots. When the morpheme is found it is copied into the first slot and the check-off monitor marks it as "used" in the target set or deletes it from the set; then the scan-copier moves to the second slot.

At the phoneme level, the same kind of ordering mechanism works with phoneme-sized target segments and ordered sequences of phoneme-sized slots. Shattuck-Hufnagel argues that words are stored in the lexicon with their phonological segments in the proper order and retrieved from the lexicon in that form, but that, even so, at some point during the production process these segments must be copied one by one into waiting ordered slots that have been computed independently. She suggests that lexical items are entered in a short-term storage buffer as they are retrieved, perhaps with the initial, medial, and final elements lined up for the syllables of the target lexical items. The slots might then be separately derived from a rule of canonical syllable structure in English and the stress pattern of the words. If the scan-copier then scans this positionally organised buffer for a particular word-initial target segment, the most likely error is the misselection of a similar word-initial target to copy.

Error generation
Each of the five error types can be accounted for as some variation on the basic mechanism of a malfunction in the segment selection process.

Copying and check-off errors combine with this malfunction to cause the range of error types.

1. Exchanges arise from misselection by the scan-copier (but intact check-off, as described earlier).
2. Anticipatory substitutions arise from misselection and then failed check-off, perseveratory substitutions from failed check-off and then misselection. "No source" substitutions are explained as copying errors, either information specifying a target is incompletely or incorrectly transferred to the slot location, or an extra word found its way erroneously into the set and was misselected (e.g. as in "Freudian" slips).
3. Additions involve misselection and failed check-off, where the misselection is of a segment for a slot that should have been empty.
4. Omissions are argued to arise from misselection of a null element followed by failed check-off.
5. Shifts are explained by two full misselections, one of a target for a null slot and the other of a null segment for a target slot.

Blend errors involve the blending of two separate words, which may either be two words that should appear sequentially in the utterance (e.g Ted Kennedy – Tennedy), or the blending of two alternative words that could fill a single slot (usually virtual synonyms, e.g. symblem from symbol + emblem). To produce these blends the scanner must jump from the slot-and-segment representation of the first word or phrase to the slot-and-segment representation of the second one. Shattuck-Hufnagel argues that the model predicts that the jump from one set of slots to the other should occur at a point where the two sequences are similar. When the scan-copier is searching for target segments under their slot descriptions and copying them into their appropriate locations, the presence of two slot sequences with a point of strong similarity should increase the chances of slippage from one set to the other. Shattuck-Hufnagel found that this was confirmed in the MIT–CU corpus.

Shattuck-Hufnagel (1979) argues that the slot-and-filler model embodies the constraints derived from analysis of a large corpus of speech errors in such a way as to permit all observed error types to be generated as the result of a small number of minor malfunctions in the normal production mechanism. The model would predict that those errors that involve more malfunctions will be less common. There was evidence from the MIT–CU corpus that this was the case. For example, exchange errors that involve only a single misselection (with a later compromise on the best available planning segment) are found to be more common (259 occurrences) than shifts that involve two separate wrong choices between a null segment and a real segment (31 occurrences). As phonemes only move into phonotactically permissible slots, there must be some aspect of the production process that marks the slot representation of an utterance for locations into which phonemes could fit without violating the phonotactic constraints of the language.

The serial ordering process for sublexical elements operates on a representation made up of abstract phonemic segments, rather than of contextually adjusted segments or even motor commands. The elements being manipulated during this process have not yet been shaped to fit their phonemic contexts, and detailed phonetic specifications are computed at a later processing stage. Error segments themselves undergo this shaping to fit their new contexts. The model deals only with errors of planning, not execution.

The role of the syllable

Shattuck-Hufnagel (1987) re-examined evidence for processing units that are between the word and phoneme levels. Once again she concludes that although a few errors involving the syllable as an error unit are found (Fromkin, 1971), in general there is very little evidence from spontaneous speech errors that favours the syllable as a movable processing unit. However, some of the structural subunits of the syllable do find support in error data, in the form of errors that involve the movement or replacement of whole onsets, rimes, nuclei, and codas, and additionally she notes that syllabic structure now plays a more significant role in generative phonological theory (nonsegmental phonology).

Error evidence for suprasegmental sublexical structure:

1. *Susceptibility: Certain structurally defined classes of segments are differentially susceptible to errors.*   Of the 1520 consonantal errors in the corpus, 66% occurred at word onsets, whereas only 33% of consonants occur at word onset in running speech. Shattuck-Hufnagel argues that it is word-onset position that is relevant rather than syllable onset, as 56% of the consonant errors in polysyllabic words involve word-onset segments (19% of consonants are word onset in the same sample). She uses these data to claim that word-onset consonants are processed differently from other consonants during speech production planning and that this special processing makes them particularly prone to disruption.

Segmental errors occur in all positions but interaction errors (e.g. exchanges, substitutions with an identifiable source) have a special affinity for word-onset consonants. Of interaction errors, 82% occur in word-onset position, compared to only 43% of noninteraction errors. Similar effects were found for errors elicited using tongue twisters such as "from the leap of the note to the nap of the lute", but this effect disappears when the same words are produced in a list (e.g. "leap, note, nap, lute"), with word-final consonants having an increased likelihood of error (compared to in the phrases). Thus she suggests that in phrasal planning, word-onset consonants are processed in a way that leaves them open to confusions, whereas consonants in other positions are somewhat protected against confusion errors. When the protective representation imposed by phrasal planning is withdrawn, final consonants are at least as likely as initial consonants to participate in interaction errors.

However, as Butterworth (1992) points out, the two sets of stimuli differ in more than just the presence of phrasal organisation. The "phrasal" lists contain an additional eight unstressed syllables, which may act as a buffer between the critical items. Butterworth suggests that in the same way as the likelihood of interactions between words is conditioned by proximity, perhaps the type of interaction is also conditioned by it. He suggests that Shattuck-Hufnagel should have also tried lists such as "the from leap the of note the to nap the of lute".

2. Error units: Certain structurally motivated sequences of adjacent segments appear as discrete error units more often than unmotivated sequences do.   Error evidence offers some support for the word onset as a representational unit, even though counter examples to this claim do occur in both directions. Onsets break apart into their constituent segments, e.g. Did the grass clack? (glass crack), and onset segments also combine with the following vowel to form C(C)V- units, e.g. cassy put (pussy cat). Shattuck-Hufnagel feels that evidence for word-based or syllable-based suprasegmental units other than the word onset is equivocal, although -VC (rime) error units occur fairly regularly, e.g. hever _ardly (hardly ever), and certain segment sequences that would violate syllable structure are not found at all as error units.

Other authors have also addressed the issue of whether the relevant distinction is between syllable onset and rime or between word onset and rest of word. Davis (1989) pointed out that many of the words that are involved in speech errors and most of the stimuli used in experiments contain a single syllable where the distinction between syllable and word onset cannot be made. Fowler, Treiman, and Gross (1993) used a speeded phoneme shift task to examine this distinction between word and syllable onsets. Subjects were presented (visually) with two nonwords (e.g. mupnav lefbok) and had to transpose a specified consonant (printed in upper case) from the second nonword into the corresponding position of the first nonword and say the result as quickly as possible. Subjects were faster and more accurate at shifting word initial consonants (e.g. resulting in "lupnav") than syllable-initial consonants (resulting in "mupbav"). However, they argue that although these results suggest that there is a division between word onset and rest of word, these may not be the only constituents of polysyllabic words. Further experiments using trisyllabic stimuli did give some support for a role for syllable structure as well as word structure (at least for stressed medial syllables of trisyllabic words). Subjects were faster to shift the initial consonant than a final consonant and a -VC than a CV- within these syllables. Fowler et al. suggest that this is consistent with the idea that syllables are comprised of onsets and rimes. Treiman, Fowler, Gross, Berch, and Weatherston (1995) continued this research using auditorily presented stimuli and conclude that although word-based structure is not the only structure in stimuli of more than one syllable, it is important. In contrast, the extent to which onset/rime structure emerges in the rest of the word may depend on the task and the nature of the stimuli.

Shattuck-Hufnagel (1987) concludes that if suprasegmental (and subsyllabic) structure beyond the word onset plays a role in constraining errors, it appears that it is a different role from that of defining the independently represented and movable planning units, i.e. the individual phonemic elements that commonly become misordered in sublexical errors.

3. Position-similarity constraints: Pairs of segments that occur in structurally similar locations often interact in an error, whereas pairs of segments in structurally different slots rarely do. As with the evidence from error susceptibility and error units, almost all the evidence regarding position similarity supports word-onset position and very little supports the representation of other aspects of suprasegmental structure.

As many spontaneous errors occur in words that carry main stress on the first syllable (94% of pairs of interacting word-onset consonants occur before a primary stressed vowel, e.g. borrow a s<u>how</u> s<u>n</u>ovel (snow shovel)), Shattuck-Hufnagel (1987) performed an error-elicitation experiment to investigate the independent effects of stress and word onset. Lists of four words were used that had confusable pairs of consonants (e.g. p/f, l/r) that either (a) shared word-onset position but not stress (repeat load lot repaid) or (b) shared stress but not word onset (parade load lot parole). The onset consonants that shared word position were found to promote twice as many errors as those that shared stress.

A further experiment (see also Shattuck-Hufnagel, 1992) was performed with two more sets of lists (in addition to the comparisons already described) where confusable consonants shared both stress and position, or neither stress nor position. This experiment made it clear that there was also an effect of lexical stress on the probability of error, as significantly more errors occurred on the stimuli that shared both stress and word position than on the stimuli that shared word position alone. The same pattern was found when the four words of these lists were uttered in phrasal contexts or were used in a sentence-generation task (Shattuck-Hufnagel, 1992). However, in an unusual step—but it seems important that more experimenters should adopt this step—she also examined the patterns of performance shown by individual subjects. In this analysis less than half of the subjects (who made large numbers of errors) showed the overall error pattern of the group (an error ranking of: both word and stress position > word position > stress position > neither). Similar problems are found in an analysis examining the reliability of the effect across stimuli

Thus, whereas Shattuck-Hufnagel (1987) concludes that although stress does have an effect the main effect is one of word onset, in her 1992 paper she notes that "these equivocal results [from the analysis of individual subjects and stimuli] suggest that any claims about the relative power of the two position constraints would be premature" (p.237)—although one wonders whether a stronger effect of stress might have been obtained if all the words in the list had been two-syllable words rather than only the key (interacting) words.

An amended scan-copier model

Following the results of these experiments Shattuck-Hufnagel (1987) suggests a two-stage model of phonological encoding with two separate processing mechanisms that produce sublexical (phoneme) errors, each governed by a separate position-similarity effect. For one of these processes, the sublexical representation consists of two parts—the onset consonants of the word and some (unspecified) representation of its remainder. The second processor has access to all the individual segments of each word. During the time the words are represented in terms of the onset plus the rest of the word, most of the errors that occur involve word-onset consonants. In contrast, during the processing that takes place while words are represented in terms of all their individual segments, errors are distributed more evenly across positions in the word.

Shattuck-Hufnagel hypothesises that phrases involve integration of phonological and syntactic information, which is accomplished by building metrical structures that determine the prosodic shape of the utterance (Selkirk, 1984). One step during this integration involves the separate transfer of phonological information about word-onset consonants. As they play no role in the determination of the relative prominence of syllables or of any other metrical elements, it is possible to delay their integration into larger metrical structures until a later processing stage. She also assumes the process operates initially on open-class words separately from closed-class words (see Garrett, 1980).

Shattuck-Hufnagel (1987) breaks down the process into the following steps:

1. Selection of a set of candidate open-class words from the lexicon. Selection can be made by transferring lexical items into a short-term store or by marking their lexical representations temporarily. These candidate lexical items provide the set of phonemic segments among which final selection for the utterance will be made, and interaction errors can occur. The form of each lexical item specifies its segments and their serial order.

2. Construction of syllabic structure and other apparatus for assigning main lexical stress to the open-class lexical items. These processes incorporate the rest of the word minus the onset, word-onset consonants are ignored until later.

3. Transfer or association of the nononset portions of content morphemes, now organised into the metrical structures that govern lexical stress, to the emerging phrasal framework. The phrasal frames define two classes of components, word-onset locations (which at this point remain empty) and locations for the rest of each word (filled).

4. Transfer/association of word-onset consonants into the word-onset locations for content words. All segments of the content words of the phrase are now in place.

5. Transformation of this representation with its accompanying hierarchical organisation into a complete string of discrete fully specified segmental elements, including those of grammatical morphemes, and subsequently into a pattern of motor commands characterised by substantial temporal overlap in the effects of adjacent segments. This process presumably involves many steps, among them one that is subject to single-segment errors at any position in the word. The influence of suprasegmental structure on interaction errors is not clear at this point, but noninteraction errors that are distributed more evenly across word positions may occur here. Planning for a list differs in that it goes directly from step 2 to step 5 (hence accounting for the different pattern of errors).

Shattuck-Hufnagel (1992) notes that this model is not entirely adequate as it fails to account for the fact that lexical stress also plays a role in constraining interaction errors. She therefore proposes that within the word-onset scan set (when they have been "separated" from the remaining segments of the word) lexical stress is one of the factors constraining similarity between candidate segments. Thus, when two onset segments share lexical stress there is a higher probability of misselection between them.

THE TIME COURSE OF PHONOLOGICAL ENCODING WITHIN A WORD

The late insertion of word-onset consonants into word frames seems a less than satisfactory way of accounting for the speech error data. Is there any independent evidence that this is the case? Meyer (1990, 1991) ran a series of experiments that were designed to investigate the time course of phonological encoding using an implicit priming paradigm that made use of a paired-associate learning task. Subjects learnt five pairs of common nouns at a time (e.g. dog-cat; prince-king; thief-cop); the first member of a pair was then presented (e.g. dog) and the subject had to name the second member of the pair as quickly as possible (e.g. cat). The experimental word pairs were tested under two conditions, homogeneous and heterogeneous. In the homogeneous condition the response words of each pair were systematically related in phonological form (as in the earlier example where the response words all begin with /k/, i.e. cat, king, cop), whereas the response words of heterogeneous test blocks were unrelated in form.

Meyer (1990) studied encoding of successive syllables in a word, using this technique. The production of bisyllabic words was found to be speeded when homogeneous sets had common initial syllables, but not when they shared the second syllable. Experiments using trisyllabic words showed that a facilitatory effect could be obtained from information regarding the second syllable, provided that the first syllable was also known. She concludes that these findings suggest that the syllables of a word are encoded strictly sequentially, according to their order in the word.

Phonological encoding within the syllable was also studied by Meyer (1991) using the same implicit priming technique for paired-associate recall. Priming effects on the reaction times were only found when the primes included the onsets of the response words. Word-initial and word-internal syllable onsets produced priming effects of about equal strength (in other words, words in groups that shared syllable onsets were named faster than those that were in unrelated groups). Meyer takes this to suggest that these (implicit) primes facilitated the phonological encoding of the response words rather than their articulation, and that onset and rime of a syllable are phonologically encoded sequentially. However, she does not take this to mean sequential activation of syllables, citing the speech error literature, which indicates that segments of several words must be activated simultaneously, merely that they are selected or encoded sequentially. Meyer (1991) concludes by saying "I assume that sequential encoding involves the selection of phonological segments and segment sequences, the creation of syllable frames, and the insertion of the segments and sequences into the slots of the syllable frames. The association of phonological segments and syllables can be viewed as the integration of two complete and fully ordered representations of different aspects of word forms" (p.88).

Meyer and Schriefers (1991) obtained further evidence that word forms are created in a left-to-right fashion using a picture-word interference paradigm. Subjects were presented with pictures of common objects, which they named as rapidly as possible. They were also (auditorily) presented with interfering words (IWs), which were either phonologically related or unrelated to the targets. For monosyllabic targets, these either shared the same onset and nucleus or nucleus and coda as the target, and for bisyllabic words they shared either the first or second syllable. The IWs were either presented so that the phonemes they shared with the target began exactly at the picture onset or slightly before or after the picture onset. When the IWs were presented before picture onset, naming was faster in the related than the unrelated condition but only when the shared segments were word initial. When the IWs were presented later there was facilitation for utterance initiation in the related condition regardless of the position of the shared segments. Meyer and Schriefers argue that the reason the effect of shared word-initial segments occurs before the effect of word-final segments is because the encoding of the beginnings of words happens before the encoding of the ends. This supports the conclusions from Meyer (1990, 1991) that the onset and rime of a syllable (see also Sevald & Dell, 1994), and the syllables of a word are encoded in succession.

This view is entirely compatible with the slot-and-filler model as described by Shattuck-Hufnagel (1979), although the data regarding the time course of encoding within a syllable would seem to throw doubt on some aspects of the amended model (Shattuck-Hufnagel, 1987, 1992). In particular, Shattuck-Hufnagel (1987) suggests that encoding of word-onset consonants occurs after the encoding of the rest of the word, which seems to be incompatible with Meyer's (1991) data. Meyer (1992) also argues that this separation of word onset from the rest of the word is not particularly plausible linguistically. Specifically, all syllable onsets are irrelevant for the determination of the metrical structure of an utterance, not just word onsets (Selkirk, 1984). "If metrically relevant information is to be processed first, syllable rimes should precede onsets. Yet, in Shattuck-Hufnagel's model the complete 'rest of the word', including rimes and word-internal syllable onsets, is associated to its position before the word onset" (p.193).

INTERACTIVE ACTIVATION ACCOUNTS OF
PHONOLOGICAL ENCODING

Dell's (1986, 1989) interactive activation model, described briefly in Chapter 1, is compatible in many ways with the slot-and-filler model. Dell revised his 1986 model to incorporate serial encoding within a syllable, as a result of Meyer's (1990, 1991) data (previously he had assumed simultaneous encoding of onset, nucleus, and coda). The network has two parts, a lexical network and a word-shape network (see Fig. 2.1). This captures the idea that it is profitable to separate the phonological structure of a word into two components, as argued earlier: (1) a frame or a sequence of slots that specifies the abstract shape of the word and the number and kinds of syllables and phonemes it contains; and (2) a separate representation of the actual sounds of the word that are associated with those slots.

The lexical network connects word (or morpheme) nodes with their sounds, from the word level to the phoneme level with excitatory and bidirectional connections, allowing positive feedback between levels (Dell, 1989). At the phoneme level, phonemes are specified for syllable position—initial (onset), vowel, final (coda). Stress is not represented within this model. Dell (1986) also has syllables, rimes, and features as independently represented levels, which are not considered in the later paper. Each word node in the lexical network connects to a word-shape "header" node, representing the pattern of phoneme categories for the word (CVC, CV, etc.), which in turn connects to a sequence of categories.

The word that is currently being phonologically encoded is flagged as being the "current" word. That is, an arbitrary amount of activation (100 units) is added to that word's node. Upcoming words in the same phrase that are already flagged are primed by adding a lesser amount of activation (50 units). During each time step, every node sends some fraction of its activation to nodes that it is connected to (both top-down and bottom-up). When activation reaches its destination node, it adds

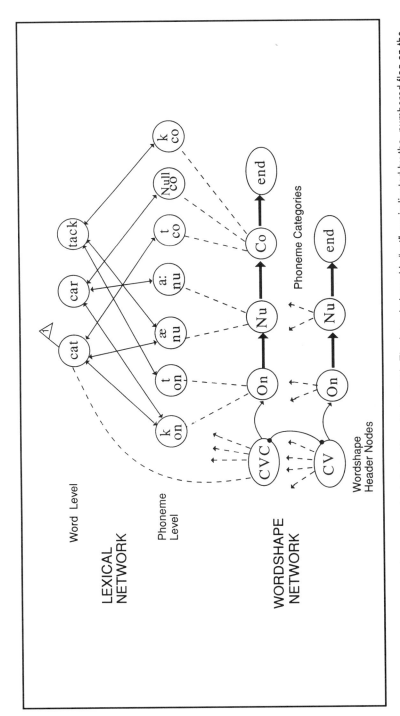

FIG. 2.1. Dell's lexical wordshape networks (adapted from Dell, 1989). The intended word is "cat", as indicated by the numbered flag on the word node. The broken lines indicate connections between the lexical and wordshape networks. The arrows between phoneme category nodes in the wordshape network (on: onset, nu: nucleus, co: coda) indicate their sequence of activation.

63

to that node's activation. Also, during each time step each node's activation decays by a fraction towards its resting level. The resting level is assumed to be zero for phoneme nodes and varies with frequency for word nodes.

After a certain number of time steps have passed (determined by the speech rate), the most highly activated phonemes are selected. How many phonemes, what kind of phonemes, and in what order, depends on the word-shape network. Activated word nodes are assumed to send activation to their respective header word-shape nodes. The most highly activated header wins the right to select a phoneme for each of its category nodes. Dell (1989) suggests that selection could be achieved by any of several mechanisms. For example, the phoneme category nodes could be activated in series (as suggested by Meyer, 1991). When activated, each node would send an increasing amount of activation to all the phoneme nodes in its category until one of them (the one with the highest activation level to begin with) reaches some kind of selection threshold. This kind of categorically triggered selection has been suggested by Stemberger (1985, see later).

One important aspect of Dell's model is the occurrence of post-selection feedback. After selection, the activation levels of the phoneme nodes are set to zero, that is, "post-selection inhibition". This helps prevent unwanted reselection or stuttering and is analogous to Shattuck-Hufnagel's check-off monitor. However, turned-off phonemes quickly rebound from zero because of other activated nodes in the network connected to them. At this point the word "flagged" as the "current word" will also be updated, and a new word selected.

Phonological errors happen when the wrong phoneme is more active than the correct one of the same phoneme category (initial phoneme, final phoneme) and is selected. There may also be errors where the wrong word shape is chosen (e.g. CCVC as opposed to CVC), leading to addition or deletion of sounds.

Once a sound has been anticipated it is subject to post-selection inhibition (like any selected sound). However, the replaced sound is still active and if it remains sufficiently active it could be selected the next time its phoneme category comes up, because the correct sound was "turned off" by its use in the previous word.

Dell (1989) outlines three sources of interference that may cause the wrong sounds to be more active:

1. Spreading activation from intended words creates its own interference by activating many (semantically and phonologically related) words and phonemes that are not really involved in the utterance.

2. Previously spoken words and upcoming words in the same phrase are active and therefore are sources of interference, particularly if the speech rate is fast.

3. It is assumed that unintended words are activated by extraneous cognition and perception, consistent with the speech error literature (e.g. Motley & Baars, 1976).

Errors are most common when the model tries to say many words quickly. Under these circumstances various sources of interference combine and conspire to direct activation to the wrong phonemes at the wrong time.

Built-in features of Dell's model

Dell lists those features built into the model to account for empirical effects in the speech error literature and distinguishes these from phenomena whose existence the model predicts. Built-in features are:

1. Anticipatory priming: Upcoming words in the same phrase are primed. The primary motivation for anticipatory priming is the existence of anticipatory errors.

2. Syllabic position encoding of consonants: Within the model there are separate phoneme nodes for pre- and post-vocalic consonants, which correspond to categories in the word-shape network. This accounts for the positional constraint on phoneme errors. Onsets and codas rarely slip with one another. Dell does note that although this separation accounts for the speech error data, it only does so at considerable cost. He concludes that the model's mechanism for handling syllable-position effects is not very satisfactory as the network will no longer recognise that a phoneme in pre-vocalic position is related to an identical phoneme in post-vocalic position (e.g. the /k/ in "cat" and "back"). Although, if a feature level is included (Dell, 1986) that is common to both onset and coda consonants, then presumably feedback from the feature level to the phoneme level would lead to activation of the phoneme in both positions to a greater extent than other phonemes that would not share all the features.

3. Selection of phonemes: That phonemes are selected rather than features is motivated by the observation that phoneme slips are more common than feature slips (Shattuck-Hufnagel, 1979; Stemberger, 1982). Although selection takes place at the level of phonemes, the model does have a feature level that has the effect of making similar phonemes more likely to slip with one another.

4. Post-selection inhibition: As mentioned earlier, this prevents unwanted repetition and allows for exchanges. Its motivation is therefore similar to that for the check-off monitor (Shattuck-Hufnagel, 1979).

5. *Frequency-sensitive resting levels:* These were incorporated into the model to account for data showing that low frequency words are more vulnerable to phonological errors than high frequency words. This was found to be true in spontaneous speech errors (Stemberger & MacWhinney, 1986) and in induced errors (Dell, 1989).

6. *Bottom-up excitatory connections:* The presence of bottom-up connections allows for interactive positive feedback between the word and phoneme levels, producing familiarity biases and similarity effects.

The lexical bias, an example of the familiarity bias, refers to the tendency for phoneme errors to be real words. Baars, Motley, and Mackay (1975), using an error elicitation paradigm, found that initial consonant misorderings that created words (e.g. dean bad – bean dad) were nearly three times more likely than slips making nonwords (e.g. deal back – beal dack). They account for this bias in terms of a pre-articulatory editor that is "better" at detecting nonword errors than real words.

In Dell's model, lexical bias happens because the interactive flow of activation between words and phonemes ensures that a pattern of activation that corresponds to a word is a stable pattern. If the pattern corresponds to a nonword, particularly one that does not share many properties with words, it tends to change until it does. Thus, because of the model's feedback properties there is no need for a special editor as suggested by Baars et al. (1975).

Other familiarity biases include the fact that phonemes that are common in the vocabulary tend to replace those that are less common (the phoneme-frequency effect), and tendencies to produce meaningful and contextually appropriate phrases, e.g. "get one" – "wet gun" is more likely to occur after presentation of "damp rifle" (Motley & Baars, 1976). The phoneme-frequency effect is produced by the model because phonemes that are present in many words, particularly in common words, receive additional input as activation reverberates between words and phonemes. The latter, more "Freudian" type of biases, cannot be produced by Dell's model as it stands, as it does not represent the relevant syntactic, semantic, and pragmatic knowledge. Dell (1989) says "if the model did represent this knowledge—a very big 'if'—its connectionist properties would provide a natural mechanism for producing these familiarity biases as well" (p.151).

The bottom-up connections also give an account of similarity effects between targets and intruding material in errors. For example, two sounds are more likely to participate in an error if their neighbouring sounds are identical—the "repeated phoneme effect". Thus "deal beak" (where the vowels are shared between the two stimuli) will slip to "beal deak" more than "deal back" (where the vowels differ) will slip to "beal dack". Wickelgren (1969) explains this by the representation of each sound reflecting the sounds that are supposed to be adjacent to it. Thus a sound resists movement into a new context unless the new adjacent sounds are identical to the old ones.

Dell's model produces the repeated phoneme effect differently, through the interactive spread of activation between words and phonemes. For example, when the intended phrase is "deal beak", both words connect to the same vowel node /iː/. When "deal" is flagged as the current word (with the addition of 100 units of activation) it will highly activate the node for /iː/. However, "beak" is also activated as it is the next word to be produced (with the addition of 50 units of activation), and in turn also activates /iː/. Nevertheless, due to the higher activation level of "deal" activating /iː/, the feedback from /iː/ to "beak" will be greater than it would otherwise be. Thus, the shared phoneme between "deal" and "beak" will cause their relative activation levels to become closer (the activation level of "beak" increasing) via the shared phoneme node /iː/. Dell (1989) describes it as the shared phoneme acting as a "siphon" and tending to equalise the activation levels of the two words. As a result of this equalisation, there is a greater chance of each word's phonemes being selected while the other is being encoded.

Predictions arising from Dell's model

Based on the characteristics built in to the model, Dell (1989) makes predictions as to phenomena that should be found to occur in relation to speech errors:

1. Non-adjacent repeated phoneme effect: The repeated phoneme effect is mediated in the model by word nodes rather than a phonemic adjacency mechanism (as described earlier). It therefore predicts that any repeated phoneme can induce other phonemes to slip—in other words, that this phenomenon is not restricted to phonemes adjacent to the repeated phonemes.

This was tested experimentally by Dell (1984), using a modification of the paradigm used by Baars et al. (1975). Subjects see word pairs at a one-per-second rate, with the instruction to prepare to say each pair as they see it. Eventually they see a series of question marks that signal the subject to speak. They must say aloud the last word pair that they saw either "as quickly as possible" or before a deadline (a tone). All critical stimuli pairs are preceded by three to five pairs of interference stimuli that bias for a reversal of initial consonants. For example, subjects would see "ball doze" then "bash door" then "bean deck" then the target pair "darn bore" followed by a signal to speak, which would predict the error "barn door". In this particular experiment critical word pairs in one group either shared a vowel (mad back) or did not (mad bake), and pairs in a second group either shared a final consonant (boot coat) or did not (boot comb). For pairs in the first group, the expected adjacent-repeated-phoneme effect was found in the rate of initial consonant misorderings with 8.0% errors when the vowel was shared versus 4.5% when the vowel was not shared. A significant effect was also found in group 2, where 6.3% misorderings occurred when the final consonant was shared versus 2.4% when it was not.

Dell (1984) also analysed a set of naturally occurring initial consonant exchanges. The adjacent (second-position) phonemes of the words involved in the exchange were found to be identical in almost 30% of the errors, and the nonadjacent (third-position) phonemes were identical nearly as often (around 24% of errors). This compares with less than 10% that would be expected to be identical by chance. Thus the model's prediction seems to be confirmed.

2. Speech rate interactions: The model will make more errors at a fast rate, due to the fact that the spreading of activation takes time. As many error effects are due to activation reverberating between levels, the model predicts different patterns of errors at different rates. For example, the lexical bias effect should decrease at faster speech rates (as it is dependent on reverberation between levels, which takes time).

Dell (1986) tested this prediction and found that the lexical bias effect (proportion of errors that were words) interacted significantly with the deadline given for response in the predicted direction. Of course, the alternative explanation given for the lexical bias effect in terms of an output editor might also predict the same rate dependency. Either the editor becomes less "efficient" at detecting errors at fast speech rates or perhaps it is unable to be employed at all.

3. Error type interactions: Within Dell's model exchanges are double errors, with two erroneous selections having to occur to cause them. Thus any error-causing agent should show its influence on exchanges more than on anticipations and perseverations, as because of their greater complexity, exchanges "need" more error-correlated agents to instigate them.

This prediction is not made by Shattuck-Hufnagel's (1979) scan-copier mechanism, where exchanges are the most simple type of error involving only one malfunction, whereas for anticipations and perseverations to occur an additional malfunction is necessary. Dell claims that in all experiments, except for one involving lexical bias, the manipulated variable had a greater effect on exchange probability than it had on anticipations and perseverations, supporting the predictions made from his model.

4. Lack of a frequency effect for homophonic words: High frequency words are less error-prone than low frequency words. However, the model predicts that this is not the case for homophones, where the high and low frequency homophone should have the same error rate. In Dell's terms, the low frequency homophone "inherits" the relative invulnerability of its high frequency counterpart. For example, the homophones "him" (high frequency) and "hymn" (low frequency) are predicted to elicit the same proportion of errors. This is because the low frequency homophones activate the same network structures (i.e. the same phoneme nodes) as their high frequency counterparts. Thus, when "hymn" becomes active it activates its component phonemes, which in turn feed back to "him", which will reinforce the activation of these phonemes and contribute to their successful selection. Dell (1989) reports the result of an experiment testing this prediction, which found that initial-consonant error rates were identical for high and low frequency homophones. However, as Dell points out, a final experiment demonstrating that comparable nonhomophonic low frequency words had a higher error rate is necessary to make the results more conclusive.

Although Dell's (1986, 1989) interactive activation model accounts for a number of error phenomena, there are other phenomena that it is unable to handle. The model combines a highly parallel lexical network, which activates all the phonemes of a syllable in parallel, with a separate word-shape network that imposes a serial order on these phonemes. However, in this form the model cannot account for the fact that syllable-initial and word-initial consonants are five times as likely to participate in phonological errors than final consonants. Similarly, the model is unable to account for Meyer's (1991) finding that advance knowledge of the phonological properties of words increased production speed only if the knowledge concerned a continuous string of segments including the initial segment. Dell (1989) concludes "I believe that the model must be changed to accommodate these initialness effects, as they are fundamental to its domain" (p.160).

Stemberger's (1985) model and more on lexical bias
The interactive activation model described by Stemberger (1985; see Chapter 1 for figure and description of the architecture) accounts for most of the speech error phenomena in the same way as Dell. However, although his explanation of the phenomenon is the same, Stemberger (1985) questions the strength of the lexical bias effect.

Although Dell and Reich (1981) found a strong lexical bias in their corpus, Garrett (1976) used a different calculation of chance and found no evidence for such a bias. Stemberger (1985) used Dell and Reich's method for calculating chance and did find a significant lexical bias, although much weaker than Dell and Reich's. He notes that this weak bias may actually be due to perceptual effects. When the error is a word, the listener can note semantic as well as phonological anomalies and may thus be better at detecting them than nonwords. Stemberger suggests that the large lexical bias in Dell and Reich's corpus implies that at least part of the lexical bias arises in perception. Stemberger (1984) argues that if a corpus of errors is carefully collected, perceptual biases should be small, but that they are more likely to be exaggerated with casual collection. Dell and Reich's corpus was collected by students with little training as part of class projects. This contrasts with the corpus analysed by Garrett, which he collected himself. Stemberger suggests that this may account for the different findings.

A strong lexical bias is found in experimentally induced errors using the Baars et al. (1975) paradigm described earlier. These experiments make use of phonological priming to facilitate error production. Stemberger argues that, in his interactive activation model, priming exaggerates any weak lexical bias by increasing the strength of the feedback earlier in time (activation is present before lexical access of the critical items begins), and thus priming reinforces lexical outcomes from an earlier point. The model can therefore account for the difference in magnitude of lexical bias in the two conditions, whereas, he claims, pre-articulatory output editors cannot easily explain this. Indeed, if the naturally occurring lexical bias is weak (as Stemberger claims) the nature of the editors would need to be adapted to allow for this. Perhaps an account could be formulated in terms of the degree of subjects' vigilance in the two conditions. Under experimental conditions subjects may attend more to the monitoring of their speech, resulting in a greater lexical bias than in conversation, when less attention may be paid to monitoring.

Stemberger (1985) also details three types of error due to feedback from the feature level to the segment level that Shattuck-Hufnagel's model has difficulty accounting for:

1. *Noncontextual substitutions:* The replacement of one phoneme with another where no source is evident in the context. As with Dell's model, a target segment activates its features, which feed activation back up to the segment level and give activation to competing segments that share those features. Noncontextual substitutions occur in Stemberger's model when one of these secondarily activated phonemes

inhibits and replaces a target phoneme. Shattuck-Hufnagel (1992) is forced to assume that the source of a noncontextual substitution is from an unexpected entry in the short-term lexical candidate store. She gives the example of "plime the tree" for "climb the tree", where the assumption is made that "play in" is the source of the error, which is an "unexpected entry".

2. *Noncontextual additions:* The addition of a phoneme to a word where no source for the error is evident in the context. Again, competing phonemes are given activation through feedback from the feature level. Rather than inhibiting and replacing one of the target phonemes, a secondarily activated phoneme causes the syllable structure to be modified to allow a new phoneme, and is accessed in that new position. A high proportion of these errors (67.5%) differ by only one feature from another phoneme in the word, as Stemberger would predict. Shattuck-Hufnagel's model has no direct explanation for noncontextual additions or substitutions, although Stemberger (1985) finds that the latter are at least as common in his corpus as exchange errors. Shattuck-Hufnagel (1987) gives a rather general explanation in terms of incomplete or inaccurate copying of a segment into a slot, but with little detail as to how precisely this might occur.

3. *Feature errors:* Misordering of a feature rather than an entire phoneme. Although Shattuck-Hufnagel (1979) admits that these do occur, she argues that it is rare for a feature error to occur that cannot be explained other than by recourse to a feature level. She does, however, acknowledge that features may have a role in phonological encoding, but does not specify what this might be. Stemberger argues that his model not only can account for feature errors but also predicts (correctly) that anticipations and perseverations are more common than exchanges in feature errors. For example, in the error "clear blue" – "glear plue" the phonemes /k/ and /b/ activate their features, and this activation feeds back up to /g/ and /p/. These secondarily activated phonemes are usually inhibited but anticipations and perseverations may result if one of the alternatives wins out in one position. Exchanges where both alternative phonemes win out are possible but less common.

SUMMARY

In this chapter we have discussed in detail the motivations for two influential models of phonological encoding. Both of these models take a slot-and-filler approach, which, as will become apparent, is common to the majority of current accounts.

In order that the reader gained full insight into the motivation behind the development of these models we examined in detail Shattuck-Hufnagel's original motivation for her model, which was based on an analysis of the factors that influence the occurrence of speech errors. We then described her scan-copier model. The different error types (e.g. exchanges, anticipations, perseverations, omissions, etc.) are accounted for by a combination of errors in copying segments into slots and checking-off when they have been used.

In 1987 Shattuck-Hufnagel revised her original model on the basis of evidence regarding the greater susceptibility of word onsets in errors compared to other phonemes. This revised model treated word onsets separately from the remainder of the segments in the word. Word onsets were inserted into the slots late in the phonological encoding process (and substantially after the insertion of the other phonemes). We argued that this seemed a most unsatisfactory way of accounting for the data as other evidence (e.g. Meyer, 1991) pointed to a strictly left-to-right sequential encoding within a syllable.

We then looked at Dell's model as an example of interactive activation accounts of phonological encoding. Like Shattuck-Hufnagel, Dell designed his model to be able to account for phenomena affecting speech errors. He gives impressive demonstrations that the model can do just that, then proceeds to derive further predictions from the model regarding factors affecting speech errors that have not been examined in the past. These predictions are then shown to be upheld by the data. This is a most impressive demonstration of the power of connectionist implementations of models of language. The model is set up to account for one set of data and then, using the same parameters, novel predictions are derived against which the model can be tested. However, in Chapter 1 we discussed the time course of lexical access and evidence that necessitated modifications to this model. Thus, we should not forget that a model which can account for both types of data has not been implemented. Until this is done we cannot truly be sure whether this model can do all it claims and simulate all aspects of speech production. Indeed, Dell is open in acknowledging some of the weaknesses of the model. This is not to say that Shattuck-Hufnagel's model fares any better: In the final section we have listed some errors that Stemberger points out are problematic for her model.

Thus, in summary, both Shattuck-Hufnagel and Dell claim that their model can account for the patterns found in the speech error data; however, neither can account for all the data entirely satisfactorily (at least not in their present form). Nevertheless, they are an influential and useful basis for developing theories of phonological encoding.

CHAPTER THREE

More phonological encoding: Motor control and monitoring

OVERVIEW

In this chapter we continue the discussion of models of phonological encoding and extend it to other aspects of speech production. In Chapter 2 we described the motivation behind the development of these models and two possible architectures that they might take. Here we look at two more models, which are closely related to each other and both explicitly use a slot-and-filler mechanism (MODIFIED SLOT-AND-FILLER APPROACHES). Both the models also have the advantage of incorporating the phonological encoding mechanism into a more general model of speech production. Thus, in Chapter 1 we discussed the models for retrieval of lemmas proposed by Levelt (1989) and Butterworth (1989), and here we extend those models to include phonological encoding. In Chapter 1 we also described Morton's logogen model, which has been particularly influential in the neuropsychological literature. We suggest that although this model does not incorporate any kind of phonological encoding mechanism, there is no reason why phonological encoding could not be "added on" to the model (THE LOGOGEN MODEL AND PHONOLOGICAL ENCODING). We follow Ellis (1979) in a discussion of how the response buffer could relate to phonological encoding (THE ROLE OF THE RESPONSE BUFFER) and propose models that combine the logogen model with subsequent phonological encoding procedures. We then move on to discuss evidence for the presence of "buffers" (mechanisms by which information can be held in memory until required) at other levels of processing (ARTICULATORY BUFFERING).

In the penultimate section of this chapter we briefly discuss how the results of phonological encoding might be translated into the muscle movements necessary to produce speech (SPEECH MOTOR PROGRAMMING). Finally, we examine the evidence that speakers monitor their output and the level of processing at which this monitoring might occur (MONITORING AND FEEDBACK). We conclude by presenting a model that incorporates all the different levels of processing discussed in the previous chapters.

MODIFIED SLOT-AND-FILLER APPROACHES

Two further accounts of the process of phonological encoding are those of Levelt (1989, 1992) and Butterworth (1992). These both take the slot-and-filler approach as their basis. The key features of these theories will be discussed here, but the reader is referred to Levelt (1989) in particular for a complete description.

Levelt (1989, 1992)

In common with all slot-and-filler accounts, Levelt distinguishes between two kinds of phonological information—segmental and metrical. Each of these is "processed" by independent procedures ("spell-out" procedures). Levelt (1989) notes that phonological encoding seems like a wasteful process—the metrical and segmental information is stored together, why then go through the process of "separating out" the two types of information only to recombine it to retrieve stored syllable plans? Surely it would be easier just to store the syllable plans for each word. He argues that the reason for this is to be found in the generation of connected speech. When we speak, words frequently "run together", causing what is known as "resyllabification". For example, "I don't know" is rarely produced as three separate words. It is far more likely to resyllabify into two phonological words "I" and "dunno". Therefore the syllables that appear in the lexicon for a particular item may not be those that are required in the final utterance, hence the need for phonological encoding.

Segmental information contained in the stored phonological form (lexeme) relates to the phonemes of the word (consonants, consonant clusters, vowels, etc.). Levelt and Wheeldon (1994) note that theories differ regarding the degree of specification of these representations. It may be the case that at this level only underspecified phoneme

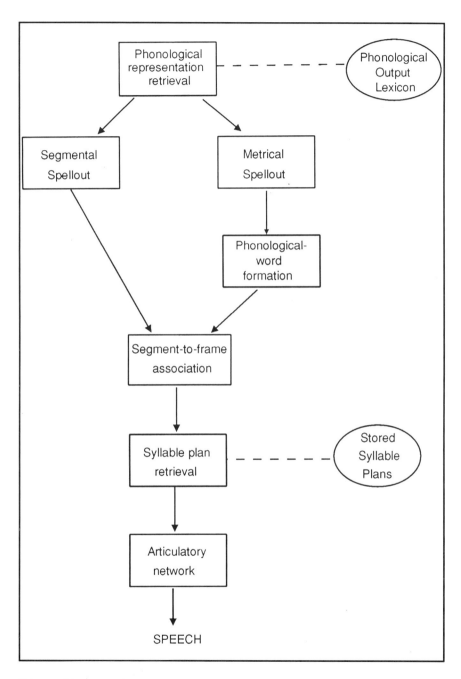

FIG. 3.1. Diagrammatic representation of Levelt's model of phonological encoding (adapted from Levelt & Wheeldon, 1994).

representations are stored, with any predictable features added later by the use of universal or language-specific rules.

Metrical information relates to the word's "frame". Crucially in Levelt's account, metrical information is retrieved at a very early stage. The full metrical pattern as it is stored in the lexicon becomes available at this stage, consisting of the number of syllables and the lexical stress levels of these syllables. No segmental information is available at this level of representation. The metrical spell-out is crucial for the construction of frames at the phonetic spell-out level as it determines the number of syllables to be retrieved (from the store of syllable plans). Levelt (1992) suggests that this early availability of metrical information is supported by the tip-of-the-tongue literature, where knowledge of number of syllables and stress pattern are available without access to most or all of the segmental information.

Having specified the metrical frame (the slots) as a result of metrical spell-out, the segments must be associated with those frames. This is the procedure described as segment-to-frame association (see Fig. 3.1), which is clearly a form of slot-and-filler mechanism. Segments are associated in a left-to-right fashion with the metrical frame of the phonological word. However, rather than having slots for individual segments, Levelt (1992) proposes the use of "more global syllable frames, that is, frames only specified for weight, not for individual segmental slots" (Levelt & Wheeldon, 1994, p.245). The details of this theory are not important for our purposes, what is important is that the one-slot-one-segment idea is given up and broader frames are used. For example, frames might be specified only for onset and rime, or as onset, nucleus, and coda, with no specification of the internal structure of each element of the frame.

After associating segments with slots, the phonological encoder will use them to address phonetic plans for syllables. These specify the articulatory gestures to be executed by the articulators. Levelt (1989, 1992; Levelt & Wheeldon, 1994) argues that the skilled language user has an inventory of syllable plans. These stored programmes are not completely fixed and will have free parameters (e.g. pitch movement, duration), which will have to be set from case to case. He suggests that it is unlikely to be the case that all of a language's possible syllables are stored as some of these may be quite rare and used infrequently. Speakers are probably able to form new but well-formed syllables by analogy. Levelt and Wheeldon (1994) describe a series of experiments as evidence for the storage of syllable plans. They found that naming latencies were found to be slower for words consisting of low frequency syllables than for words consisting of high frequency syllables (independent of word frequency). Thus, they argue that retrieval of syllable plans from the syllabary is frequency sensitive.

So, in summary, Levelt's model involves four different processes.

1.   The metrical structure is retrieved from the stored phonological representation and spelt out, making available the word's frame.
2.   The segmental structure of the lexical item is also spelt out, giving a sequence of phonemes.
3.   The segments are inserted into the syllable frames.
4.   The filled syllable frames are used to retrieve stored syllable plans for articulation.

Butterworth (1992)

Butterworth (1992) describes a model (see Fig. 3.2) which, as he acknowledges, is very similar to that of Levelt (1989). As with the majority of models, the starting point of phonological encoding for Butterworth is retrieval of the Phonological Lexical Representation (or lexeme), which contains sufficient information to specify the syllabic structure and stress pattern of the word and the segmental contents of the syllables. This phonological information is condensed or abbreviated and needs elaborating for output. This elaboration may involve adding information on the basis of general rules of phonology that the normal speaker is assumed to know.

Butterworth also incorporates a slot-and-filler device (which he calls "segment-to-frame association"), whose slots are defined by the spelling out of the syllabic structure and prosodic structure of each syllable. Information regarding the segmental content is then spelt out and inserted into the appropriate slots. Unlike Levelt, Butterworth does not consider the morphological structure of the planned word. He assumes that words are retrieved as complete units and not derived on-line from morphemic components (e.g. happiness would be stored/retrieved as a single lexical item rather than as happy and -ness). Information about morphology and lexical rules are brought into play only when word search fails to retrieve a phonological lexical representation meeting the retrieval specification. (This might occur in the case of a polymorphemic word that is rarely used or new to the speaker.)

Butterworth also includes control processes that check the output of subsystems in phonological encoding. This is achieved by running through the process twice and comparing the results (Butterworth, 1981) and as such the control processes serve as editors at each level. However, they also provide access to back-up devices that can be invoked when problems arise. Butterworth suggests that one way this might

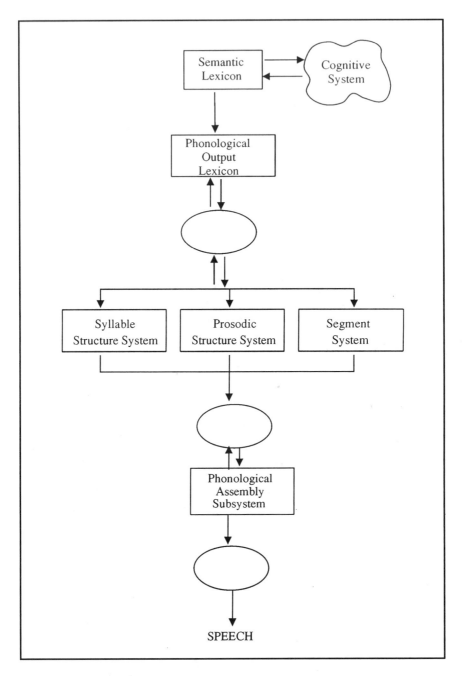

FIG. 3.2. Butterworth's model of spoken word production (including phonological encoding; adapted from Butterworth, 1992). Ovals represent "control processes" at every level.

happen in phonological encoding is for default values of phonological parameters to be generated when information cannot be retrieved from the phonological lexical representation. For example, if a syllable specification is unavailable, then perhaps a default pattern is generated; if a stress pattern is unavailable, then the default strong-weak will be generated for an English two-syllable word; or if a segment value is unavailable, a default segment is generated, perhaps using any features that are available for that segment as the basis for the derived default segment. (See also the discussion in Chapter 5 relating the "neologism generating device" and this default mechanism.)

THE LOGOGEN MODEL AND PHONOLOGICAL ENCODING

In Chapter 1 we described a model of lexical access that has been widely used in the (neuro)psychology literature—Morton's logogen model. This model does not directly address the issue of phonological encoding and therefore could be compatible with any of the theories outlined earlier. These models take as their input the stored phonological form of a word. In the logogen model this becomes available as the result of an output logogen reaching threshold and firing. This phonological form is then "held" in the response buffer until it is required for output. How might the response buffer relate to the processes of phonological encoding that translate the retrieved phonological form into a phonetic plan for output?

The role of the response buffer

Ellis (1979) discusses, in depth, the role of the response buffer in speech production and in short-term memory. He argues that the response buffer is involved in both short-term memory for phonemically coded material and phonological storage in speech production. He predicts that if this is the case, then "the same forms of phonemic error should be detectable in both speech and short-term memory, and they should be influenced by the same variables in the same way" (p.170). This prediction appears to be upheld. For example, the probability of two items transposing in short-term memory declines sharply as the distance between the items increases and this is also true in sound exchange errors; transpositions and substitutions in memory tasks and in speech errors tend to involve pairs of phonemes with similar distinctive feature descriptions; similarity of context (e.g. following vowel) also influences exchanges in both short-term memory (the "phonological similarity effect") and speech errors.

Morton and Smith (1974, cited in Ellis, 1979) assigned a phonemic rather than a phonetic level of coding to the response buffer. There is support for this from the speech error literature in that phonemes participating in exchanges are accommodated to their new contexts. For example, Nooteboom (1972, cited in Ellis, 1979) observed that the lip rounding that would normally be present on the phoneme /k/ at the beginning of "quite" was no longer present when the /k/ moves to the initial position of "tolerate" in the error "to tolerate quite a lot – to colerate quite a lot". Similarly, Fromkin (1973b) notes that affricates such as "ch" and "j" (/t∫/ and /dʒ/) which are single phonemic units, move as units in speech errors, although at the phonetic level they are clusters, whereas consonant clusters at the phonemic level (such as /gl/) are frequently split in speech errors. These observations have been taken to imply that these segmental errors occur at a level of coding prior to the application of phonological and co-articulatory rules that determine the precise phonetic form of an utterance.

The response buffer seems to be intimately related to the level of phonological encoding that has been discussed earlier. It could be equated with the mechanism by which the activated phonological forms from the lexicon (or the output of those logogens that have reached threshold) are "held" prior to phonological encoding or spell-out. In this sense it is compatible with most of the accounts of phonological encoding described earlier (with the exception of the interactive activation accounts, which would assume interaction between the semantic and lexical levels as well as with those levels of processing involving phonological encoding).

Figure 3.3 shows one possibility where the speech output logogen system has been combined with a phonological encoding procedure based on Butterworth (1992). The phonological representations are retrieved from the phonological output lexicon and may be held at the level of the response buffer (together with other retrieved representations) until they are required. This condensed or abbreviated representation is then "spelt out" as described by Butterworth (1992). The Phonological Assembly Subsystem is essentially a slot-and-filler device that results in a series of syllable plans used to retrieve stored motor plans for syllables (Levelt, 1989, 1992; Levelt & Wheeldon, 1994). At each level there is a buffer where the results of that level of processing can be held until processing begins at the subsequent level (see the discussion in the next section).

As was discussed in the previous chapter, the logogen model has only one stage of lexical retrieval, whereas psycholinguistic research seems to point to two stages of lexical retrieval (e.g. Kempen & Huijbers, 1983). Thus, Fig. 3.4 shows the same model but adapted to accommodate this

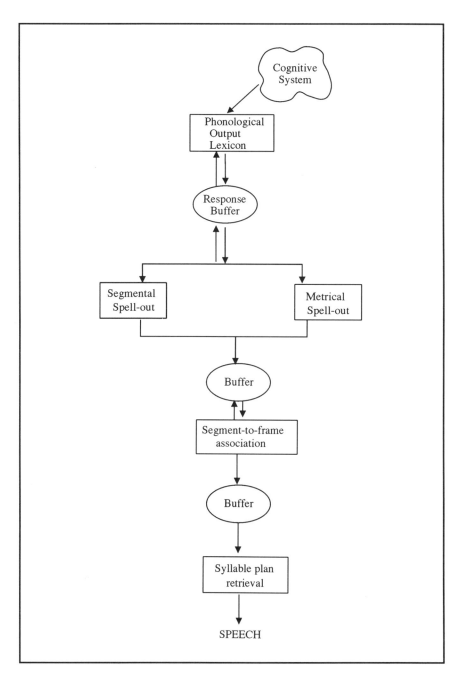

FIG. 3.3. Model of speech production incorporating phonological encoding procedures into the logogen model.

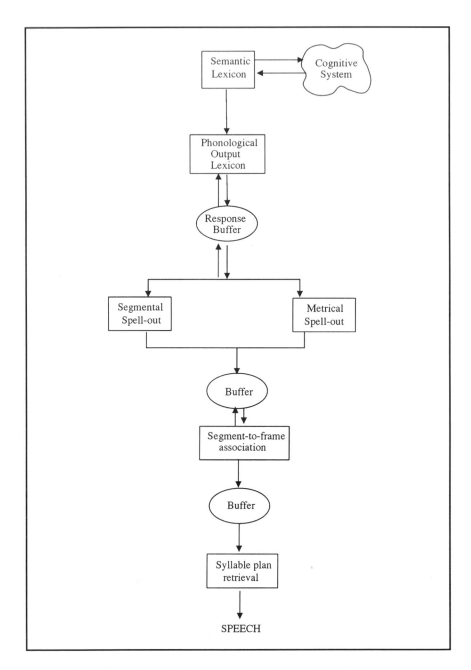

FIG. 3.4. Model of speech production incorporating phonological encoding procedures into the logogen model but also drawing the distinction between general conceptual semantic representations and a lemma level—lexical semantics or a semantic lexicon.

research by the inclusion of a semantic lexicon or lemma level, making it similar to Butterworth (1989, 1992).

ARTICULATORY BUFFERING

There is also support for an additional buffer after completion of phonological encoding. For example, Monsell (1987) distinguishes a sublexical output phonology buffer (which roughly equates with the response buffer) from an articulatory buffer. These two buffers are part of two separate feedback loops from output to input, evidence for which will be described later.

Similarly, Levelt (1989) argues that the phonetic plan, which specifies the articulatory gestures for successive syllables, may become available at a rate that is not exactly tuned to the actual rate of articulation (as specified in the plan). Thus, sustaining fluent speech will require a storage mechanism that can buffer the phonetic plan (the speech motor programme) as it develops. Levelt suggests that this buffer can presumably contain a few phonological phrases at a time, and that it must contain a minimal amount of motor programme in order for speech to be initiated (probably as much as a phonological word).

The next experiments we will describe examine the length of time it takes to begin saying a word (voice-onset latency) under different conditions. Two basic variants are used—either immediate production of the word on presentation of the stimulus or delayed recall. In the latter condition, subjects are presented with a stimulus and told to get ready to say it, but only to produce it after a signal. Under these circumstances the time it takes to say the word is assumed to reflect only those aspects of speech production that cannot be prepared in advance. Quite what these are is clearly a matter of debate, but generally it is agreed that lexical access (of lemma and phonological form) can occur in advance—and the results held at the level of the response buffer. However, these experiments argue for "holding" of a more peripheral representation and hence address the issue of the nature of this more "articulatory" buffer.

When single words or digits are read aloud, the voice-onset latency, measured from the onset of the stimulus, increases with the number of the syllables in the utterance (Eriksen, Pollock, & Montague, 1970, cited in Levelt, 1989). Klapp, Anderson, and Berrian (1973) found that two-syllable words showed significantly longer latencies (14msec) than one-syllable words (matched to them for number of letters) in reading aloud. As there were no differences in latencies on a categorisation task, the discrepancies between the one- and two-syllable words could not have been due to a difference in word-perception times. Klapp et al. (1973) concluded that the syllable latency effect was due to the preparation of the articulatory response. Confirming this, a syllable latency effect was found when subjects were required to name pictures requiring one- or two-syllable word responses (e.g. clock, camel). However, when the subjects saw a word to read but were told not to say the word until a signal appeared 3 seconds after stimulus onset, no differences were found between response latencies for one- and two-syllable words. Therefore, Klapp et al. concluded that the syllable latency effect was due to a difference in time taken to phonologically encode one- and two-syllable words and not a difference in initiation time (time to retrieve an item from the articulatory buffer). (Klapp and Erwin (1976) measured the utterance duration of the one- and two-syllable words and found virtually no difference. This seemed to exclude the possibility that the difference in encoding time was due to a difference in temporal duration of the words, i.e. how long it actually took to pronounce the words.)

Keele (1981) suggests that the planning difference stems from the hierarchical nature of the articulatory programme (phonetic plan). In particular, that the relative timings of syllables in polysyllabic words have to be established by a prosody generator. This could result in a greater programming load for two-syllable words as compared to one-syllable words attributed to the extra time needed to compute the durational relations between the syllables of the bisyllabic words. An alternative explanation is put forward by Levelt (1989). In the phonetic spell-out of a phonological word, syllable programmes are addressed one by one in serial order. Thus, the number of syllables in a phonological word will determine the duration of phonetic spell-out. Assuming that only plans for whole (phonological) words are delivered to the articulator and that execution can only start once it has received the whole word, monosyllabic words will become available for articulation earlier than polysyllabic words.

Other investigations of response latency give insights into the mechanisms of articulatory unpacking and execution. Sternberg, Monsell, Knoll, and Wright (1978) showed subjects lists of words presented one after another and then asked the subjects to recall the words as quickly as possible following a signal presented 4 seconds after the end of the list. They found that as the number of items in the list increased, the response latency increased by about 10msec per additional item. In this task, subjects had time to prepare (phonologically encode) the response and only had to retrieve a prepared phonetic plan from the articulatory buffer and initiate its execution. Sternberg et al. therefore interpreted this result as a retrieval effect. They suggest that in order to retrieve an item from the articulatory buffer, the speaker draws an item at random from all those contained in the buffer and inspects it to see if it is the correct one. If it is not, then another will be drawn until the correct item is retrieved. Thus, the more items in the buffer the longer (on average) retrieval will take.

In another experiment, Sternberg et al. compared the subjects' performance on matched lists of one- and two-syllable words. They found that two-syllable lists were about 4.5msec slower to be initiated than one-syllable lists. Sternberg et al. suggest that perhaps experiments such as those of Klapp et al. (1973) have not been sensitive enough to detect differences as small as this, hence the earlier claims of no effect. This effect was, however, also found in a similar experiment with single Japanese words by Wydell (1991). She found a 17msec mean difference between response latencies for delayed naming of three- versus four-syllable katakana words (a syllabic, phonemically transparent script) and an 11msec difference between three- and four-syllable kanji words (a logographic, phonemically opaque script).

By way of explanation of these differences in initiation times, Sternberg et al. speculate that having retrieved an item from the buffer, the speaker then has to unpack it further to make its constituent motor commands available for execution. Two-syllable words require more unpacking than one-syllable words as some unpacking of the second syllable has to occur before the first syllable can be initiated. It might also, at the next level, take more time for a cluster to be unpacked than a single consonant. They suggest that this unpacking is followed by a command and execution stage, where the motor commands are issued to the neuromotor machinery and the response is executed. The duration of a word is its execution time. The motor units in the articulatory buffer are argued to be phonological phrases rather than words. Thus, Sternberg et al. found that when a three-word list was presented with function words between the nouns (e.g. "bay-rum-cow" presented as "bay and rum or cow") it still behaved like a three-word list in terms of latency. They suggested that motor planning units in the articulatory buffer were "stress units", which correspond to small phonological phrases, each containing one stressed element. Levelt (1989) suggests a very similar account, where the articulatory buffer is successively filled with phonological words, but that larger units (phonological phrases) are formed when the buffer is heavily loaded.

Levelt (1989, p.421) provides a useful summary of his proposed stages in speech motor control:

1. Assembling the programme: This is the stage of phonological encoding, with a phonetic plan as output, which is a detailed motor programme, delivered phonological word by phonological word. When the task requires, phonetic plans can be stored in the articulatory buffer. The preferred units of storage are phonological phrases.

2. Retrieving the motor programmes: When the speaker decides to start a prepared utterance, its motor units (i.e. the phonetic plans for the phonological phrases) are retrieved from the articulatory buffer. The time needed to retrieve each unit depends on the total number of units in the buffer.

3. Unpacking the subprogrammes: Once retrieved, the phonetic plan has to be unpacked, making available the whole hierarchy of motor commands. The more complex a motor unit, the more time unpacking takes.

4. Executing the motor commands: At this stage the motor commands are issued to the neuromotor circuits and executed by the musculature. Syllables can be drawled to absorb retrieval latencies.

SPEECH MOTOR PROGRAMMING

How precisely do the articulatory or motor programmes represented in the phonetic plans become realised as coordinated muscle activity? The phonetic plan is still an abstract level of motor programme. In order for the programme to run, its articulatory features must be realised by the speech articulatory musculature. Levelt (1989) describes a strong tendency in the literature to include all, or most, of the fine detail of neuromuscular activity in the phonetic plan, which would therefore prescribe the full detail of individual muscular contractions. However, models of this type have difficulty in accounting for the adaptation observed to different peripheral contexts (for example, accurate pronunciation can be achieved with food in the mouth). Levelt suggests that it is, therefore, attractive to assume that the commands in the phonetic plan involve only the context-free or invariant aspects of motor execution. He proposes that the context-dependent neuromuscular implementation of the programme is left to a highly self-regulating neuromotor execution system that translates the programme codes into appropriate neuromuscular activity. This leads to the rejection of some theories of the nature of speech motor commands on the basis that they are not able to account for this adaptability. I will briefly outline some theories of speech motor control, starting with mass-spring theory, which suffers from the problem that it cannot cope with the need for compensation in particular contexts. (For example, greater lip movement is needed to achieve bilabial closure for [b] when the jaw has been clamped open).

Mass-spring theory in its simple form has been used to explain motor control in speech by, among others, Lindblom (1963) and later Fowler, Rubin, Remez, and Turvey (1980). The theory treats the two muscles that control a limb's position (e.g. biceps and triceps for the elbow joint) as springs that "want" to reach their normal resting position (zero position). A muscle's target length is set (using the spindle system) and each muscle will then strive for that length, until an equilibrium is reached between the pulls of the different muscles controlling a movement. However, the mass-spring model does not predict compensation when an articulator's movement is interfered with, as the interfering force is simply added to the set of forces with which an equilibrium is established. The eventual steady-state position will be different from the case where there is unhampered movement, but there will be no adequate compensation for this difference.

Other theories agree that motor commands are abstract and relatively invariant, with only the executive apparatus adapting the motor commands to the context, although they still differ regarding the precise nature of the motor command codes. Some theories suggest that the speaker's codes are auditory or acoustic images of the intended sound structure. Stevens (1983) characterised these as a set of distinctive features, which are acoustic goals that the speaker tries to achieve. For each of the sounds in a syllable, a small set of such acoustic goals must be realised. In this view, the relation between motor programmes of speech and perceptual analysis of speech sounds is not arbitrary but systematic. Levelt (1989) notes that this systematicity has often been stressed, but is usually interpreted in the reverse way. For example, Liberman, Cooper, Shankweiler, and Studdert-Kennedy (1967) made this reverse move in their motor theory of speech perception. However, although "one should be sympathetic to the view that there are quite systematic relations between perception and production of speech sounds ..., one should be worried when students of perception conjecture motor targets while students of production surmise perceptual targets" (Levelt, 1989, pp.441–442).

A problem for acoustic or auditory theories of motor commands is how they actually control articulatory movements on the basis of an acoustic target. Perkell (1980) suggests one solution to this problem. Although the "distal" goals of speech motor programming are indeed sensory-distinctive features (e.g. voicing, nasality), the speaker has learned how these goals can be attained by realising orosensory goals. Each distinctive feature corresponds to a particular aspect of articulation that can be sensed by the speaker (e.g. "obstruency", a feature of stop consonants, can be realised by reaching the goal of increased intra-oral air pressure). Perkell assumed subsequent stages of motor control at which the abstract motor commands are reorganised and translated into neuromotor commands controlling the contraction patterns of the articulatory muscles. The neuromotor commands depend not only on the orosensory goals but also on feedback from the articulators. This feedback (including proprioception, orosensory, and auditory feedback) allows for compensation for aspects of physical context.

Lindblom, Lubker, and Gay (1979) also address the issue of how an auditory goal is translated into actual control of movements. They do this in a more direct way using "model-referenced control". The speaker has an internal model of his own vocal apparatus. For each configuration of the model, the resulting sensory image can be derived and compared to the goal image. Model-referenced control is particularly useful for dealing with compensation phenomena. When an articulator is hampered in its movements, another can "take over" so that the goal image is nevertheless reached and the intended sound produced.

An alternative theory that is currently popular in speech motor programming is coordinative-structures theory (e.g. Fowler et al., 1980; Saltzman & Kelso, 1987), which supposes that the executive system consists of a hierarchy of task-oriented structures. Each such coordinative structure is a group of muscles temporarily set to function as a unit. The phonetic plan is a string or hierarchy of articulatory tasks specified in a context-free way. Each articulatory task requires a different coalition of cooperating muscles—a coordinative structure. Within a coordinative structure the muscles are restricted in the ways they can operate (from the range of possible movements) with only a few degrees of freedom left to the system. These restrictions (combined with the degrees of freedom) guarantee a particular kind of result (e.g. lip closure). That result is obtained whatever the initial states of the individual muscles or the external conditions. Both model-referenced control and a mass-spring account of movement control are essential aspects of coordinative-structures theory. Thus, the elementary articulatory elements of a coordinative structure are mass-spring systems, but they are joined together to operate as a whole that can perform a particular phonetic task. Saltzman and Kelso (1987) contrast with Fowler et al. (1980) in assuming that there is a feedback mechanism, necessary for compensation to occur. Coordinative-structures theory has also been developed into a broader phonological theory—articulatory phonology (see Browman & Goldstein, 1991, 1992, for a review).

As outlined earlier, there are a number of theories of motor speech control, which differ both in the nature of the commands and in their modelling of motor execution. There increasingly seems to be a consensus that whereas speech motor commands (phonetic plans) are relatively invariant, the executive motor system can take care of adaptations to the immediate context. Most theorists also seem to consider the syllable to be the unit of speech motor execution. Levelt (1989) concludes "a syllable ... is a production unit designed for optimal co-articulation of its segments. As a consequence, a maximum of perceptual distinctiveness is produced by means of a minimal amount of articulatory effort" (p.454).

Levelt (1992; Levelt & Wheeldon, 1994) favours a theory based on "gestural scores" (Browman & Goldstein, 1991) as the phonetic representations of syllables accessed from their mental syllabary. These abstract gestural scores specify the task to be performed (not the motor patterns to be executed) on five tiers (glottal and velar system, tongue body and tip, lips). The gestural score specifies that, for example, the lips should be closed but not how this should be achieved. Levelt and Wheeldon (1994) suggest that the computation of how the task is to be achieved is performed by "a coordinative motor system that involves feedback from the articulators" (p.245) similar to that proposed by Salzman and Kelso (1987).

MONITORING AND FEEDBACK

Having discussed how speakers might produce a word, there is one final aspect of speaking that plays a vital role—monitoring of how well what we are saying matches what we intended to say. Speakers monitor and often self-correct almost any aspect of their speech from context to grammar to properties of phonological form and articulation. There are two major classes of monitoring theory which were mentioned briefly earlier. These are editor theories, which put the monitor outside the language production system, and connectionist theories, where the mechanism for error detection is internal to the language production system. Both theories have their strengths and both are hard to disprove.

Connectionist theories have no mechanisms external to the speech production apparatus that are involved in speech control. The system's self-control is due to the same inherent feedback that occurs during the process of speech production. That is, the bottom-up priming from lower-level nodes to higher-level nodes in the network. Although they do not have editors, Stemberger (1985) and Dell (1986, 1989) do not exclude other types of feedback (e.g. through the comprehension system). Errors arise when the "wrong" node becomes activated, as described earlier. Errors will be detected by backward priming to the conceptual level. Thus if "red" becomes more highly activated than the target "green", activation will spread back to the conceptual level, where the concept node RED will have an increase in activation. This is then (somehow) "perceived" as erroneous and corrective action (as yet undefined) can begin.

Editor theories involve feeding the result of speech production through an editor or monitor that is external to the production system. This device can be distributed, in that it can check "in-between" results at different levels of processing. The major problem with this kind of account is reduplication. That is, if an editor is to evaluate the output of a particular level of processing, then it needs to incorporate the same kind of knowledge as that processing level.

In contrast, the editor proposed by Motley, Camden, and Baars (1982) could not inspect intermediary output but only pre-articulatory output, with editing following phonological encoding. One source of evidence for a pre-articulatory editor comes from partially intercepted errors. For example, "to the left side of the purple disk is a v- a horizontal line" (Levelt, 1989, p.474). In this correction, execution of the erroneous word "vertical" had begun before speech could be halted, but too little of the word was pronounced for the error to have been detected via the external loop (audition). However, this editor, despite not being distributed, would still seem necessarily to involve reduplication.

Butterworth (1981, 1992) advocates a monitoring system that avoids reduplication by running through a process (e.g. lexical retrieval) twice and comparing output. This can occur at various levels (e.g semantic lexicon, phonological output lexicon). Another way to avoid reduplication is to equate the editor with the language comprehension system. Thus, internal feedback loops will pass the output of the speech production system to the speech comprehension system for evaluation without it being articulated (as well as being able to evaluate speech after it is uttered by listening to one's own output). Some sort of subvocal speech rehearsal loop is a standard and central constituent of models of working memory (e.g. Baddeley, 1983) but until relatively recently there has been little attempt to specify the relationship between this loop and lexical theories (Franklin, 1989a; Howard & Franklin, 1987, 1990; Monsell, 1987). Monsell (1987) addresses the issue of the level(s) at which any feedback loop(s) might operate.

Monsell (1987) describes data from a series of priming experiments which demonstrated that silent phonological generation primes later auditory identification. Auditory Lexical Decision was not only primed by hearing the word and being required to access its meaning, but was also primed when subjects were given a description of the meaning of a word and were required to either silently generate, say, or mouthe the word. They concluded that generation of a phonological word form for output (as in the latter experiments) activates entries in whatever lexicon is used for auditory lexical decision. This could be either because a common phonological lexicon is involved in both input and output (Allport, 1985; Funnell & Allport, 1987) or because the output form is fed into the input analysis pathway by means of a feedback loop. Silent mouthing facilitated auditory lexical decision as much as saying the word aloud and more than the silent generation of phonology. The common lexicon account would not appear to be able to readily explain this observed difference in the strength of the priming effect. Monsell (1987) suggests that generation of a relatively peripheral articulatory code (as in mouthing a word) produces a qualitatively different and more substantial activation of the input pathway than the mere generation of phonology. This leads to his proposal of at least two different feedback loops from output to input.

Gipson (1986) corroborates this finding, demonstrating that tasks that required silent generation of a word's phonology (from a written pseudohomophone—a nonword that sounds like a real word, such as BRANE) facilitated accuracy of later auditory identification of that word in noise (within a list). However, tasks that involved saying the number of syllables in a printed word or in the name of a pictured object did not prime later auditory recognition of the word. This is despite the fact that syllable judgements are assumed also to involve generation of phonology (although some authors might argue that access to the complete phonological form was not necessary for accurate performance). Monsell (1987) explains this lack of priming in terms of the requirement to speak a word other than the target word (the number of syllables) blocking activation of the target word's entry in an input lexicon via a feedback loop. He argues that the common lexicon account provides no obvious account of the lack of priming in this task compared to other phonology-generation tasks. Monsell also considers further evidence addressing the common lexicon issue such as dual-task studies (e.g Shallice, McLeod, & Lewis, 1985), neuropsychological evidence (e.g Bramwell, 1897/1984; Howard & Franklin, 1988), and speech error data (e.g. Fay & Cutler, 1977). As was discussed in Chapter 1, he concludes that "there seems to be no evidence positively favouring a common lexicon model, but several fragments favouring separate pathways" (Monsell, 1987, p.297).

Mouthed output has been found to have similar effects to auditory input with regard to recency and suffix effects in immediate serial recall as well as in priming. Thus, typically, the last item of an auditory sequence is better recalled than the corresponding items of a visual sequence, and this recency effect is eliminated by an irrelevant spoken suffix. Nairne and Walters (1983) and Greene and Crowder (1984) found that visually presented lists said aloud or actively (silently) mouthed produce auditory-like recency and suffix effects. However, these effects were not found when subjects were required to imagine the experimenter saying the items (Nairne & Pusen 1984). Monsell (1987) also found a similar contrast when subjects were required to recall a list of visually presented words that they also had to monitor for a rhyming pair. Although phonological coding was thus enforced, an auditory-like recency effect was observed only when the subjects were also required to mouth the words silently as they were presented. Monsell (1987) therefore adopts Crowder's (1983) proposal of two internal pathways sending information from speech-production to input-processing modules. These comprise an inner pathway, which transmits relatively abstract phonological codes, and an outer pathway, which sends information from processes determining articulatory gestures to a more peripheral mechanism for perceptual analysis of articulatory gestures (including lip-read information). Figure 3.5 shows Monsell's preferred model including these "feedback" loops, and Fig. 3.6 shows the same loops incorporated into the model developed earlier in this chapter based on Patterson and Shewell (1987), Butterworth (1992), and Levelt (1992; Levelt & Wheeldon, 1994).

SUMMARY

This chapter continued the review of current models of phonological encoding which was begun in Chapter 2. We discussed the models proposed by Levelt (1989) and Butterworth (1992), both of which explicitly incorporate phonological encoding mechanisms into models that also describe the processes by which lexical access occurs. This, of course, is also true of the model described by Dell (1986, 1989) that was described in Chapter 2. Although the precise details of these three models differ, they all incorporate some kind of "slot-and-filler" mechanism to spell out or unpack the phonological information retrieved from the lexicon. This mechanism entails a separate spell-out of the syllable (and stress) pattern of the word, which then is filled by the appropriate segments from the segmental representation of that word. This comprises the phonetic address that retrieves the phonetic plan for the articulation of that word (or syllable), which can then be held in a buffer prior to articulation.

We then discussed how phonological encoding procedures might be combined with another model of lexical access—Morton's logogen model.

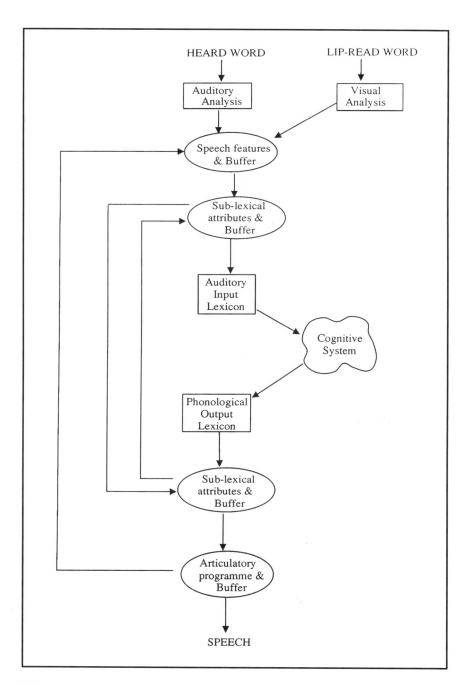

FIG. 3.5. Monsell's model of speech comprehension and production, incorporating two "internal" feedback loops (adapted from Monsell, 1987).

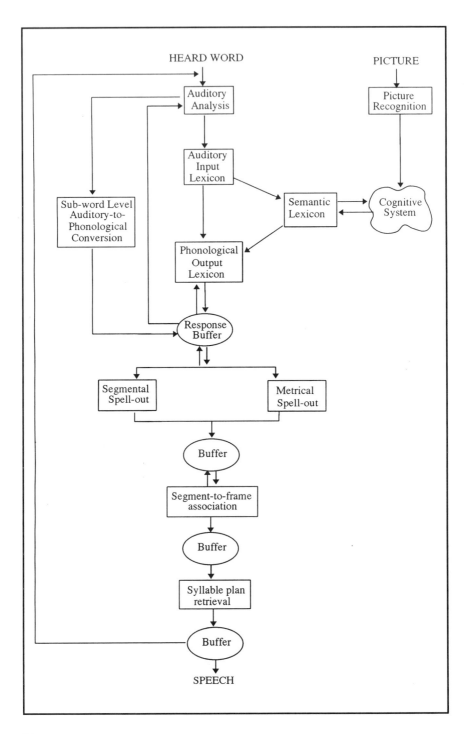

FIG. 3.6. (opposite) Composite model of single word production. This model incorporates two levels of lexical representation—the semantic lexicon (equivalent to a lemma level) and the phonological output lexicon (equivalent to a lexeme level). Subsequent to retrieval of the phonological form various phonological encoding procedures are implemented (as suggested by Levelt, 1989, 1998, and Butterworth, 1992), culminating in the retrieval of syllable-based articulatory plans. Two feedback loops are incorporated, as suggested by Monsell, 1987. No claims are made regarding the nature of the auditory comprehension or picture-recognition processes depicted.

We concluded that phonological encoding procedures should be added subsequent to the level of the response buffer (where the stored phonological representation is held after retrieval). In Fig. 3.3 we gave a diagrammatic representation of a possible architecture for a model that combined the logogen model with phonological encoding procedures. However, we noted that as there seems to be strong psycho-linguistic evidence for two levels of lexical access (semantic/lemma and phonological form), an adaptation of the logogen model to include an additional lemma or lexical-semantic level was preferable. This resulted in the model in Fig. 3.4, which was similar to Butterworth's (1989, 1992) model with the addition of a level of syllable plan retrieval as suggested by Levelt (1989).

This model is further elaborated by discussion of a "late" buffer for the products of phonological encoding, which is linked to "feedback" routines used for monitoring of speech production by the comprehension system. The final composite model is sketched in Fig. 3.6. The majority of the (speech production) components of this model are those that have been clearly motivated from the experimental evidence described in Chapters 1 to 3. However, there are a number of points on which the evidence remains unclear—particularly in terms of the nature of the spread of activation within the model. The figure here shows my preference for a purely feed-forward spread of activation from the lexical semantic level to the phonological form (see also Harley, 1993). However, this may prove to be mistaken and there may be two-way interaction between these levels. This model also does not show anything about the nature of lexical access itself—are there distributed or localist representations, are there cascades throughout the system or "thresholds", and can "partial" information be accessed? What seems clear is that whatever mechanism is used to access the phonological form, this is then processed using a serial slot-and-filler mechanism of some kind. This model also incorporates "buffers" at almost every level of processing, whereas only two have been motivated in the text—the "response buffer" and the final pre-articulatory buffer. The other buffers may prove unnecessary—their role here being to "hold" information at any stage of processing while it is being acted on. For example, in the case of the buffer for segment-to-frame association, where the "spelt-out" phonemes and their metrical frames are held during the insertion of segments into frames, perhaps the response buffer can perform this role with spell-out occurring "on-line".

This model is clearly not theory-neutral in a number of key respects (indeed I would argue that a theory-neutral model is impossible to sketch given the current diversity in model architectures). The final example of this is that it incorporates separate input and output lexicons and uses feedback loops to the input processes to monitor output.

However flawed this sketch may prove to be, it should at least provide an *aide memoire* for the reader of the key levels of processing involved in spoken word production, which will be of particular use when discussing patterns of acquired speech production disorders in the chapters that follow.

PART TWO

The breakdown of spoken word production in aphasia

Introduction

In Part 1, we discussed theories of spoken word production. These theories were mostly developed with the aim of explaining various patterns of speech errors produced by normal subjects, and evaluated in terms of their ability to account for these patterns. However, some authors (e.g. Butterworth, 1989, 1992; Monsell, 1987) have also used neuropsychological data as support for one theoretical account as opposed to another. This is a key role; I would argue that a model of language processing cannot be considered adequate unless it can account for patterns of impaired performance in addition to the "normal" speech error and experimental data. The use of neuropsychological data in this way rests on the assumption that patterns of language breakdown reflect the structure of the normal language system. Thus, "the differences between normal language mechanisms and the set of language mechanisms available to aphasics are [considered to be] subtractive—that is, the aphasic is simply lacking some of the components available to normal language speakers, rather than inventing new ones" (Saffran, 1982, p.318). Although this assumption is by no means universally accepted, it is the basis of the cognitive neuropsychological approach and as such implicit in much of what follows (see Shallice, 1988, for a detailed debate of this issue). This assumption also leads to models of spoken word production increasingly being used to determine the loci of deficits in the spoken word production of aphasic people (e.g. Howard & Orchard-Lisle, 1984; Kay & Ellis, 1987).

In Part 2, we aim to review the literature concerning deficits of spoken word production in aphasia in relation to the theoretical issues raised in the previous chapters. In the past much of the literature has been concerned with relating the type and cause of naming breakdown to aphasic syndrome categories (such as Broca's, Wernicke's, or conduction aphasia). The difficulty with this approach is that a syndrome label is not necessarily a reliable indicator of the locus of difficulty in name retrieval. Thus, in "group studies which end up combining patients with different loci of impairment into the same group ... The resulting mean values for each group become both uninterpretable and uninformative" (Ellis, Kay, & Franklin, 1992). Therefore the emphasis here will be on those studies that primarily involve investigation of a single case or a series of single cases, which enable a detailed examination of patterns of deficit.

GENERAL FACTORS AFFECTING APHASIC NAMING

One motivation for studying disorders of naming and word retrieval in aphasia is to understand better the psycholinguistic processes involved (e.g. Morton, 1985). Two general approaches can be distinguished. One focuses on the types of errors aphasic subjects make in naming tasks (e.g. Butterworth, Howard, & McLoughlin, 1984; Howard & Orchard-Lisle, 1984) and will be discussed further in the chapters that follow. However, although useful, this approach suffers from the disadvantage that apparently similar errors may have different causes (see Shallice, 1988).

The second approach is described by Shallice (1988) as the "critical-variable approach". This seeks to establish the variables that affect the probability that a task will be correctly performed by an aphasic subject, and to draw from this conclusions about the levels at which the processes are breaking down (e.g. Gardner, 1974; Rochford & Williams, 1962, 1965). It has been suggested that a variety of different factors may play a role, including frequency, familiarity, word length, age of acquisition, operativity, imageability, and concreteness. (See Chapter 1 for a summary of the effects of these variables on nonaphasic subjects' performance.)

Word frequency
Of all the variables studied, it was the effects of word frequency that initially appeared to be one of the most stable and replicable of results from studies of groups of aphasic subjects. Newcombe, Oldfield, and

Wingfield (1965) found a linear relationship between the latency of correct naming and the logarithm of the picture name's frequency for aphasics, as there was for normal subjects. This has been confirmed by a number of studies that have found a relationship between naming accuracy and word frequency for aphasic subjects (Butterworth et al., 1984; Goodglass, Hyde, & Blumstein, 1969; Howard, Patterson, Franklin, Morton, & Orchard-Lisle, 1984; Howes, 1964; Rochford & Williams, 1965).

Nevertheless, despite these seemingly robust effects, not every aphasic subject exhibits an effect of frequency on word production (e.g. HW, Caramazza & Hillis, 1990; Howard et al., 1984). Indeed, Nickels and Howard (1995b) studied 27 aphasic subjects and found that frequency was a significant predictor of performance for only two subjects (when the effects of other variables with which frequency is correlated were taken into account). This seems in stark contrast to the robust effects reported elsewhere. They suggest that the results reported previously have been based on the results of experiments where frequency was confounded with other variables (especially length, e.g. Butterworth et al., 1984), and no attempt was made to determine the amount of variance accounted for by frequency alone (by use of multiple regression analysis, for example). Nickels and Howard do not claim that frequency cannot or does not have an effect on aphasic naming but simply that these effects are neither as common nor as robust as had been assumed in the past.

The presence of an effect of frequency on spoken word production has been used by some authors as support for their hypotheses regarding the nature of the deficit for a particular aphasic subject (e.g. Ellis, Miller, & Sin, 1983; Kay & Ellis, 1987). However, the difficulty with this approach is that there is very little consensus as to precisely where frequency effects originate. Thus, Shallice (1987) argues that frequency is a property of the semantic system, whereas Ellis et al. (1983) suggest that frequency effects may be located in the links between semantics and phonology (see also McCann & Besner, 1987; Vitkovitch & Humphreys, 1991). Both of these contrast with Morton (1970; Ellis et al., 1983), who argues that frequency effects result from variation in the thresholds of the lexical representations (logogens). This is functionally equivalent to Dell's (1986, 1989) argument for variable resting levels of activation for the word-level nodes. In view of the variety of loci proposed it seems unwise to place too great a reliance on frequency effects as support for a particular locus of a deficit, except in distinguishing pre-lexical access and post-lexical access deficits (as most theories do agree that frequency effects in production are localised at or before lexical access occurs, as discussed in Chapter 1).

Familiarity

As was discussed in Chapter 1, Gernsbacher (1984) argues that it is "experiential familiarity" and not printed word frequency that is the important variable, particularly given the unreliability of objective frequency measures for low frequency items. Funnell and Sheridan (1992) also argue for the importance of familiarity in predicting the naming success of an aphasic subject, suggesting that it is not sufficient to control for frequency alone.

It is important to note, however, that the nature of "familiarity" differs between studies. Gernsbacher (1984) asked her subjects to rate how familiar they were with each of a list of written words, and seemed to have given no guidance regarding in what sense "familiar" should be interpreted. This contrasts with Funnell and Sheridan (1992), who used the ratings of Snodgrass and Vanderwart (1980), who define familiarity as "the degree to which you come into contact with or think about the concept". They, therefore, require subjects to rate pictures on the basis of "how usual or unusual the object is in your realm of experience". Finally, Brown and Watson (1987) use the ratings from Gilhooly and Logie (1980), which are rated on the basis of how often a subject believes he or she sees, hears or uses that word.

Given the variety of types of rating employed, it is difficult to draw any conclusions regarding the precise nature of familiarity. Nevertheless, it does correlate highly with frequency of use (both spoken and written word frequency; Brown and Watson, 1987), and may therefore reflect subjective frequency. It is clear that printed word frequency counts should not be the only measure of frequency taken into account when studying naming (as has been common in the past), and that some measure of familiarity can provide useful insights into naming and naming breakdown.

Age of acquisition

Furthermore, both frequency and familiarity correlate highly with the age at which children learn words, and Rochford and Williams (1965) suggest that word-frequency effects in aphasic naming may in fact be attributable to rated age of acquisition (AoA). In a study of 18 aphasic subjects, Feyereisen, van der Borght, and Seron (1988) show that rated AoA, rated picture familiarity, and word frequency are all good predictors of naming accuracy, but all three variables are highly intercorrelated. When either familiarity or AoA are taken as covariates, there is still a significant effect of frequency, suggesting that there is an effect of frequency independent of AoA. Unfortunately, Feyereisen et al. do not test for an effect of AoA when frequency is taken as a covariate.

Thus, these data do not demonstrate unequivocally whether AoA or frequency is the critical variable affecting performance.

However, Hirsh and Ellis (1994) present a single-case study of an aphasic subject, NP, whose naming was influenced by the AoA of the targets even when word frequency, imageability, and length were taken into account. Similarly, Nickels and Howard (1995b) found that AoA was a significant predictor of naming performance for eight of their aphasic subjects (even when frequency, word length, imageability, etc. are taken into account). Hirsh and Ellis favour an account that places AoA effects at the level of phonological word-form retrieval (like, for example, Gilhooly & Watson, 1981, for normal subjects). Nickels and Howard note that there is a variety of factors that may determine the age at which children acquire words (for a review, see Markman, 1989). For instance: names for basic-level objects are easier to acquire (Rosch et al., 1976); names for parts of objects are harder to acquire than those for whole discrete objects (Markman & Wachtel, 1988); young children avoid using names for items that are difficult to articulate (Schwartz & Leonard, 1982). Some or all of these factors may also be important for aphasic word retrieval. They suggest that it may be this common causation that is responsible for the correlation between naming performance and rated AoA, and that under this account it would not seem sensible to seek a single locus for AoA effects on the accuracy of aphasic word retrieval.

Imageability and concreteness

Differences in imageability and/or concreteness are also known to affect aphasic performance in a number of tasks. Thus, in comprehension, Franklin (1989b) demonstrates that many aphasic subjects perform worse on comprehension tasks with abstract/low imageability words than concrete/high imageability words. Additionally, the effect of imageability/concreteness on the reading aloud of deep dyslexic subjects is well documented (Coltheart, Patterson, & Marshall, 1980) and similar effects of imageability/concreteness can be found in word repetition (Howard & Franklin, 1988).

Marcel and Patterson (1978) found that for normal subjects visual word recognition was affected by imageability but not by concreteness. This pattern was also found to be true for some aphasic subjects by both Marcel and Patterson (1978) and Richardson (1975). They conclude that imageability effects are semantic in nature and this has been generally accepted as the locus of these effects.

Goodglass et al. (1969) demonstrated that some aphasic subjects show an unusual reliance on concrete words in their spontaneous speech. However, little work has been done on imageability/concreteness effects in picture naming, partly due to the fact that the range of imageability/concreteness that can occur within a set of picture names is inevitably restricted, as picturable items are necessarily highly imageable. Nevertheless, Nickels and Howard (1995b) find significant effects of imageability on picture naming for two subjects and concreteness for one subject, even when the other variable (concreteness/imageability) is included as a covariate. In every case aphasic subjects are better able to name items higher in imageability/concreteness; no aphasic subject has yet been reported who shows the reverse pattern for picture naming. However, Warrington (1981) describes a subject (CAV) with "concrete word dyslexia" (he was better at reading abstract words than concrete words), and two subjects have been described who had worse comprehension for concrete words than abstract words (AB, Warrington, 1975; SBY, Warrington & Shallice, 1984; see also a recent report by Breedin, Saffran, & Coslett, 1994).

Operativity

Gardner (1973, 1974) presented evidence for the importance of a factor he calls "operativity". He showed that aphasic subjects were somewhat better at naming the items that he designated "operative" (manipulable, discrete, firm, and experienced by several sensory modalities—e.g. book, screwdriver, finger) than those he considered "figurative" (hard to grasp and normally only visually experienced—e.g. wall, cloud, hip) even when word frequency was accounted for.

The examples demonstrate that this is not a well-defined concept, and it is not clear that operativity has an independent effect. Indeed, Feyereisen et al. (1988) found that although operativity significantly affected aphasic naming performance, when AoA and familiarity were introduced as covariates there was no longer a significant effect. The effects of operativity also disappeared when the rated degree of tactile experience of the object was introduced as a covariate. Feyereisen at al. conclude that frequency and AoA are better predictors of aphasic performance than operativity. However, as in the case of familiarity, these results are made more difficult to interpret due to slight differences in the definitions of operativity used across the two studies (Feyereisen et al. defined operativity as "the extent to which one can act upon or with the item").

Nickels and Howard (1995b) also studied the effects of operativity on aphasic naming, using ratings based on a definition derived directly from Gardner. Their findings failed to support Feyereisen et al.'s conclusion that there was no effect of operativity on aphasic naming independent of that of age of acquisition. Indeed, 7 of their 27 aphasic subjects showed significant effects of operativity even when age of acquisition, familiarity, frequency, and other variables were taken into account. They argue, however, that it is unclear what the origin of the operativity effect might be, suggesting that it is vital to tease apart the relative importance of the different dimensions involved in the rating (e.g. manipulability, firmness to the touch, availability to several sensory modalities). For example, if the key aspect of the rating is the availability to a number of different sensory modalities, it may be that the semantic representations of high-operativity objects are distributed across a number of sensory modalities, and as a result are less susceptible to localised cortical damage.

Howard, Best, Bruce, and Gatehouse (1995) investigated the contribution of the different facets of operativity in a group of 18 aphasic subjects. Overall operativity effects were rare but the elements of operativity each had effects for some of the aphasic subjects, but in different directions. "Availability to multiple senses" and "separability from the surrounding context" tended to aid naming performance, whereas highly manipulable items were named less well. Howard et al. discuss the relevance of these results for models such as that of Allport (1985), which predicts that items that are experienced by multiple sensory modalities will be more resistant to localised brain damage. They suggest that their results provide only weak support for such a claim.

Animacy

Many aphasic subjects show better naming and comprehension of inanimate than animate items (e.g. animals, plants, fruit, vegetables, and food). The majority of these have recovered from *Herpes simplex encephalitis* (e.g. De Renzi & Lucchelli, 1994; Sartori & Job, 1988; Silveri & Gainotti, 1988; Warrington & Shallice, 1984), although Laiacona, Barbarotto, and Capitani (1993) describe an aphasic subject showing such a pattern who had suffered closed head injury.

Funnell and Sheridan (1992) demonstrated that in their aphasic subject a perceived animacy effect was due to a confound with picture familiarity (see also Stewart, Parkin, & Hunkin, 1992). However, Laiacona et al. (1993) and Farah, McMullen, and Meyer (1991) have both demonstrated that even when effects of familiarity, frequency, and visual complexity have been partialled out, there can still be a significant deficit for animate items. Nevertheless, Howard et al. (1995) suggest that further confounds also need to be considered (e.g. word length, imageability, age of acquisition, and operativity).

Fewer cases have been reported where aphasic subjects are better at naming animate than inanimate items. Warrington and McCarthy

(1983, 1987) report such an effect in comprehension for two subjects, and Sacchett and Humphreys (1992) describe a subject who was also more impaired in naming inanimate items (even though these are more familiar and less complex than the animate items). Howard et al. (1995) found that if only word frequency and familiarity are controlled (as is common in many studies), a substantial proportion of their group of aphasic subjects were better at naming animate items. However, when other variables were also controlled (including word length, imageability, age of acquisition), only one aphasic subject continued to show a significant effect. Howard et al. show that the animacy effect for this subject could be wholly attributed to an advantage for items known to multiple senses rather than a true category effect. Thus, animacy is another variable that may prove to be a complex combination of subfactors rather than a unitary variable.

Word length
Apart from frequency, the other variable that has shown relatively consistent effects on aphasic naming performance is word length (number of syllables or phonemes). Most authors have found that where there are length effects, aphasic subjects are less accurate with longer words (e.g. Caplan, 1987; Ellis et al., 1983; Goodglass, Kaplan, Weintraub, & Ackerman, 1976; cf. Dubois, Hecaen, Angelergues, Maufras de Chatelier, & Marcie, 1964). Once again, however, not every aphasic subject shows an effect of word length on naming (e.g. EST, Kay & Ellis, 1987). Moreover, Best (1995) has recently described an aphasic subject who shows a reverse length effect—he is better at naming longer words.

Most authors agree that length effects are likely to originate from procedures subsequent to lexical access. There are two main classes of theories: those that propose a deficit in phonological encoding (e.g. Caplan, 1987) and those proposing a buffering deficit (e.g. Miller & Ellis, 1987). A deficit in phonological encoding could predict effects in terms of either phonemes or syllables, depending on whether the syllable is viewed as a unit of phonological encoding or not. A buffering deficit comprises a problem in maintaining a representation in a buffer store. This could be a deficit at any level, depending on the location of buffers within the particular model. These predictions will be examined more closely in Chapter 6.

Summary
It is clear that a variety of factors may play a role in determining how hard an aphasic subject might find the retrieval of a picture name. As many of these factors are strongly intercorrelated, it is difficult to disentangle their effects (Gilhooly & Watson, 1981). Indeed, as already

mentioned, until recently many studies suffered from the flaw of having failed to take account of the intercorrelations between variables. Thus, some of the significant effects found may be due to the confounding of intercorrelated variables and may not in fact be independent effects of the specific variable under scrutiny. This is illustrated in the study by Feyereisen et al. (1988) described earlier, where operativity was not found to have a significant effect independent of AoA or familiarity. This has clear methodological implications—it is essential to use sets of stimuli matched on these variables (often a difficult task, given how highly some of the variables intercorrelate) and/or regression statistics, in order to discriminate between the effects of the different variables.

Nickels and Howard (1994) argue that it is not sufficient to examine the effects of variables on correct responses, but that the same analyses should be performed on each error type. They argue that as aphasic subjects frequently produce errors of more than one type, an investigation of the effects of variables affecting correct responses alone may confuse independent effects on each error type. They give the (hypothetical) example of a subject who produces semantic errors when naming low imageability stimuli and phonological errors when naming low frequency stimuli. They suggest that the domain of the effects of a particular variable can only be established by studying their effects on individual error types. Nickels (1995) demonstrates that the production of semantic errors tends to be influenced by imageability (see also Nickels & Howard, 1994) and phonological errors by frequency and/or word length.

It is not yet possible to attribute unequivocally the effects of many of the variables discussed earlier to different levels of processing. Indeed, some variables may (as we have argued) turn out to be effects of combinations of subfactors that have independent effects on representations and processing. Alternatively, other variables may have effects at multiple levels of processing (e.g. word length may influence processing at a number of different points in phonological encoding). The nature and extent of the effects of variables on performance will also vary with the architecture and processing assumptions of a particular theoretical model (see the discussion in Chapter 4 and Nickels, 1995).

LEVELS OF BREAKDOWN IN APHASIC NAMING

Benson (1979) distinguished two types of anomia—"semantic anomia" and "word selection anomia". This distinction has been influential in discussions of the breakdown of word retrieval in aphasia (anomia), which have often centered on two papers, Howard and Orchard-Lisle

(1984) and Kay and Ellis (1987). Each of these papers provides a detailed single-case study of an aphasic subject who has impaired picture naming. Ellis et al. (1992; Ellis & Young, 1988) use these two subjects, JCU (Howard & Orchard-Lisle, 1984) and EST (Kay & Ellis, 1987), to illustrate the division between semantic and phonological (word selection) levels of impairment in naming.

The discussion of spoken word production disorders in aphasia that follows will also take this division as its starting point. It was made clear from the outset that this book does not purport to discuss in detail the nature of semantic representations, but is focusing on the processes involved in lexical retrieval and word production subsequent to this level. The same principle holds here in the discussion of aphasic naming impairments. We will not dwell in detail on the nature of semantic breakdown except in the most general sense—that an aphasic subject may have a semantic impairment (alluding briefly to more general semantic impairments with regard, for example, to semantic dementia). Notably category-specific semantic disorders (that is, those subjects who show deficits confined to certain categories of words) will not be directly addressed (except for those disorders specific to word production, which will be discussed in Chapter 5). For example, one of Warrington and Shallice's (1984) subjects, JBR, was markedly better at comprehending and producing words describing inanimate objects than those referring to living things. (For further discussion see Funnell & Sheridan, 1992; Shallice, 1988, Chapter 12). Nor will the issue regarding single versus multiple semantic systems be addressed. This is hotly debated, with some authors proposing that there is a modality-independent semantic mechanism common to all lexical processes (e.g. Hillis, Rapp, Romani, & Caramazza, 1990; Riddoch, Humphreys, Coltheart, & Funnell, 1988) and others distinguishing between different modality-specific semantic systems: e.g. (minimally) visual and verbal semantics (but possibly, tactile, olfactory, etc.; e.g. Shallice, 1987, 1988). I will not enter into this debate, on the aforementioned grounds that the aim of this book is to focus on lexical processes. However, we will follow many models (but not Morton's logogen model) in drawing a basic distinction between lexical semantic representations and more general "conceptual" semantics (for some authors this may be subserved by the level of structural descriptions in visual processing, e.g. Hillis et al., 1990).

Thus, Chapter 4 focuses on the production of semantic errors in aphasic subjects, their causes, and factors affecting their production. This is followed by a discussion of disorders of lexical retrieval in Chapter 5, and phonological errors, phonological deficits and beyond in Chapter Six.

CHAPTER FOUR

Semantic deficits and semantic errors

OVERVIEW

A striking symptom of aphasia is the substitution of a word by one that is similar in meaning—a semantically related response. This may occur even with what seem like the most simple of targets—"chair" may be produced when aiming for "table". Some aphasic people are immediately aware of their error (and may reject the response with a shake of the head or frustrated "NO!"), whereas others seem unaware that anything is wrong. The underlying cause of the semantically related response (which, as a short-cut, we shall call a semantic error) is often a deficit in the semantic system. In the literature the analysis of a patient's deficit has frequently been described within the logogen model (see Chapter 1). This model does not discriminate between central "conceptual" semantics and lexical semantics, and therefore a possible dissociation between deficits in the two systems is frequently lost.

The chapter starts with some case studies of patients who produce semantically related responses. It begins with a discussion centred around the patient "JCU" described by Howard and Orchard-Lisle (1984) (SEMANTIC ANOMIA). This leads on to consideration of patients with profound semantic memory impairments, often with a progressive disorder (e.g. semantic dementia) (DISORDERS OF SEMANTIC MEMORY). These patients show deficits that are far more severe than the majority of subjects that have an acute onset of aphasia (as a result of stroke or head injury) and are providing insights into the nature of language processing when semantic representations are lost over time.

The emphasis of the chapter then changes, with the focus turning to semantic *errors* (rather than semantic *deficits*) with a discussion of the level of breakdown that might result in these errors (WHERE DO SEMANTIC ERRORS COME FROM?). Semantic errors in word production frequently co-occur with the same kinds of errors in comprehension (for example, pointing to a picture of a chair when asked to point to the picture of a table). We begin with a review of the studies that have examined these co-occurrences (THE RELATIONSHIP BETWEEN SEMANTIC ERRORS IN COMPREHENSION AND PRODUCTION) and follow it with one study that reports two patients who produce semantic errors in spoken naming but do not make these errors in comprehension (OUTPUT SEMANTIC ERRORS). This section then turns to examine what influences the likelihood of a semantic error occuring (FACTORS AFFECTING THE PRODUCTION OF SEMANTIC ERRORS) and the nature of the errors themselves (SUBDIVISIONS OF SEMANTIC ERRORS). We look at different types of error that may occur and methodological issues regarding the classification of semantic errors (versus circumlocutions or semantic rejections). Finally, we discuss in detail the origins of semantic errors within each of the major classes of theoretical models (MORE ON THEORETICAL ACCOUNTS OF THE PRODUCTION OF SEMANTIC ERRORS).

"SEMANTIC" ANOMIA: JCU (HOWARD & ORCHARD-LISLE, 1984)

Howard and Orchard-Lisle's patient, JCU, was a "global" aphasic with limited comprehension and spontaneous speech that was restricted to recurrent utterances. Her picture naming was extremely poor, with only 5/30 items correctly named in the naming section of the Western Aphasia Battery (Kertesz & Poole, 1974). However, when given phonemic cues (i.e. the first sound of a target; e.g. /t/ for tiger) she correctly named a further 18 items (of a possible 25). Howard and Orchard-Lisle investigated in detail the effect of these phonemic cues on JCU's naming and found that not only were correct cues highly effective, but also that JCU could be induced to make a semantic error when given the initial phoneme of a coordinate of the target as a cue. (For example, when JCU was shown a picture of a tiger she was given /l/ as a cue, which was derived from the coordinate, lion.) Howard and Orchard-Lisle argued that this effect of "miscueing" suggested that the semantic information used in addressing the output lexicon was sometimes incomplete, resulting in activation of semantically related items in addition to the target.

Further evidence for a semantic deficit came from the observation that whereas JCU spontaneously rejected 86% of her responses when they were unrelated to the target, she only rejected 24% of her semantic errors. This was investigated in further detail by asking JCU to judge whether a spoken word was the correct name for a picture. She correctly accepted 98% of correct names and rejected 99% of unrelated names, but incorrectly accepted 55% of her semantic errors (produced by miscued naming) as correct names. Howard and Orchard-Lisle conclude that JCU's semantic errors in comprehension and production can be accounted for by hypothesising that she was only able to use an incomplete semantic representation for both tasks.

Hillis et al. (1990) describe a patient, KE, who was also described as having a semantic deficit. This impairment resulted in semantic errors in all single-word production tasks, independent of modality. Thus, when attempting to orally name a picture of ARM, KE made the semantic error "finger", and for the same stimulus he produced "leg" when attempting written naming, "ear" when reading aloud, and "hand" when writing to dictation. KE also made a high proportion of semantic errors in auditory and written word-picture matching tasks.

Although Howard and Orchard-Lisle's patient, JCU, was impaired in verbal comprehension tasks (with both written and spoken stimuli), she performed normally in a nonverbal picture-association task. Butterworth et al. (1984) argue that this pattern cannot be explained in terms of a single, modality-independent, semantic or conceptual deficit within a unitary semantic or conceptual system (as found in the logogen model). However, within models that propose "partially independent modality-specific semantic systems" (Warrington, 1975) this pattern can be accounted for by a deficit within one (verbal) semantic system but intact functioning of other (visual) semantic system(s). Within Butterworth's (1989) "semantic lexicon" model a deficit at the level of the semantic lexicon with unimpaired semantic/conceptual representations would also give JCU's pattern of impairments.

Thus, JCU's deficit can be considered a lexical-semantic deficit; however, there are other patients who show similar patterns of deficit (semantic errors in comprehension and production) who have more general semantic deficits. These patients are impaired not only on semantic tasks involving written or spoken words, but also on tasks solely consisting of nonverbal material. An example of an assessment designed to test semantics nonverbally is Howard and Patterson's (1992) Pyramids and Palm Trees Test. In this assessment, subjects are required to choose which of two coordinate pictures (e.g. a pine tree and a palm tree) is semantically associated to a stimulus picture (e.g. a pyramid). It is argued that consistent correct performance is only possible if the pictures are correctly recognised and full semantic information about them is retrieved. Nickels and Howard (1994) used the Pyramids and Palm Trees Test with a group of eight patients who produced semantic errors in naming and had impaired verbal comprehension. Of this group, three patients performed within normal limits on the task, suggesting an impairment of lexical-semantics with a sparing of semantic information for nonverbal material. The remaining five patients all performed outside the normal range (although above chance) and could therefore be described as having a more general semantic deficit. Nevertheless, none of these patients could be said to have a gross conceptual deficit; they all functioned appropriately in the real world, recognising and using objects appropriately (they were not agnosic). However, patients have been described with more severe deficits in semantic knowledge, as will be discussed in the next section.

DISORDERS OF SEMANTIC MEMORY

The term semantic memory is generally applied to the component of long-term memory that contains knowledge of objects, facts, and concepts as well as words (Tulving, 1972; equivalent to the general nonverbal semantics or conceptual semantic knowledge discussed earlier). Warrington (1975) was the first to clearly define selective impairments of semantic memory in her description of three patients (AB, EM, and CR). These three patients all presented with cerebral atrophy, progressive anomia, and impaired word comprehension. Warrington demonstrated that they showed a loss of vocabulary both for comprehension and production, and also poor recognition of objects. Other aspects of language (e.g. syntax and phonology) and perceptual skills were relatively intact.

Since then, a number of patients have been reported with similar patterns of breakdown and described as having semantic memory impairments. These have often been patients with progressive neurological conditions, although others have been reported, usually with extensive diffuse cortical damage, for example following *Herpes simplex* viral encephalitis (e.g. Sartori & Job, 1988; Warrington & Shallice, 1984). Patients with dementia of the Alzheimer type (DAT) often show this pattern of impairment (e.g. Bayles & Tomoeda, 1983; Hodges, Salmon, & Butters, 1990, 1991, 1992), although some authors argue that the deficit is one of access to information rather than a loss of semantic memory knowledge (Nebes, 1989). Additionally, in DAT there are almost always further cognitive deficits—initially deficits in episodic memory and eventually broader deficits including visuospatial and "frontal" deficits. In contrast, patients have been described with progressive deficits restricted to language, often described as progressive aphasia (e.g. Mesulam, 1982; Poeck & Luzzatti, 1988). However, Hodges, Patterson, Oxbury, and Funnell (1992) suggest the term "semantic dementia" (Snowden, Goulding, & Neary, 1989) may be more useful as it avoids assumptions about underlying pathology associated with "progressive aphasia".

Hodges et al. (1992) use the term "semantic dementia" to refer to patients with five key features:

1.   Selective impairment of semantic memory causing severe anomia, impaired spoken and written single-word comprehension, reduced generation of exemplars on category fluency tests, and an impoverished fund of general knowledge.
2.   Relative sparing of other components of language output and comprehension, notably syntax and phonology.
3.   Normal perceptual skills and nonverbal problem-solving abilities.
4.   Relatively preserved autobiographical and day-to-day (episodic) memory.
5.   A reading disorder with the pattern of surface dyslexia.

They describe five patients who show these features. The degree of semantic impairment is striking; for example, when asked "Have you ever been to America?", one patient, PP, replied "what's America?", and asked "What's your favourite food?", replied "food, food, I wish I knew what that was" (yet she was able to remember appointments and keep track of family events).

PP also showed a clear distinction between intact perceptual and semantic abilities. For example, she could match a photograph of an object to an unusual view of that object (e.g. photographed from above or from one end) rather than a visually similar distractor. Yet she was unable to name or identify (to verbal command) any of the same objects. She was also unable to perform an object-decision task (Humphreys & Riddoch, 1987), where subjects are required to classify drawings into real or unreal items, where the unreal items are made by combining two halves of a real item (e.g. the head of a mouse with the body of a lion). She was also at chance on the Pyramids and Palm Trees Test (see earlier); all of the aphasic subjects tested by Nickels and Howard (1994; and indeed every aphasic person I have ever tested) scored well above chance, despite scoring worse than normal controls.

On a picture-sorting test (from the Semantic Memory Test Battery, Hodges, Salmon, & Butters, 1992) all five patients were able to sort pictures accurately using the broadest distinction (living vs. man-made) but scored more than three standard deviations below the controls when using the most subtle distinction involving subordinate or attributional information (e.g. British vs. foreign animal; fierce vs. nonfierce animal). PP was also impaired on the intermediate level task—sorting into categories (e.g. household item vs. musical instrument vs. vehicle; land animal vs. sea creature vs. bird), although the other four patients were unimpaired. Thus, all these patients showed preserved superordinate category knowledge (e.g. living thing) with impairments involving subordinate/attributional knowledge (e.g. fierce or not). This pattern parallels that found in DAT (Hodges et al., 1992) and described by Warrington and her colleagues (e.g. Warrington, 1975; Warrington & Shallice, 1984).

WHERE DO SEMANTIC ERRORS COME FROM?

The relationship between semantic errors in comprehension and production

A number of authors have addressed the issue of the relationship between semantic errors in comprehension and those in production (Butterworth et al., 1984; Caramazza & Hillis, 1990; Gainotti, 1976, 1982; Gainotti, Miceli, Caltagirone, Silveri, & Masullo, 1981; Gainotti, Silveri, Villa, & Miceli, 1986). Howard, Patterson, Franklin, Morton, and Orchard-Lisle (1984) found a similar pattern with a group of aphasics to that shown by JCU: The patients erroneously accepted 49–80% of their (mostly semantic) errors as the correct name for the picture. Gainotti (1976) and Gainotti et al. (1981) found that those aphasics that produced at least one semantic error in naming made more semantic errors in comprehension.

Nickels and Howard (1994) found an exact correspondence between those aphasic patients (of a group of 15) who performed outside the normal range on tests of comprehension of high imageability words (including word-picture matching, synonym judgements) and those who produced more semantic errors than normal elderly subjects in picture-naming. Similarly, Butterworth et al. (1984) found that the incidence of semantic errors in comprehension correlated significantly with their incidence in naming, although, unlike Gainotti et al. (1981), they found no relationship between the number of neologisms produced in naming and semantic deficits in comprehension. Despite the strong relationship between comprehension impairment and naming failure, pictures that had elicited semantic errors in comprehension were no less likely to be named than those that had not. Therefore, the semantic deficit is unlikely to be the permanent loss of particular lexical items or semantic information related to these items, at least for their group of patients (for further discussion of this issue see Gainotti, 1982; Shallice, 1987, 1988). Butterworth et al. explain these results in terms of a variable inability to retrieve or use a full semantic specification in both comprehension and naming. They hypothesise that for each word, there is a semantic representation that consists of a set of "items of information" and that the patients are sometimes forced to operate on the basis of some of these items of information but not others. This semantic representation does not have to be in terms of a hierachical set of features (Collins & Quillian, 1969; Katz & Fodor, 1963); for example, Howard (1985) argues for an unordered set of propositions or meaning postulates on the basis of which a reasoning system can perform deductions and inductions.

Kremin (1986, 1988; Kremin, Beauchamp, & Perrier, 1994) is unusual in arguing that there is no necessary correspondence between deficits in comprehension and naming deficits. She reports two patients (AND, ORL) who she claims have intact naming despite comprehension deficits and uses these data to argue for a "direct, nonsemantic" route for picture naming. However, the numbers of stimuli used in testing were small and comparisons were not made using the same items. Furthermore, it is always difficult to be sure whether or not the complexity of the task requirements in the comprehension assessments may be a possible reason for failure for both these two patients and those reported later (Kremin et al., 1994; particularly as the majority of the patients were subjects with dementia). For these reasons Kremin's proposal has not been widely accepted.

"Output" semantic errors

Patients who produce semantic errors do not always have semantic deficits. Gainotti et al. (1986) contrast two types of anomia, anomia with and without lexical comprehension disorders. They found that there was no difference between the two groups in terms of severity of the naming deficit, although the groups were significantly different in terms of the numbers of semantic errors produced, with the comprehension-impaired group producing more errors. However, all the patients (except for one in the group without comprehension disorders) produced some semantic errors.

Caramazza and Hillis (1990) describe two aphasics (RGB and HW) who also made predominantly semantic errors in spoken naming. However, neither subject made semantic errors in written naming and they were argued to have unimpaired comprehension for written and spoken material. Caramazza and Hillis propose that the locus of the deficit for these patients is at the level of activating the representation of the target word in the phonological output lexicon. They suggest that semantic errors occur when the target phonological representation is inaccessible and the most highly activated semantically related item will be output instead (although they do not specify exactly how this mechanism would work).

This argument is similar to the "response blocking" explanation for semantic errors suggested by Morton and Patterson (1980). In their account, the output logogens for certain items have outputs that are blocked, or at least have greatly raised thresholds (although which items are blocked may fluctuate). The correct and full semantic code is sent from the cognitive system to the output logogen system. The appropriate output not being forthcoming, the logogen nearest to threshold activation is selected, which would be semantically (but not phonologically) related to the target. Morton and Patterson also put forward another possible explanation—the correct code is produced by the semantic system but is distorted in transmission to the output logogen system. This account would be difficult in practice to discriminate from response blocking.

Caramazza and Hillis do not attempt to distinguish the precise nature of the deficits for HW and RGB, saying "we remain silent on whether the impairment is in transmission of information from the semantic system, in access to the output lexicon, or within the output lexicon itself" (footnote 3, p.114). Perhaps the two patients actually have different deficits within this range of possibilities, for although they share some characteristics, there are ways in which they differ. For example, HW produces up to 34% phonological errors and does not show a frequency effect in the proportion of semantic errors produced, whereas the other patient, RGB, never produces phonological errors and does show a frequency effect.

Factors affecting the production of semantic errors

Nickels and Howard (1994) examined the factors affecting the production of semantic errors in picture-naming for their group of eight patients that produced more semantic errors than normal elderly controls. These patients also showed comprehension deficits, and it was hypothesised that they might be expected to show effects of semantic variables such as imageability on the production of their semantic errors. For the group as a whole there was indeed a significant effect of imageability on the production of semantic errors, such that the lower the imageability of the target the more likely it was that the patient produced a semantic error. No significant effects were found of word length (in syllables), or frequency (either written word frequency or familiarity taken as a measure of spoken word frequency). Analysis of the individual patient data identified four patients as showing the pattern of the group, a significant effect of imageability alone in predicting the occurrence of semantic errors. The remaining four patients fail to show a significant effect of imageability (and for three of these patients there is not even a trend towards an effect). Nickels and Howard suggest that the absence of an imageability effect could be consistent with a deficit at the level of Butterworth's semantic lexicon (or lexical-semantics) rather than a central semantic deficit.

However, even for those patients where imageability does have a significant effect it is by no means certain that it is actually how imageable an item is (how easily a mental image is created of that item) that affects performance. Imageability ratings may instead reflect other factors, such as "richness" of semantic representations, and it may be this, rather than imageability *per se*, that affects naming.

Using the hypothesis of "underspecification" of semantic information addressing the lexicon, Nickels and Howard suggest that imageability effects may occur in at least two ways: Either underspecification of semantic information addressing the lexicon is more likely for lower imageability targets, or the effects of underspecification may be less disruptive for higher imageability targets (which may have "richer" semantic representations and so be less harmed by partial specification; Plaut & Shallice, 1993).

However, within the logogen model, underspecification of semantic information addressing the lexicon predicts a frequency effect in the production of semantic errors—Nickels and Howard fail to find this. Therefore they provide an amended account, which predicts an interaction between frequency and imageability rather than a main effect of frequency. For two of the patients who show imageability effects there is some evidence for this interaction where low imageability low frequency stimuli are particularly prone to the production of semantic errors. The account of this interaction is as follows: Initially it is the imageability of the target that influences whether or not a full semantic specification for that word is likely to be retrieved. If the full semantic specification is retrieved, then this addresses the output lexicon and the phonological form of the target is retrieved, with spoken word frequency having no influence on the accuracy of retrieval. However, for lower imageability words underspecification of information addressing the output lexicon is more likely (for the possible reasons given earlier). This underspecification leads to the activation of a range of semantically related words in the lexicon. The word that is most highly activated will be retrieved. As higher frequency items have higher resting levels of activation (or lower thresholds), higher frequency targets are more likely to be successfully retrieved than lower frequency targets (lower frequency targets are more likely to result in a semantic error with production of a higher frequency competitor). Thus, a frequency effect is observed for low imageability targets but not for high imageability targets.

Subdivisions of semantic errors

Shared-feature and associative errors

Howard and Orchard-Lisle (1984) argue that JCU uses partial semantic information in lexical access. They predict that such a deficit would result in errors that share semantic characteristics (features) with the target (e.g. superordinates or coordinates) but not associates of the target that do not share semantic features; that is, in Coltheart's (1980) terminology "shared-feature" rather than "associative" errors. For example, the semantic specification of the target "racquet" might include characteristics such as "instrument for hitting a missile, used in ball games, parts comprise a handle and stringed head, etc.". Underspecification of this semantic representation could result in a shared-feature error such as "bat" (which would share the first two elements of the semantic specification but not the third) but should not result in associative errors such as "tennis".

As predicted, the majority of JCU's semantic errors are shared-feature errors (69%; e.g. bike → "car", rake → "shovel", toe → "foot"). This pattern is also shown by the patients in the studies by Butterworth et al. (1984) and Howard et al. (1984), for whom 85% and "the majority" (p.272) of semantic errors, respectively, are shared-feature errors (coordinates and superordinates). Nevertheless, patients also make significant numbers of associative errors (8% of semantic errors for the aphasic group tested by Butterworth et al.; 31% of JCU's semantic errors, e.g. match → "light"). These are not easily explained by the use of partial semantic information, and Howard and Orchard-Lisle (1984) are forced to suggest that these arise at a level prior to that of the use of an incomplete address to the lexicon.

Coltheart (1980) also argues that shared-feature errors and associative errors should be viewed as two distinct types of semantic error, and that these two error types may require different explanations. Thus, he proposes that shared-feature errors arise because some of the semantic features of the stimulus are lost or not used during the process of deriving response from stimulus via semantic representation (Marshall & Newcombe, 1966)—which is equivalent to the under-specification account discussed earlier. In contrast he proposes that associative semantic errors arise because the "internal lexicon" incorporates an associative network. When the lexical entry for a word is activated, the entries for other words linked to this entry by the associative network are also activated (Weigl & Bierwisch, 1970). Coltheart proposes that if the procedure by which a correct choice is made from this set of associatively related words is disabled, then the response produced would often be an associate of the stimulus (although he does not make it clear at what level this associative network is located, it could be within either the semantic system or the output lexicon). This could be an explanation for JCU's production of associative errors, and perhaps some of her unrelated word errors might also be explained in these terms, as associates of semantic errors.

However, a problem with this account is the need to propose two separate deficits to account for the occurrence of these two types of error, with so many patients seeming to show both types. Analysis of the semantic errors produced by the eight patients studied by Nickels and Howard (1994; in Nickels, 1992b) showed that every patient produced both shared-feature (between 55% and 75% of their semantic errors) and associative errors (between 20% and 42% of semantic errors). To assume two separate deficits for every patient seems unparsimonious; it would be preferable if a hypothesis could be developed that could account for the occurrence of both types of error with a single deficit.

A final point of note is the nature of "associative" errors. In experimental psychology "associative" relationships are commonly contrasted with "semantic" relationships (within category), most commonly in terms of the different priming effects observed when prime and target differ in these dimensions (see Neely, 1991, for a review). Whether or not two items are associated is determined with reference to "word association norms" (Postman & Keppel, 1970), where subjects are required to indicate the first word that comes to mind when presented with a stimulus. Some of the "associative" semantic errors produced by JCU and other aphasic patients are indeed of this type, e.g. tea → "cup" (JCU); motor → "car", free → "enterprise" (from Coltheart, 1980, table 6.1). However, other associative errors do not occur in the association norms, e.g. grass → wind, saddle → ride, saxophone → soul (from Nickels, 1992b). Huber (1981) and Rinnert and Whitaker (1973) both examined this issue, with rather different conclusions. Rinnert and Whitaker found that over 50% of aphasic semantic errors were those found in word associations given by normal subjects, whereas Huber found only around 20% in common. Huber concludes that his findings do not support Rinnert and Whitaker's conclusion that semantic paraphasias are more like than unlike word associations.

Nevertheless, this distinction should not be obscured and perhaps further analysis subdividing these "associative" errors may prove fruitful (Rinnert & Whitaker, 1973). Similarly, the subdivision of shared-feature errors into superordinate (e.g. cat – animal), coordinate (e.g. cat – dog) or (the rare) subordinate errors (e.g. cat – tabby) may also prove of interest in the analysis of semantic deficits.

Single- versus multiword responses

The focus of this chapter has been on single-word responses that are semantically related to the target—so-called "semantic errors". Most investigators distinguish between these single-word responses and multiword responses or circumlocutions (e.g. Caramazza & Hillis, 1990; Goodglass & Kaplan, 1972). These multiword responses appear to be attempts to define or describe the target when the patient is unable to produce the name. For example, when attempting to name a picture of a pair of pyjamas, RGB (Caramazza & Hillis, 1990) responded "what you wear at night"; similarly, Caramazza and Hillis's other patient, HW, responded "for going to school" to a picture of a bus. Thus, these circumlocutions are rarely described as "errors". Indeed, the patient who produces circumlocutions is often contrasted with the patient who produces single-word semantic "errors".

However, inferences about the patients' deficits based on the distinction between these response types may be unwise. It may be that the different response types are more a reflection of processing at the level of the sentence (and beyond) than the deficit underlying picture-naming. For example, the "fluent" aphasic may produce "it's like a radio" when attempting to name a picture of a record player (EST, Kay & Ellis, 1987), and the "nonfluent", "agrammatic", "Broca's type" aphasic may produce "radio". Nevertheless, it may be the case that the nonfluent patient was aiming at the same underlying utterance ("it's like a radio") but due to his or her difficulty in sentence production could only succeed in the single-word utterance "radio". Thus, it would be a mistake in this case to label the single-word response an error but accord the multiword response a different status.

Indeed, Goodglass and Kaplan (1972) urge that "verbal paraphasias" (single-word semantic errors) that are unintended should be distinguished from "one-word circumlocutions" in which the patient deliberately chooses an approximation to his intended idea because of his word-finding difficulty (p.8). In other words, they are suggesting a distinction between automatically occurring error processes and strategic responses to a deficit. Unfortunately they do not provide any criteria on which to base this distinction and in practice this is difficult. Although it is possible to draw a distinction between semantic "errors" and semantic "rejections" (where a patient produces a response followed by "no" or a shake of the head), whether or not a patient rejects the response may reflect many factors, including the patient's perception of the task requirements, the experimenter's response to the patient's attempt, and his or her own personality. One solution may be to require the patient to rate how confident he or she is that the response is accurate, and classify responses on this basis. The important point, however, is that it may be methodologically flawed to attempt to relate single- and multiword responses and/or semantic errors, and semantically-related responses (with or without rejection by the patient) to different levels of breakdown.

More on theoretical accounts of the production of semantic errors

In Chapter 1 we discussed the occurrence of semantic errors in the speech error corpora (Fromkin, 1971, 1973a), and described a number of theoretical accounts of the origin of these errors. In this chapter we have examined the production of semantic errors in aphasic speech (and specifically in picture naming), and during the course of this a number of theoretical positions have been mentioned. This section aims to summarise these positions and draw attention to their limitations.

It may be that one cause of the semantic errors produced by aphasic subjects is simply an exaggeration of the normal error-producing mechanism (perhaps, for example, by increasing the levels of "noise" within the system). Alternatively, specific damage to the component processes of spoken word production in the aphasic subject may produce causes of error different from those that result in the production of errors by normal subjects. Thus, for each model in turn, we will recap the production of semantic errors within the intact model, describe possible deficits resulting in semantic errors, and discuss the predictions regarding the effects of variables associated with the stimulus (such as frequency, imageability) on the probability of a semantic error occurring.

Logogen model (Morton, 1970)

"Normal" semantic errors: As described in Chapter 1, in the logogen model conceptual/semantic information from the semantic system activates all words in the phonological output lexicon that represent that information. This results in a range of semantically related items being activated at any one time. The item whose activation level first reaches threshold is produced. Semantically related errors may result when random noise or variation within the system causes another (semantically related) word to have higher levels of activation than the target. For example, this may be due to a temporary lowering of a threshold due to the recent firing of a logogen, or partial activation of a logogen from interfering stimuli (e.g. distracting stimuli in other sensory modalities).

CF5 2YB   UWIC

semantic errors: (i) Semantic deficits: loss or degradation ᴏʀ semantic information within the semantic system leading to underspecification of information addressing the output lexicon (e.g. JCU, Howard and Orchard-Lisle, 1984). A range of semantically related items will be activated but due to the underspecified nature of the input to the lexicon no item will be fully activated or reach its threshold. The lexical item likely to be accessed will be that closest to threshold. There would seem to be a need for an automatic or strategic lowering of all thresholds if no logogen fires in order to enable a response even when no one logogen has fulfilled its complete semantic criterion and reached threshold (cf. Morton & Patterson, 1980). This semantic defict will also result in semantic errors in comprehension and written naming.

(ii) Post-semantic deficits: deficits in activating the representation within the phonological output lexicon in the context of preserved semantic information (as demonstrated by good comprehension and modality-specific semantic errors). This could be due to deficits "in transmission of information from the semantic system, in access to the output lexicon, or within the output lexicon itself" (Caramazza & Hillis, 1990, footnote 3, p.114). Morton and Patterson (1980) are somewhat more specific in the nature of these mechanisms (when discussing the origins of semantic errors produced by some deep dyslexic patients). They suggest that in a transmission error the correct semantic information is generated but is in some way degraded during its transmission to the output logogens or word-level nodes. They also suggest a "raised threshold" account, which argues that a logogen has a temporarily raised threshold that blocks an output and therefore the logogen nearest threshold is selected (which will be semantically related to the target). Morton and Patterson suggest that which items are blocked may fluctuate, although presumably permanent blocking (or even "loss") of a particular item is also a possibility.

Effects of variables: (i) Frequency: A frequency effect for the production of semantic errors is predicted for normal semantic errors and with semantic and post-semantic deficits, as described earlier.

An underspecified semantic representation will activate a range of semantically related items (as also occurs in the intact model), and the lexical item likely to be accessed will be that which reaches threshold first. Because high frequency items have lower thresholds, they need less additional activation to be selected. For high frequency targets, even if the address is underspecified they may be successfully accessed, whereas for lower frequency targets a semantically related word of higher frequency may be accessed instead. Therefore, not only is a frequency effect predicted in naming accuracy but also the semantic errors should be of higher frequency than their targets.

Unfortunately, Nickels and Howard (1994) failed to find any evidence for an effect of frequency on the production of semantic errors despite the strong prediction from the logogen model that this should occur (but see the earlier discussion regarding the possibility of an interaction between imageability and frequency).

(ii) Imageability: A semantic deficit might predict an effect of "semantic" variables such as imageability on naming and the production of semantic errors. Thus, correct responses will be more likely to occur with higher imageability targets and semantic errors with lower imageability targets. In contrast, an effect of imageability on performance is not predicted for post-semantic deficits.

Nickels and Howard (1994) found evidence for imageability effects on the production of semantic errors in patients with semantic deficits; however, other patients (who also made semantic errors in comprehension and therefore could be described as having semantic deficits) did not show significant effects of imageability (although confirmation of this result through replication would be preferable given the relatively small sample of errors analysed). Thus, it may be the case that semantic deficits may dissociate into different subtypes with and without an influence of imageability on performance.

Two-stage model of lexicalisation: Semantic lexicon model (Butterworth, 1989)

Normal semantic errors: Just as in the logogen model, Butterworth (1989) argues that within the semantic lexicon model normal semantic errors can be the result of random errors in the semantic system (caused by interfering stimuli). This would result in an erroneous semantic search criterion addressing the semantic lexicon, which may access an address for a word but this will be semantically related to the target rather than the target itself. An alternative possibility is an "addressing error"; the correct semantic search criterion is generated by the semantic system, but an error occurs when this is matched to the appropriate entry in the semantic lexicon. As the entries in the semantic lexicon are held to be arranged according to their meanings (Butterworth, 1981), an addressing error will yield a near neighbour, related in meaning to the target (but not necessarily phonologically related).

Aphasic semantic errors: Butterworth (1989) argues for three distinct loci of damage within his model that could result in the production of semantic errors.

(i) Semantic deficit: damage to the semantic system resulting in incomplete or erroneous semantic specifications of the word to be retrieved, just as was described earlier for the logogen model.

(ii) Access to semantic lexicon: an impairment in accessing the semantic lexicon from the semantic system given intact output from the semantic system. This deficit, which consists of a failure to match the semantic search criteria with the correct entry in the semantic lexicon (and is one possible mechanism for semantic errors in normal subjects), would be very difficult to dissociate from a "transmission" error in which the semantic criteria are in some way distorted or degraded in transmission from the semantic system to the semantic lexicon. This deficit does not necessarily involve a comprehension impairment, as access to the semantic system from speech recognition may be intact.

(iii) Semantic lexicon: The final locus for a deficit resulting in semantic errors is damage to the semantic lexicon (in Butterworth's model, equivalent to a lemma level). This will lead to the retrieval of incorrect addresses for the phonological lexicon, which will be the addresses of words semantically related to the target. This level of impairment will also result in comprehension deficits on linguistic tasks (e.g. synonym judgements, word to picture matching with semantically related distractors). However, performance on nonlinguistic tasks (e.g. Pyramids and Palm Trees Test, category-sorting using pictures) need not be affected as the semantic system can be unimpaired even in the presence of a semantic lexicon deficit. Thus, as pictorial stimuli gain direct access to the semantic system, performance will remain intact on tasks using only pictures. However, as words can only access the semantic system via the (damaged) semantic lexicon, comprehension will be impaired on all tasks involving words.

Effects of variables: (i) Frequency: Butterworth has not implemented frequency within his model and therefore no frequency effects are predicted. However, in his slightly different two-stage model, Levelt (1983) argues that frequency is associated with retrieval of the phonological form of the target. Thus, even if frequency were implemented within Butterworth's semantic lexicon model at the level of the phonological output lexicon, no effect would be predicted in the production of semantic errors (but an effect might be expected for phonological errors).

This is more in keeping with Nickels and Howard's (1994) results, where frequency did not predict the occurrence of semantic errors. However, their finding that there may be an interaction between frequency and imageability effects in the production of semantic errors would not seem to be compatible with this account.

(ii) Imageability: It is assumed that imageability ren. characteristic of the semantic system within this model and hence . deficits at this level may be affected by imageability. However, furthe. evidence is clearly required regarding the extent to which imageability may (additionally/alternatively) be a factor affecting lexical-semantic levels of processing. If the semantic lexicon is not influenced by imageability, then semantic errors resulting from deficits at this level would not be predicted to be affected by this variable.

Connectionist models

Normal semantic errors: In the interactive activation (IAA) models of Dell (1986, 1989) and Stemberger (1985) errors arise in much the same way as in the logogen model, as in these models conceptual/semantic information also activates all words that ever represent that information. A word will reach a sufficient level of activation (across the network as a whole) to be produced by summing activation from large parts of its semantic structure. Once again, random noise within the system can result in a nontarget being selected for production. Noise can be from external sources (Dell, 1986) or from random variation in the resting level of activation of units and the systematic spread of activation to nontarget units from other semantically related units.

The reverberation of activation between levels in IAA models also predicts that a relatively high proportion of the errors will be mixed errors, which is argued by some authors to be the case in normal corpora (e.g. Butterworth, 1981). Mixed errors are those that bear both a semantic and phonological relationship to the target e.g "a book with the most magnificent dialogue" → "... magnificent dialect" (Fromkin, 1973a, p.262). In contrast, the logogen model predicts only chance occurrence of these errors, unless an editor mechanism is employed as described by, for example, Butterworth (1981) or Motley and Baars (1976).

A second type of connectionist model are those models that, like stage models, involve only feed-forward processes, but unlike stage models (but like IAA models) do not require processing to be complete at one level before processing can begin at the next. Plaut and Shallice's (1993) multilayered perceptron model is a (primarily) feed-forward connectionist model, where activation is transmitted in cascade from semantic units to intermediate units to phonological units. (Although in the version of the model depicted in Fig. 4.1 there is feedback from phonological to intermediate units, the crucial factor for the discussion here is that there is no feedback between semantic and intermediate

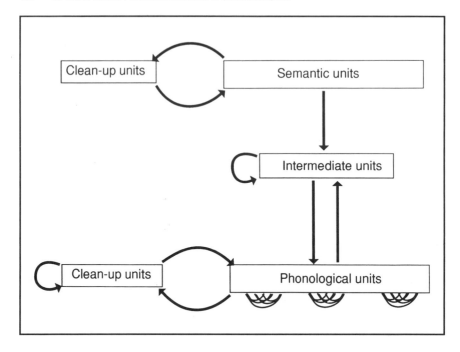

FIG. 4.1. Plaut and Shallice's connectionist model (output component, adapted from Plaut & Shallice, 1993). Recurrent connections are included at the intermediate and phonological clean-up levels to facilitate the development of strong phonological attractors. At the phonological level there are intra-phoneme connections.

units.) This allows the final state of each unit (i.e. the response) to be computed in a single pass through the network.

This model was developed to simulate the performance of deep dyslexic patients, and was an extension of the work by Hinton and Shallice (1991), including abstract words in the net's "vocabulary" (Plaut & Shallice, 1991, 1993) and adding an output network (Plaut & Shallice, 1993). It is the output portion of the model that concerns us here. This involves the transmission of activation from semantic units (sememe units) to phoneme units via intermediate units.

Plaut and Shallice do not discuss the occurrence of normal speech errors in the context of their model, but it is reasonable to assume that some of the same conditions that result in semantic errors in all the other models might also result in errors in this model (e.g. interference from external stimuli).

It is also possible for models to be "hybrids" combining feed-forward and interactive mechanisms. For example, Harley (1993) describes a model that allows only feed-forward activation from the semantic to the lexical level but also incorporates feedback connections between the lexical and phonological levels (see Fig. 1.5, p.36). Once again semantic errors can result from external interfering stimuli or from random noise (in particular affecting the connections between the semantic and lexical levels).

Aphasic semantic errors: As in all the models, the semantic errors produced by aphasic subjects may also be caused by these same error mechanisms, with the system simply being "noisier" and therefore more error-prone (Harley & MacAndrew, 1992). Indeed, one of the ways connectionist models are "lesioned" is by the addition of noise to the network (e.g. Harley & MacAndrew, 1992; Hinton & Shallice, 1991). Alternatively, the semantic errors produced by aphasic subjects may be due to causes different from those that result in the production of errors by normal subjects; that is, when the model is damaged or "lesioned".

Lesioning of connectionist networks can take many different forms: Noise can be added to weights on the connections (either throughout the network or between particular levels) or to the resting levels of activation of nodes (again either throughout the network or at a particular level); a subset of nodes and/or connections can be removed; decay rates (in those models which employ them) can be pathologically increased or decreased; or spreading rates of activation can be raised or lowered.

Plaut and Shallice (1993) and Harley and MacAndrew (1992) both examine the effects of different types of lesioning. Harley and MacAndrew find that their model is extremely resistant to disruption with increased decay rate, increased random noise in the resting levels of activation, and loss of inhibitory connections. All of these types of lesion still resulted in the target being the most highly activated; it was only lesioning by adding noise to the (excitatory) semantic to lexical connections that an error occurred. This illustrates one of the features of connectionist models, which is often described as an advantage for the description of neuropsychological data—graceful degradation (Rumelhart & McClelland, 1986). That is, when a network suffers damage it does not catastrophically fail, but rather shows a slow decline in performance that is proportional to the degree of damage. With the currently limited data from simulations with lesioned models it is difficult to predict the effects of different lesions on performance. Although different lesions may produce different effects (see Martin & Saffran, 1992, for a discussion, although without simulation), Plaut and Shallice (1993) demonstrate that for their model different lesions each produced the full range of error types (although the relative proportions varied). Most importantly, the effects of a lesion at one level (in IAA models) will spread to affect the network as a whole, as activation reverberates between levels.

Effects of variables: As discussed earlier, it is difficult to predict the precise performance of these models when "lesioned" (by, for example, adding noise, removing nodes or connections, resetting weights) without actual simulation. Similarly, the word characteristics that are of interest here are not always implemented. For example, Plaut and Shallice (1991, 1993) implement imageability but not frequency; Dell (1986, 1989) does implement frequency but not imageability (although Martin and Saffran (1992) do discuss the implementation of imageability within this same model). However, from the specifications of the models there are some general principles that can be drawn regarding how they could behave when lesioned.

(i) Frequency: Both Dell, (1986, 1989) and Harley (1993; Harley & MacAndrew, 1992) represented frequency by variations in the resting level of activation of the nodes at the lexical level (so that higher frequency words have higher resting levels of activation). Thus, high frequency words are more likely to produce a stable pattern of activation across the network and be selected than low frequency words, even under noisy conditions. Moreover, as Monsell (1991) points out, in connectionist models, which learn their weights by back-propagation (e.g. Plaut & Shallice, 1993), frequency effects are an inevitable consequence of greater learning experience with higher frequency words.

(ii) Imageability: Where it is represented (Harley & MacAndrew, 1992; Martin & Saffran, 1992, for Dell's model; Plaut & Shallice, 1993), imageability is implemented in terms of "richness of semantic representations". Higher imageability words have more semantic nodes or features associated with each item than low imageability words. Therefore, the semantic representations of high imageability words are "more likely to support the spread of priming activation through the system" (Martin & Saffran, 1992, p.265). It appears that these models predict that imageability effects will occur in the production of semantic errors when the network is lesioned even if this is subsequent to the semantic level.

Thus, Harley and MacAndrew demonstrated that the effect of weakening the semantic-lexical connections was "moderated ... by the richness of the underlying semantic representation for each item" and conclude "this further predicts that high imageability words should also be preferentially preserved in ... aphasia" (p.382). It seems likely that any network that implements imageability in this way should make the same prediction; as activation spreads through the network the "support" will be greater for higher imageability words in comparison with lower imageability words, and this support should continue to give an advantage under conditions of damage. When Plaut and Shallice (1993) lesioned their network, they did indeed find that high imageability words were less affected than low imageability words for every lesion except one. When they lesioned the "clean-up" units within semantics they found the reverse effect—low imageability words were better preserved than high imageability words (see the Introduction to Part One for descriptions of aphasic subjects that show this pattern). They argued that this was because high imageability items had a greater overlap of semantic features than low imageability items and so relied more on clean-up to stabilise the pattern of activation. Of course, although it is interesting to show that a model can produce both positive and negative effects of imageability, changing the featural representation (which was generated by the experimenters) could change the model's performance.

In conclusion, for those models that implement frequency and imageability in the way described, "those words that are most robust under noisy conditions are going to be the more frequent and imageable words in the language" (Harley & MacAndrew, 1992, p.382). Although Nickels and Howard's (1994) results do not appear to support these predictions (effects of frequency on the production of semantic errors and correct responses are surprisingly absent, and not every patient shows an effect of imageability), they did find some evidence for an interaction between the effects of frequency and imageability (although not for every patient). Clearly further simulations are required to define more precisely the performance of these models when lesioned in different ways and the effects frequency and imageability have on error production under these conditions.

SUMMARY

In this chapter we have examined the production of semantic errors in aphasic subjects. The vast majority of patients appear to produce semantic errors as the result of a lexical-semantic or conceptual semantic deficit, with a corresponding comprehension impairment. A number of patients have now been reported with profound impairments of conceptual semantics (or "semantic memory"). These patients generally have progressive disorders and may have associated (more general) cognitive impairments. Nevertheless, they provide an invaluable additional source of information to help us to understand better the nature of semantic representations through the patterns observed as these representations are lost. Our characterisation of these semantic deficits is extremely gross at present.

Although most patients who produce semantic errors also seem to make semantic errors in comprehension, we reviewed the two cases presented by Caramazza and Hillis (1990) who have a modality specific deficit—they only produce semantic errors in spoken naming. This "pure" modality-specific disorder is clearly rare, but it is common for patients to show differences in degrees of impairment between modalities (e.g. written naming to be less impaired than spoken naming). In these cases patients are often described as having a central semantic deficit and an additional output deficit in the more impaired modality (e.g. Nickels, 1992b). It would seem important for further research to be directed towards examining the features of these "output" disorders and determining how frequently they occur.

Until recently little attention has been paid to the factors affecting the likelihood of a semantic error being produced by any particular patient. This has both theoretical and clinical implications (for targeting therapy and advising patients regarding which lexical items may cause them difficulty). We discussed the study by Nickels and Howard (1994), which looked at this issue in some detail. They concluded that target imageability was the most important influence, but that even this variable affected error production for only half the patients. However, this should only be regarded as a preliminary study in an area where further research is vital, using larger numbers of patients and larger stimulus sets to determine the true range of effects that can occur. Moreover, little attention has been paid to the different types of error that occur, despite the fact that this is of relevance to theories of the nature of semantic representations and their retrieval.

The chapter concluded with a detailed examination of three different types of model of speech production—logogen model, two-stage models, and connectionist models. We studied how each model accounts for semantic errors in "normal" speech errors and following damage, including the predicted effects of variables on performance (such as frequency and imageability). All three types of model could account for the production of semantic errors with ease, and it is currently difficult to distinguish between them on this basis. (However, none of the three models could account for Nickels and Howard's findings regarding the effects of variables on production).

It is clear that the precise nature of the semantic deficits needs to be identified through more detailed studies of the factors affecting the errors and the characteristics of those errors themselves—can the "semantic deficit" be dissociated into several subtypes (even excluding the category-specific semantic disorders)? If we are currently combining several different "semantic" disorders, then clinically we may be unable to target our therapy with sufficient accuracy. Nickels and Best (1996b) found that the same therapy resulted in rather different outcomes with three patients who seemed similar in terms of all having "semantic" impairments. They suggest that one possible reason for these differences could be the very gross description of "semantic disorder" that is currently employed. Perhaps with further refinement of our understanding of semantic disorders we will be able to subdivide the patients further, and better predict the outcome of therapy.

CHAPTER FIVE

Deficits of lexical retrieval

OVERVIEW

In this chapter we will discuss the wide range of phenomena that have been associated with deficits in retrieval of the phonological form of a lexical item.

Patients with this level of deficit have intact processing at the semantic level but yet fail to retrieve the phonological form of the target in output. This level of deficit will characteristically be modality-specific, and written output will be unimpaired (in the absence of an additional deficit). In addition, patients should be unable to perform tasks that require access to the phonological form of the word without overt pronunciation—so-called "silent phonology" tasks (e.g. homophone judgements)—or at least they should perform these tasks no better than they can name the same stimuli. These deficits may be due to loss or damage of the lexical representations themselves or impairments in the procedures and processes involved in retrieving these representations for phonological encoding.

Although these points are clear, it will become apparent that the features of such a deficit in lexical retrieval are far from certain. Several different patients will be described; the anomic symptoms of all these patients are argued to be due to impairments in lexical retrieval and yet the symptoms differ widely. We have already discussed Caramazza and Hillis' patients, HW and RGB, who produce semantic errors in oral naming, due (the authors assert) to deficits in retrieval of the phonological form. As we will see, they are very different to other patients with the same proposed level of deficit.

We begin with a discussion of a patient, DRB, who shows an effect of imageability/concreteness on his naming. This pattern is usually attributed to a semantic deficit; however, DRB has intact semantics (ABSTRACT WORD ANOMIA). From there we move to a brief review of category-specific disorders, again more commonly associated with semantic deficits, but for these cases argued to be the result of a post-semantic impairment (CATEGORY-SPECIFIC ANOMIA). Patients have now been reported with deficits specific to fruit and vegetables, proper names, and nouns and verbs.

We then discuss patients whose overt errors tend to be phonologically related to the target, beginning with patients who produce phonologically related real-word errors, often called "formal paraphasias" (FORMAL PARAPHASIAS: RB, NC, AND MF). We discuss at some length methodological issues relating to whether or not these real-word errors should be considered separately from other phonologically related (nonword) errors or whether they just happen to words by chance (JARGON HOMOPHONES OR FORMAL PARAPHASIAS?). In the following section we discuss a patient who, unlike the majority of aphasics, is better at producing long words than short words ("REVERSE" LENGTH EFFECTS: CGJ).

Many patients who produce nonword errors have been described in the literature. Here we discuss some of those cases where the deficit has been suggested to be one of lexical retrieval. We begin with a patient, EST, who produces nonword errors that are phonologically related to the target ("PHONOLOGICAL" ANOMIA) and then discuss patients who may produce nonword errors that are unrelated to their targets (NEOLOGISTIC JARGON APHASIA: KC AND RD). Finally, we discuss the effects of phonemic cues (as benefit from cues is often used as support for a lexical access deficit) (EFFECTS OF PHONEMIC CUES), and then describe a patient whose proposed deficit is one of lost lexical representations (LOSS OF STORED LEXICAL REPRESENTATIONS?).

ABSTRACT WORD ANOMIA: DRB

Franklin, Howard, and Patterson (1995) describe a case currently unique in the literature. DRB was only mildly impaired on picture-naming but had marked word-finding difficulties in spontaneous speech. This is explained in terms of his anomia being specific to abstract (or low imageability) words. They present four lines of evidence to support this position:

1. Franklin, Howard, and Patterson (1994) demonstrated that DRB could only repeat words via the semantic route. Thus, the fact that DRB is worse at repeating abstract words than comprehending them is consistent with a problem in producing abstract words. However, as Franklin et al. point out, an alternative explanation would be that the repetition task requires more specific and more complete semantic information than the comprehension task.

2. Franklin et al. (1994) also showed that DRB's written comprehension was intact, and therefore argue that any deficit in oral reading (where lexical representations must be retrieved) must be a consequence of impaired word production (naming) processes. They find that DRB shows both a regularity and an imageability effect in reading aloud, and moreover an interaction between the two. In other words, he was poor at reading aloud only low imageability irregular words, as would be predicted if he had a specific deficit in the retrieval of abstract words for production.

3. DRB's abstract word anomia was also demonstrated using a category fluency task. Both DRB and matched control subjects were asked to produce as many words as they could within a particular category in 2 minutes. The task included both "concrete" categories (e.g. animals, colours) and "abstract" categories (e.g. good qualities, religions). DRB was within the range of the normal controls for the number of appropriate responses for the more concrete categories, but produced significantly fewer appropriate responses than the controls for the more abstract categories.

4. Finally, Franklin et al. (1995) compare the imageability of the word associations that DRB and two matched control subjects gave to written words. DRB produced responses of significantly higher imageability than the controls. For example, when given the written word WRATH, DRB produced "fight", whereas the controls said "anger" and "ire". Similarly, to DEBT, DRB said "money" and the controls said "owe" and "owing".

Thus, as DRB has excellent written comprehension and therefore by implication an intact semantic system, his deficit in producing abstract words is argued to be post-semantic, specifically in "the mapping between semantics and phonology". Franklin et al. (1995) suggest that perhaps this type of impairment necessarily results in a greater vulnerability for abstract words because of differences in their representation at a semantic level, and that therefore patients with post-semantic problems in word retrieval will often show greater difficulty in retrieving abstract words.

CATEGORY-SPECIFIC ANOMIA

We have briefly alluded to category-specific disorders that are common to both comprehension and production. However, there have also been reports of some patients who have been claimed to have category-specific disorders only in word production. We will review some of these studies here, first regarding naming impairments for fruit and vegetables and then dissociations between proper names and other nouns.

Fruit and vegetables

Farah and Wallace (1992) describe a patient, TU, who was impaired at naming fruit and vegetables in comparison with other objects, even taking into account any effects of frequency and familiarity on performance. This pattern occurred with naming from object, picture, or definition, with the majority of errors being semantic. TU could accurately select the correct name to match a picture from a choice of three (using within-category distractors). On the basis of this pattern of data, Farah and Wallace suggest that TU's deficit is in the "process by which phonology is accessed from semantics" (p.619), although they also claim that TU showed consistent performance, which "implicates impaired representations as opposed to impaired access processes" (p.620). To overcome this apparent contradiction they suggest a model whereby distributed semantic representations (as patterns of activation across semantic features) are linked to distributed phonological representations (phonological features) via a layer of hidden units corresponding to semantically related words. In many ways this is similar to a semantic lexicon (or lexical-semantic representations). Farah and Wallace argue that if some of the hidden units that represent fruit and vegetables are damaged, this system would perform in a similar way to TU. This is rather a large claim in the absence of an implemented version of this model, where the effects of the lesion are simulated (predicting the behaviour of connectionist models in the absence of simulations is difficult at best). However, it is very similar to the argument made by Hart, Berndt, and Caramazza (1985) for the nature of the deficit in their patient, MD.

MD also showed a specific impairment for fruit and vegetables compared to other stimuli on picture- and object-naming and naming to definition. He was unimpaired on word to picture matching and unimpaired (but hesitant) at making judgements regarding the properties of fruits and vegetables. Although he was accurate at categorisation of words, he made errors on picture categorisation for fruit and vegetables. On the basis of this pattern of performance, Hart et al. suggest that lexical categorisation could be accomplished on the basis of strictly lexical as opposed to semantic information. They suggest that the lexical-semantic system (semantic lexicon) is organised categorically, and specifically that this is at the level of "input and output processes to and from the system" (p.440). MD's deficit is construed to be a highly selective disruption of the semantically categorised address from the lexical-semantic system to the output lexicon. However, this account would appear not to explain MD's poor performance on picture categorisation. The fact that he was "hesitant" in responding to questions regarding the properties of fruit and vegetables might suggest poorer performance for these relative to other items in verbal tasks. As Best (1994) points out, it is essential to compare performance across categories in comprehension tasks where performance has been taken off ceiling (or by using reaction time measures) before one can be sure that there is not a category effect in input as well as output. Thus, for both MD and Farah and Wallace's patient, TU, (without these additional data) it is difficult to be sure that the category effect might not arise at a central semantic level.

Proper names

McKenna and Warrington (1980) were the first to report a dissociation involving proper names. They described a patient, GBL, who had a highly selective difficulty in naming people (either from photographs or from description), especially when compared to naming of objects and towns, which was entirely normal. More recently a number of other authors have reported dissociations in patient's abilities to say proper names in the context of good comprehension. Semenza and Zettin (1988, 1989), Lucchelli and De Renzi (1992), Shallice and Kartsounis (1993), and Hittmair-Delazer, Denes, Semenza, and Mantovan (1994) all report patients with severe impairments in retrieving names of people. (Carney and Temple, 1993, also describe a patient with an impairment in retrieving people's names but this patient did have a prosopagnosia (face recognition deficit) earlier in the evolution of his disorder, suggesting that perhaps the deficit might not be modality-specific to output).

Semenza and Zettin's patients, PC (1988) and LS (1989), also had impairments involving geographical names (e.g. cities, mountains, and rivers; Hittmair-Delazer et al., 1994, also note this problem for their patient MP). They account for these impairments by hypothesising a deficit at the level of the output lexicon "which would therefore be presumed to be categorically organised" (Semenza & Zettin, 1988, p.719). However, they do refer to Hart et al. (1985) on this point, and therefore it may be that rather than the lexicon itself being organised according to semantic categories (which would seem strange for a store that is generally considered to be phonologically organised) they in fact follow Hart et al. in considering that it is the address to this lexicon that is categorically organised. Indeed, Lucchelli and De Renzi (1992) suggest just this level of impairment for their patient, TL, "access to the phonological output system from a preserved semantic system" (p.227), drawing parallels between their patient and Kay and Ellis' (1987) patient EST. Lucchelli and De Renzi go further and propose that it is the arbitrary nature of the link between proper names and their referents that makes access of their phonological forms particularly labile. Although, of course, almost all phonological forms bear an arbitrary relationship to their referents, all items labelled with a particular name will share semantic characteristics (e.g. all tables share features), whereas people with the same name will not necessarily share any semantic features (e.g. all men called Tom).

Hittmair-Delazer et al. (1994) also argue for a deficit affecting retrieval of the phonological form from an intact semantic memory, concluding that common and proper names access the lexical level from the semantic system independently from one another. They specify the deficit somewhat further, suggesting that at the lemma level, where syntactic information is also represented, nouns are divided into the two major classes—common and proper.

Shallice and Kartsounis (1993) also report a patient, WK, with a long-standing low-grade glioma affecting the left temporal lobe. He was severely impaired at producing people's names, whether in naming from photographs or from description or in a proper name-generation task. His identification of people and retrieval of person-specific knowledge was within the normal range, as was his naming of objects and geographical features. However, he showed differential success at retrieving proper names, depending on when they might have been acquired (i.e. he was poor at recalling the names of currently famous people but good at recalling names of historical figures). Shallice and Kartsounis argue that an explanation in terms of a specific semantic category deficit for proper names alone would not account for his very poor performance in retrieving other words of more recent origin (e.g. "video", "credit card"). They suggest that instead his naming deficit was related to how recently the word has been acquired rather than what it denotes—"a long-standing inability to form new associations between meaning and phonological word-forms" (p.290).

Shallice and Kartsounis note that perhaps the distinction between the deficit observed for WK and the patients reported by Semenza and Zettin (1988, 1989) and Lucchelli and De Renzi (1992) is not as absolute as it might at first appear. LS (Semenza & Zettin, 1989) failed the "difficult" pairs on the paired-associate learning task from the Wechsler memory scale, indicating a possible learning deficit, as did TL (Lucchelli

& De Renzi, 1992); Hittmair-Delazer et al.'s (1994) patient, MP, also had difficulty with these items. Furthermore, LS had problems in his job in remembering numerical labels associated with particular items of hardware, and TL had difficulties recalling telephone numbers. However, whereas all these patients had difficulty in retrieving names of currently famous people, only WK showed a dissociation between these and other proper names. Shallice and Kartsounis suggest that either WK's symptoms represent a different disorder from that of the other patients, or that "the impairment of retrieval of other proper names in such patients represents an associated deficit" (p.290).

Semenza and Sgaramella (1993) report a patient who they claim shows the opposite dissociation to the aforementioned patients—a sparing of proper names relative to other words. However, because of the patient's severely impaired word production—no correct responses on a naming test, he only produced "randomly chosen monosyllables" (p.10)—the superiority for proper names was only apparent with phonemic cues (almost perfect performance, with no improvement for objects or animals). They argue that either this deficit reflects an additional deficit in the common nouns channel (presumably within the categorically organised address to the output lexicon) or there is no category-specific disorder *per se* but rather the difference in phonemic cueing can be explained by the specific semantic function of proper names. That is, "the proper names channel would be intrinsically more efficient when helped by phonemic cueing because of the simple one-to-one relationship ... that proper names entertain with their reference (sic)" (p.260).

Cipolotti, McNeil, and Warrington (1993) also report a patient with progressive aphasia (due to progressive multifocal leucoencephalo-pathy) who had proper nouns relatively spared compared to objects, although this was apparent in written naming. Her oral naming was at floor, so it is difficult to be sure whether the effect might also have been present in oral naming prior to this point. Additionally, although her word-picture matching showed no differences between categories, it was at ceiling at the point in testing reported in this paper. However, McNeil, Cipolotti, and Warrington (1994) present further data from this patient, MED, and argue that she showed selective preservation of her ability to comprehend proper nouns at this point, no more than four days after the time of testing reported in Cipolotti et al. Thus, despite the fact that this patient was deteriorating rapidly, we cannot be sure that even at the time when she was performing accurately at word-picture matching that there may have been a subtle category-specific deficit in comprehension as well as production. This suggests that for MED the category-specific effect may originate at the semantic level.

Nouns and verbs

A number of patients have now also been reported who show discrepancies between their ability to name nouns and verbs (see, for example, Miceli, Silveri, Nocentini, & Caramazza, 1988). Some patients are better at naming verbs than nouns (including AL, Miozzo, Soardi, & Cappa, 1994; HY, Zingeser & Berndt, 1988) and others are better at naming nouns than verbs (HW and SJD, each in only one output modality, Caramazza & Hillis, 1991). All of these patients show these deficits in the context of good comprehension for both categories. This pattern of deficit has been used to argue that "grammatical category information is represented separately and redundantly in each modality-specific lexical system" (Caramazza & Hillis, 1991, p.790) and that these patients have deficits within one category at the lexical level or access to it. However, it is important to note that nouns and verbs have very different semantic characteristics, and a semantic deficit may differentially impair processing of one more than another. As was discussed earlier (Best, 1994), it is important to examine whether category-specific effects occur in tasks that are not at ceiling or at floor (using, for example, reaction time experiments compared to normal subjects) before a category-specific effect can unequivocally be attributed to lexical access/storage systems.

FORMAL PARAPHASIAS: RB, NC, AND MF

One further group of patients argued (by some authors) to have deficits in lexical access are those who produce large numbers of "formal paraphasias". These are real-word responses that are phonologically related to the target (PRW; e.g. saying "biscuit" for the target "basket") as distinct from the majority of phonologically related responses (for the majority of patients), which are nonwords. For example, Blanken (1990) reports details of patient RB, who produced a high proportion of formal paraphasias in oral naming, reading, and writing to dictation. Blanken suggests that these are due to errors in lexical selection (but with semantic, lexical, and segmental factors contributing to the outcome). As these phonologically related real-word errors are often argued to have a different source to the phonologically related nonword errors (lexical access as opposed to phonological encoding, see Chapter 6), it is important to determine that they are genuinely different, rather than just real words by chance. Thus we will spend some time discussing methodological approaches to this issue.

Jargon homophones or formal paraphasias?

One problem with assessing such data is that, on occasions, phonologically related responses will be real words by chance. That is, in Butterworth's (1979) terminology, they will be "jargon homophones". For example, if the first phoneme in the word CAT is substituted, a high proportion of the resulting "errors" will be real words (e.g. mat, hat, bat, fat, etc.; cf. lat, wat, yat, etc.). How to determine whether phonologically related real-word (PRW) errors are in fact simply jargon homophones (resulting from substitution of a phoneme) or genuine substitutions of other real words (formal paraphasias) is far from a trivial problem.

Although Blanken argues that RB's PRW errors are too numerous (compared to the incidence of phonologically related nonword errors) to be jargon homophones, he does not address this issue directly. Instead he concentrates on whether these errors are more phonologically related to the target than would be expected if they were randomly generated word substitutions. This was accomplished by generating a pseudocorpus of errors, which were matched in frequency and syllabic structure to the errors. Significant differences between the error corpus and pseudocorpus were only found in some phoneme positions, in particular for vowels and the initial consonant for monosyllabic words alone. This relative lack of difference between the target relatedness of errors and pseudo-errors is cause for concern, and may reflect the fact that some errors are not true PRW errors. The criterion for an error being classified as phonologically related to the target that was used by Blanken is indeed very lax, being only that errors and targets were "related formally by at least one sound" and the corpus may, therefore, include errors that share a phoneme by chance.

RB had relatively good written naming and showed a regularity effect in reading, suggesting the ability to use a sublexical route for reading. It is possible, therefore, that when he was unable to say the name of a word, he could use his relatively superior orthographic knowledge to improve naming. This could be achieved by converting the output orthographic code into an input code and then using the sublexical reading route to attempt to convert it to an output phonological code. The partial information from this sublexical route could act as a cue at the level of the lexicon, cueing the production of the target or a phonologically related real word (Nickels, 1992a). It therefore needs to be demonstrated that the phonologically related real-word errors produced by RB are indeed more than just a combination of real words cued by orthography, jargon homophones, and unrelated errors that by chance share a phoneme with the target.

Martin, Dell, Saffran, and Schwartz (1994) use the same method as Blanken to examine target relatedness of errors. However, they too fail to demonstrate that their patient, NC, produces more phonologically related real-word errors than would be expected if they were jargon homophones.

Another method was used by Miller and Ellis (1987) to investigate whether phoneme transpositions in neologisms were real transpositions or simply the result of random phoneme substitutions. They extracted all the error phonemes from the phonological errors and randomly reassigned them back into the vacant slots in the errors, creating a set of pseudo-errors. A similar method could be used for testing whether or not phonologically related words are jargon homophones, by taking both the phonologically related real-word and nonword (PRW and PRNW) errors produced by a patient and randomly reassigning the phonemes back into the vacant slots. The resulting pseudo-errors could then be reclassified into words and nonwords and the proportion of real-word errors compared to the number that occurred in the original corpus of errors. However, even this method may not be entirely adequate as reassignment of phonemes cannot be entirely random due to the need to adhere to the phonotactic rules of the language, given that errors are phonotactically legal in those patients described to date (e.g. English-speaking patients do not produce "unpronounceable" strings such as "fbantk"). Best (1996) devised a procedure for creating a pseudocorpus that allowed for this. Every incorrect phoneme was substituted by a phoneme randomly chosen from the set of phonemes phonotactically legal in that context. The relative proportions of real words in the pseudocorpus and real error corpus could then be compared. Using this method, she demonstrates that her patient, MF, produces phonologically related real-word errors at a rate greater than would be expected by chance.

One final method rests on the fact that shorter words have a greater number of neighbours. That is, when one phoneme is changed in a word, the probability of the resulting form being a word is substantially higher for shorter words. Thus, if the phonologically related words produced by a patient are jargon homophones, they will be more common on short words than on longer words. However, this pattern might not be as clear if the patient tends to produce short (e.g. monosyllabic) errors to long (e.g. trisyllabic) words. Thus, a null result should always be qualified by looking at the length of the errors and performing a similar analysis comparing the number of phonologically related words and nonwords that contain one, two, or three syllables. The same reasoning should predict that by chance a greater proportion of monosyllabic errors (to targets of any length) should be real words than trisyllabic errors. Franklin (1989a) used this method of analysis to examine the phonological errors produced by a group of aphasic subjects. She found a relatively high proportion of real words for three- and four-phoneme responses (9% of all responses; 75% of phonological errors), which dropped for five-phoneme words (2.5% of all responses; 24% of phonological errors). Similarly, the longer the target word, the higher the proportion of nonword responses that occurred (see also Nickels & Howard, 1995b). However, Nickels and Howard (1995b) note that this analysis might be insufficient to claim that there is no lexical bias, giving the example of theories that incorporate an editor. In these theories phonologically related real-word errors do occur by chance (and therefore occur more often with short targets) but are simply less likely to be detected by the editor than PRNW. Hence the difference in the length of the targets that result in word and nonword errors would still be predicted even with a lexical bias.

Accounts for formal paraphasias

Assuming that formal paraphasias are indeed "real" (in the absence of a demonstration that this is the case for RB and NC), what are the accounts that have been given for their occurrence?

Blanken discusses the origin of RB's real-word errors with reference to both a stage model (Garrett, 1982) and an interactive activation model (Dell & Reich, 1981). He cites Fay and Cutler (1977), who explain real-word errors in normal subjects (malapropisms) as selection errors in the phonological lexicon (within a two-stage model of lexical retrieval). However, he notes two aspects of RB's performance that he claims are not consistent with this level of breakdown. First, the fact that concreteness influenced the number of formal paraphasias in reading aloud and writing to dictation. Second, a "high proportion" of RB's formal paraphasias also showed a similarity in meaning, although there was no demonstration that these occurred at a level greater than chance (see later). He suggests that these two findings are more compatible with an interactive model of word retrieval. Nevertheless, both models would appear to have difficulty accounting for the relatively low proportion of RB's formal paraphasias that share word onsets. Both Fay and Cutler and Dell and Reich observed high agreement between word onsets in targets and errors in the normal corpora. Blanken adopts a position whereby many different influences may be affecting RB's performance; "there is some evidence that RB's formal paraphasias cannot be traced back solely to errors of lexical form selection. Instead, semantic, lexical and segmental influences on the error generation could be established. A plausible conclusion could be that RB's linguistic processing system is not disturbed in a selective manner but that his output system is working with rather slightly reduced efficiency" (p.551).

Martin et al. (1994) suggest that NC's PRW errors are in fact lexically based errors on the basis of two lines of argument. First, the fact that there was a significant tendency for PRW errors to be of higher frequency than their targets. Unfortunately, however, they did not consider the possibility that this might reflect "regression to the mean". In other words, that if the targets are of relatively low frequency, then even errors that were unaffected by frequency would tend (by chance) to be higher frequency than the targets. This seems likely, especially in view of the fact that a higher proportion of errors were of higher frequency than their targets for medium and low frequency targets than was true for high frequency targets. They also argue (on the basis of a small amount of data) that the phonologically related words are less target-related than the nonwords, as, they suggest, would be expected if the real-word errors are lexically generated, because "their phonological form is presumably driven by a different lexical node than the target". They propose that NC's formal paraphasias can best be explained by the pathologically rapid decay of primed nodes in Dell's (1986) interactive activation model of language production. Martin et al. support their claim with simulations where the model is "lesioned" in different ways. They also provide longitudinal data from NC showing a change in his error pattern (the proportion of formal paraphasias reduced relative to the proportion of semantic errors). They argue that this change in error pattern can be simulated by a gradual reduction in the decay rate towards normal levels.

Best (1996) discusses how formal paraphasias might result from damage to a number of different theoretical models. As was noted in Part 1, a single-stage model of lexical access (such as the logogen model) can only account for the occurrence of real-word errors (at a greater than chance rate) by assuming there is an editing mechanism that is better at detecting (and inhibiting) nonword errors (Motley et al., 1982). Best argues that this mechanism needs further specification before it could be accepted as an adequate account. She suggests that within a two-stage model of lexical access (such as Butterworth, 1989) formal paraphasias could have two sources. Either the correct phonological address is generated by the semantic lexicon and this is mismatched to a near neighbour in the phonological lexicon (equivalent to Fay and Cutler's selection error), or only part of the address is available and this is matched to the closest phonological representation in the lexicon (either the target or a near neighbour). As Best notes, the consequences of these two different levels of deficit are difficult to distinguish. However, although both of these two levels of deficit can account for MF's production of real-word errors at a greater than chance rate, there are other aspects of his performance that are more difficult for this model to account for. In particular, MF shows an effect of length on his naming success (although not on the production of formal paraphasias) and it is not clear that this model should predict an effect of length from a deficit at this level (see also the discussion later regarding reverse length effects). Kohn and Smith (1994b) also use an account similar to this (an impaired ability to locate entries in the phonological lexicon) for the deficit of their patient, VN, whose "picture-naming was initially empty, followed by a prominence of phonic verbal paraphasias" (p.284) (i.e. PRW) but with no length effect (unlike MF).

Best also discusses the account proposed by Martin et al. (1994), where there is pathological decay within Dell's interactive activation model. However, she notes a number of problems with this account. The first is that this interactive account predicts mixed errors (semantically and phonologically related to the target), whereas no more of MF's semantic errors are phonologically related to the target than would be expected by chance (using random reassignment to produce a pseudocorpus). Moreover, Best argues that as Martin et al.'s patient, NC, produces proportionately fewer mixed errors than MF (proportion of responses: MF semantic 0.14, mixed 0.13; NC semantic 0.10, mixed 0.06) it is unlikely that NC's mixed errors are genuine. Another problem with accounting for MF's naming in this way is that he showed no effect of frequency on naming, which is predicted by Martin et al.'s account (and indeed NC showed a frequency effect).

The final account discussed by Best proposes that the nature of MF's deficit might be a post-lexical deficit. She suggests that the phonological representation is correctly accessed but that there is a deficit at a subsequent level, where abstract phonological forms are held and assembled prior to articulation. Phonologically related errors are produced if enough of the target phonology is present in the output buffer. The preponderance of real-word errors (formal paraphasias) results from feedback from the impaired buffer to the lexical level, giving additional support for lexical items. Best suggests that an effect of length is predicted from a deficit of this type. Although this deficit can account for many aspects of MF's performance, Best does acknowledge that the exact nature of the deficit needs further specification.

"REVERSE" LENGTH EFFECTS: CGJ

Best (1995) describes a patient who, in contrast to the more usual pattern, shows worse naming of pictures with shorter names than those with longer names—a reverse length effect (compared to normal). The patient, CGJ, tended to produce "no response" errors when unable to name a picture correctly, with some semantic errors and only very occasional phonological errors. The phonological errors that he did produce tended to be real words at a rate greater than chance. Best discusses this pattern of breakdown in the context of a number of different models of word production.

In Butterworth's semantic lexicon model the phonological output lexicon is accessed by a phonological address that is systematically related to phonological characteristics such as number of syllables, initial phoneme, etc. If this address is corrupted, then rather than pointing to a single entry in the lexicon the address may now point to a number of entries. This is more likely to be the case for short words, where there is often a large number of phonological neighbours (words that differ by only one phoneme). In contrast, for long words the address may still specify a single lexical item as there may be no (or very few) other words that are phonologically similar (consider, for example, crocodile, which has no neighbours that are only one phoneme different). Thus, with a deficit of this type longer words might be more successfully produced, specifically because they have fewer phonological neighbours. Best suggests that the model seems to predict phonologically related real-word errors if the address is able to access a phonological neighbour. Alternatively, if the address is severely corrupted, or if errors are edited out, no responses might be expected.

Best also discusses the predictions from two connectionist models— Plaut and Shallice (1993) and Dell (1986, 1989). Unfortunately neither of these models incorporates words of different lengths at present and therefore predictions as to how they might behave are at best tentative. However, Best and Howard (1994b) presented data from simulations using a number of different architectures of the mapping between semantics and phonology. Many of these models did produce reverse length effects when lesioned (but failed to accurately simulate the error types). In fact, no model produced "normal" length effects (better performance with shorter words), which would appear to be a problem given how widespread these effects are in the aphasic population. In fact, this is easily accounted for by proposing a post-lexical locus for these length effects that is subsequent to the level of processing incorporated into these models at present.

"PHONOLOGICAL" ANOMIA: EST
(KAY & ELLIS,1987)

In Chapter 4 we discussed Howard and Orchard-Lisle's patient, JCU, who was described as having a "semantic anomia". Here we turn to a patient, EST, who has often been contrasted with JCU in a primary division between semantic and phonological (or word-selection) anomias (e.g. Ellis, Kay, & Franklin, 1992; Ellis & Young, 1988).

EST was a "fluent anomic" patient, who managed to mask his word-finding deficits in spontaneous speech by using more general words or circumlocutions instead of the target (see Table 5.1). However, in picture-naming tasks he was clearly impaired, producing both phonological and semantic errors, and showed an effect of frequency on the likelihood of a successful response.

In their analysis of his spoken word production impairment, Kay and Ellis (1987) argue against impairment to the entries in the phonological output lexicon on the grounds that EST sometimes retrieved a word

TABLE 5.1
Examples of EST's spontaneous speech and picture-naming responses

Spontaneous speech: *description of his career at British Oxygen (from Kay & Patterson, 1985)*

Experimenter: "So when did you come back to Newcastle?"

EST: "I've been there twice actually ... hmm ... I went, aye I went, from there I went for British Oxygen, and British Oxygen offered me a job up here ... Of course British Oxygen's closed down over 'ruddy place ... 's a tragedy really ... well, they offered me a job there ... /kʌnfəs si wɛrə jə/ like I forget what, what me name was ... I could never remember /wɛrə/ name, it 'ud a lots of words on it, lotta words on it, that was it ... assistant so and so, so and so, so and so ... (laughs) ... I've often thought many times after, what the hell I was ... the manager ... what they were trying, what they were finding out was that ... if I was okay, 'n the man, the manager was going ... going to, going t'another ... to London, you see ..."

Picture-naming *(from Kay & Ellis, 1987)*

Target Name	EST's response
grapes	eat it and 5 (letters) /græfs grif græs grif gritʃ/ not /græs/.
lobster	/lɒg lʌb lɒŋ/ is it l, o? /lɒ lɒg/ couldn't be a log ... g ... /lɒŋ/
strawberry	/sʌmbɛri/ s in it, probably 8 (letters) you get fed up with /sə sʌmbəri/
skunk	begins with an r /ræbɪn/ ... something like a rabbit.
axe	3, begins with s, not a saw ... its a hammer, its not a hammer ... same sort of ... I jumped at the wrong thing ... say a lump of wood and you wanted to chop it in two ... a chopper ... has it got 3 letters in it? A saw, not a saw.

after extensive effort and might retrieve a word in one session that he had been unable to in a previous session. Furthermore, he was better at repetition of words compared to nonwords, and word repetition was also better than naming. However, the repetition data is not necessarily very strong evidence. First, it is possible that the better repetition of words than nonwords is a result of input representations (in the phonological input lexicon) supporting repetition of words. Words will be repeated via the same route as nonwords, but nonwords suffer from not having the additional lexical (input) support. Second, although repetition was better than naming, it was still impaired.

Kay and Ellis assert that EST showed good comprehension of object names that he could not access in production, ruling out a semantic deficit as the cause of his anomia. However, it is important to bear in mind a point made by Gainotti et al. (1986) "... naming tasks are more difficult than lexical comprehension tasks, since the former require the patient to retrieve the correct word within a very large number of alternatives, whereas the latter dramatically reduce the number of these alternatives. A mild form of lexical-semantic impairment could, therefore, provoke a slight anomia at the expressive level, in the absence of detectable signs of lexical comprehension impairment" (p.30). It is difficult, then, to exclude categorically the possibility of a semantic deficit as a contributory factor in EST's (or any other aphasic's) anomia and, as Kay and Ellis acknowledge, EST does have a semantic problem with abstract words. However, in contrast to Howard and Orchard-Lisle's patient JCU, EST did not produce semantic errors when provided with a miscue for a target (i.e. given the cue /t/ when shown a picture of a lion, he did not produce "tiger"). In fact, he became quite frustrated with the task. It is unclear whether EST benefits from (correct) phonemic cues (as compared to being allowed a further attempt at naming or extra time to name).

Thus, Kay and Ellis conclude that EST had difficulty in accessing phonological forms within an intact phonological output lexicon and in the context of intact semantic representations (at least for concrete words). However, the precise nature of the deficit seems less clear. Kay and Ellis (1987) suggest a partial disconnection between the semantic system and the phonological output lexicon, which "is expressed in terms of weak or fluctuating levels of activation between corresponding representations in the semantic system and phonological lexicon" (p.626). Kay and Patterson (1985) provide a slightly different account, suggesting that "threshold levels which must be reached for the representations to become available are abnormally raised in EST" (p.96). In fact, distinguishing between these accounts could be difficult in practice.

Frequency effects

Word frequency was found to have a marked effect on EST's naming, with high frequency words having a higher probability of success than low frequency words (although no control was made for other, intercorrelating, variables such as age of acquisition). Kay and Ellis argue that this is compatible with a deficit in retrieval from the output lexicon, which in many models is frequency-biased (Morton, 1970; Dell, 1986).

However, if high frequency words are more easily activated than their low frequency counterparts, not only would we expect a frequency effect in naming success, but also that word substitutions would be of higher frequency than their targets, as has been found in normal substitutions (Levelt, 1989). Smith (1988) analysed the word substitution errors made by EST in a naming task and found no significant effect of frequency for either semantic or phonologically related word substitutions. This is clearly a problem for Kay and Ellis' argument.

Caramazza and Hillis' (1990) patient, RGB, has a greater probability of making a semantic error for mid frequency categories as opposed to high frequency categories. HW, however, showed no effect of frequency. Already we are beginning to see a dissociation—all three of these patients are claimed to have a deficit in retrieval of the phonological form and yet one fails to show the predicted frequency effect. It would be interesting to know whether RGB and HW's semantic errors were higher in frequency than their targets.

Error types

EST's errors are reported as being predominantly phonemic paraphasias that often bore a close resemblance to the target word. However, describing EST and JCU as contrasting cases of "phonological anomia" and "semantic anomia" becomes rather less clear when a broader view of their naming is considered. Thus, although phonological errors are more frequent (26%), EST produces 20% semantic errors excluding circumlocutions (Smith, 1988) and 13% unrelated word responses. Similarly, JCU makes small numbers of phonologically related word errors. The distinction between these patients' disorders seems to be more one of degree of semantic and/or phonological involvement rather than a dissociation.

Furthermore, Caramazza and Hillis' patients are described as having the same deficit as one another (and the same deficit as EST) and yet one patient, HW, produces up to 34% phonological errors and does not show a frequency effect in the proportion of semantic errors produced, whereas the other patient, RGB, never produces phonological errors and shows a frequency effect.

It would appear vital to attempt to define the models used to interpret patient data in much greater detail in order to be able to investigate the nature of the deficits in terms of these models. Certainly within the logogen model the occurrence of phonological errors as a result of a deficit in lexical access is hard to explain. In this model retrieval of representations from the phonological output lexicon is "all or nothing" (it is not possible to retrieve partial information). Moreover, in the event of retrieval of the target not being possible (whether due to raised thresholds or loss/degradation of semantic information in transmission from the semantic system to the lexicon), any error will be semantically related to the target. This is because the logogens accumulate semantic information, and are not phonologically organised. (Alternatively the patient may produce "no response" or a circumlocution/description of the target. In the event of no semantic information regarding the target being available, the error could be a word that is unrelated to the target.)

Other accounts of EST's deficits

In addition to the deficit suggested by Kay and Ellis (1987; and Kay & Patterson, 1985) there are some other accounts of EST's impairment. For instance, Ellis, Kay, and Franklin (1992) argue that although the activation reaching the output lexicon is weak, it may be sufficient for strongly associated patterns to be accessed (high frequency words). When the associative strength is weaker (low frequency words), the activation may be sufficient to access part of the required pattern. That is, some, but not all, of the phonemes of the target word may be accessed, resulting in a phonological error. Ellis et al. claim that if the association between the semantic and phonological representation were weaker still for very low frequency words (i.e. very little activation reaches the entry in the output lexicon), then no useable phonological information would be forthcoming, resulting in an omission or circumlocution.

Thus, Ellis et al. would appear to conceive of the frequency bias occurring due to different strengths of associations (links) between semantic and phonological representations (see also Vitkovitch & Humphreys, 1991) as opposed to different resting levels of activation (Dell, 1986, 1989) or variations in thresholds (Morton, 1970). (Kay and Ellis (1987) do talk in terms of resting levels of activation within the lexicon.) However, Ellis et al. do not specify the precise mechanism by which part of the phonological form of a word might become available for production.

In contrast, Ellis and Young (1988) propose a "post-lexical" deficit for EST, suggesting that "sufficient activation seems to be reaching the phoneme level to activate some but not all the phonemes in the target word". This account is in the context of Ellis and Young's model of production (based on Stemberger, 1985), where nodes in the lexicon transmit activation down to nodes at the phoneme level. The difficulty with this account is that it is almost impossible to predict precisely how a connectionist model such as Stemberger's will function when lesioned without performing the simulation. Nevertheless, intuitively it seems that lesioning this model may produce some of the features of EST's production, including the presence of both phonological and semantic errors, and an effect of frequency (although the fact that errors are not higher in frequency than their targets is a problem). In contrast, a post-lexical account within a stage model (such as the logogen model) would have difficulty in accounting for the occurrence of semantic errors (unless another deficit is proposed) and the presence of a frequency effect.

NEOLOGISTIC JARGON APHASIA: KC AND RD

Ellis et al. (1983; Miller & Ellis, 1987) and Butterworth (1979, 1985) describe two patients with "neologistic jargon aphasia", RD and KC, respectively. Both patients produced large numbers of phonologically related errors and unrelated nonword responses in their spontaneous speech (see Table 5.2). Before describing the characteristics of these patients it is necessary to discuss briefly what is meant by the term "neologism".

Defining "neologisms"
Goodglass and Kaplan (1983) distinguish between "neologistic distortions" and "literal paraphasias". The former are defined as the "introduction of extraneous phonemes or transposition of intended phonemes so that less than half of the intended word is discernible as an intact unit", whereas literal paraphasias involve "transposition or introduction of extraneous phonemes such that more than half of the intended word is produced as an intact unit" (p.36). Whereas neologisms are exclusively nonwords (or else they would be classified as verbal paraphasias by Goodglass and Kaplan), literal paraphasias can be either words or nonwords.

In the papers that will be discussed there is a great deal of inconsistency in the way these terms are used. Thus, Butterworth (1979) includes under the class of "neologisms" nonword literal paraphasias ("target-related" neologisms) and unrelated nonwords, but excludes words, which are instead classified as verbal paraphasias. This contrasts with Ellis et al. (1983; Miller & Ellis, 1987), who include as neologisms all literal paraphasias. I shall attempt to avoid further

TABLE 5.2
Examples of connected speech and naming responses for KC and RD

KC (from Butterworth, 1979)

Connected speech: interview

Experimenter: "Do you remember my face?"

KC: "I forget seeing you before, sir; I remember the other /dɔkumɛn/ ... and was /plezd/ to see the other /dɔkumɛn/ ... my brother was with me ... and he was queen that I was /hɔdl/ with our own little ... mm ... bog ... my thing of /mɔgrli?/ ... you know, and he said 'oh thank you' he'd get it redone ... and /taipld/ again. I've done one or two things with that ... with my brother ... whom you've seen with me ... and he's waiting for you. I'm so sorry to do the boy all the trouble all the time ... I would love to see anyone ... even with a ... /kwailai/ return ... so that I could coo you with my brother ... but he's so very busy ... He's so busy.

Object-naming:

Target	KC's response
Matchbox	These are ... I have them at home ... at home ... then they're lended [E: What do you call this?] /wetrisɛz wetrıksɛz/ a /bæklənd/ and another bank ... for the /bœ ndıks/ I think they are ... I believe ... they're /z œndıks/ ... I'm sorry but they're called like /flıtərz lœndɔks/.
Scissors	Yes, I know those ... I know tho ... I had them ... a week or so before, sir, they are, sir, two ... /maitrɛks/ ... you get the one one, and the smaller one ... rather larger smaller ... and then the two /waitɛks/ ... would become with the ... vice ... the /voit/ of er ... /swin/ thing ... ax ... to ... /dızid/ ... the thing as it is.

RD (from Ellis et al., 1983)

Connected speech: picture description (scout camp)
(Words in brackets are possible targets for RD's neologisms)

A /bʌn bʌn/ (BULL) a /bʌk/ (BULL) is er ... /tʃɜʃıŋ/ (CHASING) a boy or a /skɜt/ (SCOUT) A /sk/ ... boy /skʌt/ (SCOUT) is by a /bəʊn pəʊ/ (POST) of pine. A ... post ... /pəʊn/ (POST) with a er /təʊn təʊ/ (LINE?) with /wɒʃıŋt/ (WASHING) hanging on including his socks /saız/ (?) A ... a /nek/ (TENT) is by the washing. A b-boy is /swı?ıŋ/ (SWINGING) on the bank with his hand (FEET) in the /strıŋt/ (STREAM).

Picture-naming:
(No full responses are given by Ellis et al., these examples may therefore not be representative of RD's complete responses)

Target	RD's response (partial)
scissors	/sıstənz/
penguin	/senstenz/
elephant	/enələst ... kenəltən/
screwdriver	/kıstrɔ/

terminological confusion by using the following different, and I hope transparent, terms:

1. Unrelated nonword (URNW) response, which corresponds to Goodglass and Kaplan's neologistic distortion; i.e. a nonword that is phonologically unrelated to the target (the criterion for relatedness may vary from a lax criterion of one shared phoneme in any position, to a strict criterion of 50% shared phonemes); e.g. stable → noke.
2. Phonologically related nonword (PRNW) response; e.g. stable → tible.
3. Phonologically related word (PRW) response; e.g. stable → table.
4. Unrelated word (URW) response, which refers to a word unrelated semantically or phonologically to the target; e.g. stable → knife.

PRNW and PRW together comprise Goodglass and Kaplan's class of literal paraphasias, and are what many authors would describe as phonological or phonemic paraphasias (not distinguishing along the lines of lexicality but generally assuming a predominance of nonwords). These two classes are also what Ellis et al. (1983) classify as neologisms. Butterworth includes PRNW and URNW in his classification of a neologism.

KC (Butterworth, 1979) and the "neologism generating device"

Butterworth (1979) studied the distribution and duration of pauses in KC's spontaneous speech. He found the normal distribution of pauses within and between grammatical classes, but neologisms (URNW and PRNW) were significantly more likely to follow a hesitant pause than real words. In addition, the average length of pause before an unrelated nonword (URNW) was longer than that before a phonologically related nonword (PRNW).

Butterworth (1979) argues that these errors occur when there has been a partial (PRNW) or complete (URNW) failure to retrieve a phonological lexical representation. Thus, search time is dependent on the amount of information retrieved. If KC manages to retrieve the whole word, the mean delay is around 80msec. However, if he cannot retrieve a whole word but is able to retrieve part of the target, gaps in this word fragment will have to be filled in to make it pronounceable. This usually results in the production of a phonologically related nonword, or occasionally by chance a real word will result (PRW; jargon homophones) with a mean delay of 295msec. If no part of the word is available, then a device for generating neologisms operates, with a resulting mean delay of 494msec. The differences in delay are due to later options only being implemented when earlier ones fail.

Butterworth's (1979) "neologism generating device" is described as a random phoneme generator: It selects phonemes at random from an inventory of English phonemes, combines them in a phonotactically regular way, and stores them in a buffer until the point in the current utterance when the target word is required. After use, Butterworth argues that the neologism remains in the buffer, decaying slowly. When the next lexical retrieval fails and the device operates again, there may be a few phonemes from the last running of the device still available in the buffer. As the new neologism will make use of this residue, it will sound rather similar to the first but not necessarily similar to any intervening words. This accounts for the strings of neologisms sharing phonemes that Butterworth documents in KC's spontaneous speech; for example, "I've had my piece of green and my [zʌp] stuff, my bit of ['zʌplən] … But he liked it. He's so ['zɪplən] to a yards … and yet after about two [lɪklən] I had from that man …" (1985, p.88). However, if a sufficient interval elapses between runnings of the device, all the phonemes in the buffer will have decayed, in which case the new neologism will be unrelated to the first.

Butterworth (1979) also found that the mean frequencies of the initial phonemes of the "device-generated neologisms" (URNW) differed significantly from those of phonologically related nonwords (PRNW), and samples of real words from KC and normal speakers. The mean frequency for the initial phonemes of "device-generated neologisms" also did not differ significantly from the expected value if the initial phonemes had been selected at random from a nonfrequency-biased set of possible phonemes. It would be interesting to know whether the initial phonemes of PRNW errors show a similar mean frequency if those that are identical to the initial phoneme of the target are excluded. It may be the case that by including those correct initial phonemes the sample has been biased. If the incorrect initial phonemes of the phonologically related nonwords show the same frequency pattern as the device-generated neologisms (URNW), then perhaps they are also generated in the same way (but only for those "missing" phonemes). This will be discussed further later on.

The "neologism-generating device" has been criticised on the grounds that it would appear to have no role in the "normal" language production system (Ellis, 1985), although Ellis does note that normal subjects can produce strings of neologisms if required. Buckingham (1990a) argues that the mechanism is in fact merely an alternative way of describing a system of phonological knowledge that is part of all speakers' cognitive capacities. It can be used by normal speakers (in word games, voluntary glossolalia) but is "released or disinhibited under various circumstances secondary to damage to the nervous system" (p.229).

In the model described by Butterworth (1992), the neologism generator can be viewed more clearly as being incorporated into the normal language-processing system. In this model, when the phonological lexical representation has been retrieved (in a condensed or abbreviated form) the information it contains is "spelt out" by independent encoding subsystems for syllable structure, prosodic structure, and segments. Each of these subsystems also has the capability to generate a "default" pattern if part of the necessary information is unavailable. Thus, if, for example, a stress pattern is unavailable for a two-syllable word, the prosodic structure system may assign a "default" stress pattern for that word (perhaps based on the frequency in the language). Similarly, if a segment is unavailable, a default may be generated. It is clear that this model can account for both phonological errors, where part of the phonological representation is unavailable (perhaps due to loss or damage in transmission from the lexicon), and for neologisms (URNW), where no information regarding the phonological representation is available to the encoding subsystems. This may occur as the result of a lexical retrieval deficit but could also be the result of "loss" in transmission between the lexicon and the encoding subsystems. In this case, each of the three subsystems would generate a default value—together they would generate a neologism.

Thus, this model provides a mechanism by which neologisms can be "generated", which is the same system that can account for the occurrence of some phonological errors. However, might even this model, which is intuitively more satisfactory, be subject to Ellis' criticism—what role might these "default-generating" systems have in the normal language system? One possibility is that subjects in the tip-of-the-tongue state may use them when attempting to find the target. Indeed, Ellis et al. (1983; Ellis, 1985) note the similarity between the neologisms (PRNW and URNW) produced by patients and some of the responses produced by subjects in induced tip-of-the-tongue (TOT) states. For example, when one subject was given a definition "a platform for public speaking" the response was "past ... pestul ... peda ... pedestal". Butterworth (1989) argues that in TOT states, subjects may be unable to retrieve the phonological form of the target but will be able to exploit the phonological information contained in the phonological address. It may be possible that this information could be used by the encoding subsystems, which can then generate default values for the missing information.

Suggesting that neologisms (URNW) arise as a result of the same deficit that could be responsible for the occurrence of some phonological errors (PRNW/PRW) is not new (e.g. Kertesz & Benson, 1970). If all the phonemes in a word are substituted as the result of a deficit in phonological encoding, then the error will no longer bear a relationship to the target. A second alternative is that unrelated nonwords arise as the result of a phonological error "on top of" a semantic error, resulting in the target no longer being discernible. Buckingham (1977, 1987, 1990a) credits Pick (1931) with being the first to suggest this "two-stage" account (see also Brown, 1972, 1977; Lecours & Lhermitte, 1972; Luria, 1970). Buckingham suggests that the recovery of these patients can help distinguish the source of the neologisms. Those patients whose unrelated nonwords are severe phonological errors (PRNW/PRW) should resolve to produce purely phonologically related responses. Those whose errors are phonological or semantic could resolve to produce either purely semantically related or purely phonologically related responses (or some of each). In contrast, Buckingham (1987, 1990a) argues that those patients who produce neologisms due to a severe lexical access deficit may over time produce fewer neologisms but more "less bizarre markers of lexical retrieval difficulties" (1990a, p.227). He suggests that the random generator's operation gradually becomes suppressed, but as lexical retrieval is still impaired the patients produce more circumlocutions, confabulations, etc.

It seems likely that in reality these three accounts of the occurrence of unrelated nonword responses (URNW) are not in competition. Some patients may indeed produce many unrelated nonwords as a result of a severe phonological encoding deficit (see Chapter 6), some as the result of a combined semantic and phonological deficit, and still others as a randomly generated string of phonemes to substitute for failed lexical retrieval. It could also be the case that it is the same "random generator" that operates (to different extents) in at least all of these possibilities. However, there are patients who have clear lexical retrieval difficulties but do not produce neologisms (they may make no response or circumlocute when trying to name). There are a number of possibilities why this might occur. The random generator itself may be impaired, making it unable to fill a lexical gap. Alternatively, neologisms may be generated but not produced by the patient due to good pre-articulatory monitoring.

RD (Ellis et al., 1983)
RD also produced large numbers of phonologically related and unrelated nonword errors (although a higher proportion of his errors appear to be related to the target than is true of KC). Ellis et al. (1983; Miller & Ellis, 1987) follow Butterworth in accounting for this pattern of errors in terms of partial or complete failure to retrieve an output phonological representation. However, as discussed earlier, in the logogen model (Morton, 1970, 1979) the output units (logogens) have thresholds,

making them "all-or-nothing" units. There can be no state when part, but not all, of the information encoded in a logogen is available. Miller and Ellis (1987) therefore suggest that logogens should take on some of the attributes of word-level nodes in interactive activation models. They illustrate their proposal using Stemberger's (1985) model (see Fig. 1.4, Chapter 1).

This account also gives an explanation of the frequency effect shown by RD in spoken word production, with high frequency words being more likely to be correct than low frequency words. Thus, they propose that in RD and other neologistic jargon aphasics the activation that cascades from the semantic level to the lexical level "is reduced to a trickle" (Miller & Ellis, 1987, p.266). This trickle of activation is sufficient to activate lexical units for high frequency words, whose resting level of activation is already high, but lexical units for lower frequency words never achieve maximum activation. This weak lexical activation results in weak activation at subsequent levels. Thus, phoneme-level units for lower frequency words will be only weakly activated and competing (inappropriate) phonemes only weakly inhibited. A word will be produced in which only some of the appropriate phonemes are sufficiently activated to be selected, and the empty slots will be filled by inappropriate phonemes.

Miller and Ellis argue that perseveration of phonemes from one neologism to another can be explained by persisting activation at the phoneme level from previous attempts. However, they also propose that each attempt at a word will be a fresh attempt to activate lexical and phonemic units, and therefore RD's successive attempts did not tend to result in closer approximations to the target. These two claims seem contradictory, and it appears unlikely that both can hold. The persistence of activation resulting in perseveration of phonemes between neologisms would also suggest that activation would persist when making a further target attempt. The phonemes of the target would receive extra activation from the second attempt, which in combination with the persisting activation from the initial attempt would make it more likely that the second word produced would be nearer the target than the first. This is not the case with RD, but is found to occur in some patients (Joanette, Keller, & Lecours, 1980; see Chapter 6 for further discussion). Persisting activation at the phoneme level also could not account for similarities between neologisms being observed even when a number of other (non-neologistic) responses intervene.

Once again, accessing representations in the output lexicon has been proposed as the location of a spoken word production deficit, on this occasion for RD and KC. EST (Kay & Ellis, 1987) was also suggested to have this level of deficit. However, although he produces many similar errors to RD in picture-naming (PRNW, PRW, URNW), their spontaneous speech is very different. RD continues to produce many phonologically related and unrelated nonword (PRNW and URNW) responses, whereas EST produces speech that is fluent but lacking in "content" words. However, the only sample of "spontaneous" speech given for RD is in a picture-description task, which can result in very different performance to free recall due to the additional constraint of the picture (Nickels, Byng, & Black, 1991).

Ellis and Young (1988) suggest that part of the explanation of the difference between RD and EST may lie in the auditory comprehension of these patients. They argue that neologistic jargon aphasia arises through a deficit in access to the phonological output lexicon combined with a degree of word deafness. Thus, these patients, unlike EST, cannot learn by monitoring their own speech which words cause difficulties and which do not, and cannot learn to limit their vocabulary to those words they can reliably say. Certainly, RD demonstrated a severe auditory comprehension deficit in the context of relatively well preserved written comprehension. However, despite RD's successive attempts failing to get nearer to the target, he does nevertheless make several attempts at each target. This would suggest that RD is at some level "monitoring" his production and attempting to "correct" it, although on occasions he attempts to "correct" a correct response. It is certainly not the case that all neologistic patients have severe comprehension deficits. (See Chapter 6 for further discussion of the relationship between phonological errors and comprehension.)

Butterworth (1992) suggests that rather than an access deficit or corruption of the phonological lexical representations, patients like EST, RD, and KC may have a deficit in transmission of information from the lexical representations to the processes of phonological encoding. As discussed earlier, he argues that information is lost in transmission to these processes, and so during the spelling out of this information by the systems for syllable structure, prosodic structure, and segments, defaults are generated to fill in the missing information. (This account is very similar to the majority of those used to describe the deficit in conduction aphasia, which will be described in Chapter 6.) Although this account is consistent with the data from KC, EST and RD both exhibit a marked effect of frequency on naming success. It is difficult to see how a frequency effect could be accounted for with a "post-lexical" deficit, unless the model used involved interaction between levels (unlike Butterworth's). (If there was interaction between the lexical and post-lexical levels, it is possible that higher frequency words would receive greater "support" from feedback to the lexical level than low frequency words, and so a frequency effect might result.)

EFFECTS OF PHONEMIC CUES

Howard and Orchard-Lisle (1984) found that providing the initial phoneme of the target increased their aphasic patient's success in retrieving the name of a picture, as have many other authors (e.g. Li & Canter, 1987; Li & Williams, 1991; Pease & Goodglass, 1978; Stimley & Knoll, 1991; Wingfield, Goodglass, & Smith, 1990). Howard and Orchard-Lisle suggest that phonemic cues temporarily raise the level of activation (or lower the thresholds of logogens) in the phonological output lexicon for words with the corresponding initial phoneme. Thus cues are interpreted as providing sufficient additional activation to bring an entry in the output lexicon to threshold. Cues are predicted to be effective when insufficient activation is reaching the output lexicon (due to a semantic deficit or a transmission deficit between semantics and phonology) or when thresholds are abnormally raised in the lexicon. Patterson, Purell, and Morton (1983) demonstrated that the beneficial effect of phonemic cues is short-lasting, with no significant benefit persisting after 5 minutes (or 30 intervening events).

Many authors have used the response to phonemic cues as support for localisation of deficit (e.g. Henaff-Gonon, Bruckert, & Michel, 1989; Kay & Ellis, 1987). However, caution should be exercised when interpreting the results of phonemic cueing. If a patient fails to respond to phonemic cues, it cannot be assumed that this is because the deficit occurs at a level where cues are not of benefit. It may be the case that the failure to benefit from cues is due to deficits in the additional processing capacities needed (e.g. auditory processing skills). It is also generally assumed that a phonemic cue cannot be of benefit to a patient once the phonology of a word has been successfully retrieved, but, as Howard and Orchard-Lisle point out, if the deficit is at the articulatory level—a failure of initiation—then phonemic cues may be successful in improving naming by virtue of being an "initiator".

Clearly further specification is needed regarding the precise mechanisms by which phonemic cues may be effective. Monsell (1987) discusses three possible routes by which phonemic cues could provide additional phonological activation to facilitate word production.

1. Partial activation in the auditory input lexicon of the representations of all words with an initial phoneme corresponding to the cue. This partial activation is transmitted to counterparts in the phonological output lexicon via a direct (nonsemantic) link between the lexicons. This partial activation then combines with the otherwise inadequate activation from input from the semantic system to facilitate production of the phonological form.

2. The phonemic cue partially activates matching lexical entries in the auditory input lexicon, which further constrains the semantics so that a more accurate semantic representation is transmitted to the output lexicon (compared to the representation from the picture alone), thereby enabling retrieval of the phonological representation.

3. "Bottom-up" activation: Monsell extends the account from interactive activation models (Dell, 1986, 1989; Stemberger, 1985) to phonemic cues. He suggests that in these models presentation of a phonemic cue would partially activate corresponding sublexical nodes in output via a sublexical input-to-output link. This activation reinforces positive feedback loops so that activation is increased for words with that phoneme in initial position; when combined with activation from semantics there is a more rapid rise in activation for the target than for competing word nodes, leading to its selection.

This sublexical mechanism for cueing is also compatible with a revised version of the logogen model, where limited interaction is invoked between the response buffer and phonological output lexicon. This would enable a cue to cause partial activation of words in the output lexicon via a sublexical route. Nickels (1992a) argues that this is the most probable route for phonemic cues to be effective in her patient TC (see also Hillis & Caramazza, 1991b, 1995; Miceli, Giustolisi, & Caramazza, 1991). However, it may still be the case that phonemic cues are effective in different ways for other patients. Before the effectiveness (or not) of phonemic cues can really be used as a diagnostic tool more research is needed to further specify the component processes involved.

LOSS OF STORED LEXICAL REPRESENTATIONS?

Howard (1995) describes a patient, EE, who is unable to name items that he can comprehend. He is not helped by phonemic cues, shows a marked effect of rated familiarity on naming success, and is highly consistent in which words he can name (even when the effect of familiarity has been partialled out). Errors are predominantly no responses (30%) and what Howard describes as "failed word retrieval" errors (62%). The latter error type includes semantic descriptions (e.g. pillow → what you lay your head on) and rejected responses (e.g. rake → not a spade; horn → trumpet … no).

Howard suggests that EE's results are consistent with two accounts in particular. First, loss of logogens within the phonological output lexicon in Morton's (1970, 1985) logogen model would predict EE's pattern. However, what is by no means clear is why damage to the lexicon resulting in loss of representations should necessarily occur in such a way that less frequent (and familiar) items are lost. Howard discusses the alternative account of a severe access impairment (where some items are never accessible), which would clearly predict EE's frequency effect (taking familiarity to be a measure of frequency). He rejects this on the basis that EE is not aided by extra time to respond and does not respond to phonemic cues (although, of course, there may be other reasons why phonemic cues are not successful for EE, and that extra time would help in a severe access deficit is highly speculative).

The second possibility that Howard discusses, to account for EE's data, is loss of entries within the semantic lexicon in the two-stage models of Butterworth (1989) and Levelt (1989). However, this deficit also would need to provide an account of the frequency effect and, as Howard notes, would predict an associated comprehension deficit (not present in EE).

SUMMARY

In this chapter we have described a number of patterns of speech output, all of which have been attributed to a deficit "between semantics and phonology". There have been reports of patients with deficits attributed to this level who produce semantic errors (Caramazza & Hillis, 1990; see Chapter 4), phonologically related real-word errors (Best, 1996; Blanken, 1990; Martin et al., 1994), phonologically related nonword errors (Kay and Ellis, 1987), and neologisms (Butterworth, 1979, 1985; Miller & Ellis, 1987). They can show effects of word length in either direction—forward (Friedman & Kohn, 1990; see Chapter 6), reverse (Best, 1995), or not at all (Kay & Ellis, 1987). They may or may not show effects of frequency (Caramazza & Hillis, 1990; Kay & Ellis, 1987) and imageability (Franklin et al, 1995), or may show category-specific effects (e.g. Farah & Wallace, 1992; McKenna & Warrington, 1980; Miceli et al., 1988).

It seems unlikely that all these patients really do have the same deficit, although some authors would go as far as to claim that for all aphasics "anomia originates from a difficulty in accessing the formal lexical representation" (le Dorze & Nespoulous, 1989, p.382). What is clearly required is further specification of models of speech production in such a way that they can incorporate all these data. Many of the patients' deficits were analysed using models with only one level of lexical access—adopting a two-stage model (e.g. Butterworth, 1989, 1992; Levelt, 1989) might be one step in the right direction, particularly in view of the wide acceptance of this type of model in psycholinguistics.

However, the processing assumptions of the two-stage models will also need to be further specified to determine precisely which patterns are predicted after damage to the model and which are not. Without better definition of the precise mechanisms by which lexical access occurs, I fear that the range of deficits attributed to this level of breakdown will continue to proliferate.

Clinically, it is obviously preferable to be able to distinguish between these patterns of symptoms in terms of different levels of breakdown and therefore be able to develop theoretically motivated rehabilitation for each. Currently it would seem counterintuitive to apply the same therapy to these very different types of aphasia on the grounds that they originate from the same deficit. Indeed, therapy may be used as another means of determining the nature of the disorder in these patients, by observing the different outcomes of different therapies with the same patient (and the same therapy with different patients).

CHAPTER SIX

Phonological errors: Deficits of phonological encoding and beyond

OVERVIEW

In the previous chapter we discussed a variety of different disorders attributed to lexical access difficulties. Here we move further "down" the processing model and describe the types of deficit that may occur after the stored phonological form of a word has been retrieved. This begins with a discussion of the possible distinction between phonological errors that occur as a result of retrieval deficits and those that arise from phonological encoding deficits (LEXICAL ACCESS, LEXICAL STORAGE, AND PHONOLOGICAL ENCODING). Many patients who make phonological errors have been classified as having the classical aphasia syndrome "conduction aphasia". This syndrome has been the focus of much research and we discuss here the different accounts that have been proposed (CONDUCTION APHASIA).

The chapter then picks up on a point made in Chapter 5 regarding the role that comprehension and monitoring may have in the production of phonological errors. We begin by looking at studies that have examined the relationship between auditory comprehension and phonological errors in speech production, concluding that there is no simple relationship (PHONOLOGICAL ERRORS AND COMPREHENSION). The discussion therefore moves on to examine the possible role of "inner speech" as a means of monitoring speech production and whether a deficit in inner speech might account for the production of phonological errors (INNER SPEECH AND ERROR DETECTION).

We then turn to examine the features of the phonological errors themselves (CHARACTERISTICS OF PHONOLOGICAL ERRORS), in terms of the position of errors within a word (CONTEXT AND SYLLABLE POSITION), the types of errors that occur (SUBSTITUTIONS/OMISSIONS/ADDITIONS), and the occurrence of sequences of phonological errors and in particular whether these sequences get progressively closer to their targets (CONDUITE D'APPROCHE). Then we review which variables affect the production of phonological errors, just as we did with semantic errors (VARIABLES AFFECTING THE PRODUCTION OF PHONOLOGICAL ERRORS).

The final sections of the chapter examine the possibility of deficits after the level of phonological encoding—phonetic deficits or deficits in executing motor programmes. We begin with a brief discussion of whether even the more fluent aphasic patients, who seem to have well-articulated speech, might in fact make phonetic rather than phonological errors in speech production (SUBTLE PHONETIC DEFICIT IN FLUENT APHASIA). This leads to a discussion of those patients who have been described as having deficits in executing motor programmes for speech (BROCA'S APHASIA AND APRAXIA OF SPEECH). In particular we focus on the difficulty in defining what characterises the disorder and the methodological problems that arise.

LEXICAL ACCESS, LEXICAL STORAGE, AND PHONOLOGICAL ENCODING

This chapter is primarily focused on the examination of phonologically related errors in aphasic word production (phonologically related words and nonwords: PRW and PRNW). As described in Chapter 2, the phonologically related errors that occur in (nonaphasic) slips of the tongue are generally attributed to errors in post-lexical, phonological encoding processes (such as copying segments into slots in Shattuck-Hufnagel's slot-and-filler mechanism). However, when subjects are in the tip-of-the-tongue (TOT) state, they often seem to have only partial information available regarding a word's phonological form (commonly the identity of the initial phoneme and the number of syllables). These subjects also produce phonologically related real-word and nonword responses during their attempts to retrieve the target. For example, Brown and McNeill (1966) give the examples of "saipan", "sympoon" (PRNWs) and "Siam" (PRW) produced when subjects were attempting to retrieve the target "sampan". Thus, in normal subjects both real words and nonwords can occur as the result of either a difficulty in retrieving the stored phonological form of a word (as in the TOT state), or an error in the process of phonologically encoding the correctly retrieved phonological form.

The aphasia literature also discriminates between these two levels of deficit—"lexical" and "post-lexical"—as underlying the production of phonological errors. In Chapter 5, we discussed a number of patients with patterns of breakdown attributed to deficits in lexical retrieval; among these were some who produced phonological errors (e.g. RD, Ellis et al., 1983; EST, Kay & Ellis, 1987). It was noted that some models cannot easily account for the production of phonological errors from this level of deficit (see also Chapter 1). In particular, the logogen model predicts semantic and not phonological errors from deficits in accessing/retrieving phonological output representations (logogens). Furthermore, any model (including the logogen model) that incorporates "all or none" retrieval mechanisms where partial information cannot be retrieved would not be able to account for the production of phonologically related nonwords (PRNW) from a lexical access deficit (although phonologically related words may be possible). Unfortunately, the nature of the retrieval mechanism is generally rather underspecified and it is often unclear whether, in the event of inadequate activation/raised thresholds, for example, part of the representation may be retrieved. In Butterworth's model, even when lexical retrieval fails, it is possible to use the systematic correspondences between the phonological address and phonological representation for generation of a response (the mechanism proposed for responses in tip-of-the-tongue states).

"Silent phonology" tasks are one possible way of distinguishing deficits of lexical access (and storage) from (post-lexical retrieval) phonological encoding deficits. These are tasks where judgements are made on the basis of phonology without overt articulation. In order to perform the tasks accurately the phonological representation must be retrieved. These tasks include judgements of homophony (e.g. Do WRITE and RIGHT sound the same?) and rhyme (e.g. Do WHITE and BRIGHT rhyme?) and can be administered using pairs of pictures or written words (written words should be spelt irregularly to ensure lexical retrieval is required). Pseudohomophone detection (e.g. Which one sounds like a real word – BRANE or PRANE?) and phonological lexical decision (e.g. Does BRANE sound like a real word or not?) can also be used. The ability of patients to perform these types of task clearly demonstrates that they can access phonological representations, and if they are better at these tasks than they are at producing the same words, then their deficit can be localised as post-lexical. However, if a patient fails on these tasks it can be difficult to draw clear conclusions as there may be many different reasons for failure other than a deficit in retrieval of phonological representation (e.g. difficulty with holding the items in a buffer for comparison). Also, of course, many patients perform at a rather equivocal level (above chance but below normal) and this is difficult to interpret.

A further possibility for dissociating deficits of lexical retrieval and phonological encoding is the use of cross-modality and cross-task comparisons. Thus, a phonological encoding deficit should affect all modalities of output (naming, reading, and repetition) to an equivalent degree as each requires this process. However, for deficits of lexical retrieval, repetition and reading may be better than naming as sublexical phonological information (that information used in reading or repeating nonwords) can be used.

Nevertheless, because of the frequency with which patients have co-occurring deficits (e.g. in reading/repeating nonwords), in practice it can be difficult to distinguish between access/retrieval deficits and phonological encoding deficits. Much depends on the precise nature of the retrieval mechanism and how the phonological representations are stored. Some authors might argue that the presence of a frequency effect would be evidence for a lexical access deficit. However, if the model incorporated feedback from a post-lexical buffer to the lexicon (to refresh the contents of the buffer as they decay), then perhaps a frequency effect might result when this buffer is impaired. High frequency items would receive greater support from the lexical level and therefore be more resistant to the effects of decay. Clearly this is speculative, but it does illustrate how difficult it is to state categorically that a particular pattern of breakdown can only be associated with a particular level of deficit. The same holds for length effects (more phonological errors on longer words), which are typically ascribed to post-lexical, phonological encoding or buffer deficits. However, this again depends on how the phonological representations are constructed and accessed—whether, for example, longer words have "larger" representations, which are more difficult to access.

Kohn and Smith (1994a) compare two patients who make phonological errors (and URNW/URW), LW and CM, with respect to this issue. They argue that dissociable patterns can be predicted from a model that distinguishes underspecified lexical-phonological representations and fully specified phonemic representations (probably equivalent to the results of phonological encoding). They argue that both a deficit in activating lexical-phonological representations and a deficit in constructing phonemic representations should result in a word-length effect, production of both phonologically related nonwords and (depending on the severity of the disorder) unrelated nonwords, and nonword responses (PRNW/URNW) with simplified CV structure. However, each level of breakdown has "distinctive features". Thus (Kohn & Smith, 1994a, p.79):

> ... the distinctive features associated with the lexical deficit are:
> (a)   nonword errors with increased CV complexity,
> (b)   phonic verbal paraphasias (i.e. PRW),
> (c)   nonword errors missing more target phonemes and containing more nontarget phonemes than with the phonemic deficit,
> (d)   greater difficulty producing pseudowords than real words.
>
> The distinctive features associated with the phonemic deficit are:
> (a)   word fragments involving initial portions of targets,
> (b)   phonemic errors increasing from left to right,
> (c)   comparable production of pseudowords and real words

These predictions would by no means be unanimously agreed (even within the same model). For example, although many authors would support the idea that phonemic planning/phonological encoding proceeds in a left-right direction, this does not necessarily mean that errors should increase from left to right. It could be the case that there is simply a set probability for each phoneme being subject to an error, which does not change with the number of phonemes encoded. Nevertheless, Kohn and Smith find that one of their patients, LW, shows the predicted pattern for a deficit in activating lexical-phonological representations, whereas the other, CM, shows the pattern predicted for a phonemic planning deficit (cf. Kohn and Smith's, 1990, account for CM's errors in terms of an inability to clear a phonemic output buffer). Clearly, what is now required is further research to discover whether, as Kohn and Smith would predict, these features always cluster together in this way. If patients are found who show different clustering of the features (e.g. nonword errors with increased CV complexity and phonemic errors increasing from left to right), then the strength of the predictions will be thrown into doubt.

So far we have contrasted deficits in lexical retrieval and post-lexical phonological encoding. However, there is also the possibility of loss or corruption of lexical representations. Butterworth (1992) addresses in detail the issue of distinguishing between deficits of (phonological encoding) translation processes subsequent to lexical retrieval and corruption of the representations themselves, concluding that there is little evidence that the storage of phonological information in the lexicon is disturbed in any of the patients in the literature to date. Distinguishing between these two types of deficit is also far from straightforward and, as ever, depends on the precise details of the model used to describe speech production. Butterworth argues that several observations for the production of each target are necessary to observe the consistency of response. Without this, he suggests, it is not possible to distinguish deficits of storage from those of phonological encoding.

Butterworth (1992) demonstrates this using data from one patient, DJ (Butterworth, 1985). A single response where one phoneme is erroneous (producing "tenant" as /semənt/) is ambiguous regarding whether a representation is corrupted or an error has occurred during the process of phonological encoding (or for that matter, although Butterworth does not address the issue, whether the deficit is one of retrieving the phonological representation). However, by observing the production of the same word several times (e.g. /semənt/ /emnənt/ /tenəmən/ /tɜneɪt/) it was possible to see that each segment of the target word (tenant) was produced in its correct position at least once (and no error occurred more than once). Thus, it was not the case that DJ had a corrupted representation for "tenant" but, Butterworth argues, the most likely account is that DJ has "some problem in translating an intact PLR (phonological lexical representation) into a phonetic plan ... on each attempt to say the word some of the information about the segments was lost in transmission, but in a rather unsystematic, perhaps random, way" (p.269).

Butterworth also suggests that if a patient suffered corruption of stored phonological representations, then identical responses would be expected every time this item was retrieved. I would argue that this is not necessarily the case. Consider the situation where a lexical representation is so severely corrupted that some segments can no longer be identified, although the syllabic and prosodic structure is intact. In this case, when segmental spell-out occurs default segments will be generated to fill the positions of the segments that are so badly corrupted so as to be indistinguishable. The default segments need not always be the same segments and therefore the errors need not be identical (although the uncorrupted segments would always be correct). For example, for the target "leaf" the representation is corrupted to /li:#/ (with an unspecified final phoneme), and when this word is produced default segment generation could result in a variety of errors, e.g. /li:m/ /li:p/ /li:d/ /li:b/.

CONDUCTION APHASIA

When examining phonological errors in aphasic word production, the patients described are very often "conduction aphasics". Goodglass and Kaplan (1983) define conduction aphasia as "the syndrome in which repetition is disproportionately severely impaired in relation to the level of fluency of spontaneous speech and to the near normal level of auditory comprehension ... The outstanding speech difficulty is the correct choice and sequencing of phonemes, so that literal paraphasia repeatedly interferes with production" (p.86).

It is clear that the distinction between conduction aphasia and neologistic jargon aphasia (as described in Chapter 5, but often subsumed within the category of Wernicke's aphasia; e.g. Ellis et al., 1983) can be difficult to maintain (especially for those neologistic jargon aphasic patients who have good comprehension). Both groups of patients can produce phonologically related word and nonword errors (PRW and PRNW; literal paraphasias) and unrelated nonword (URNW) responses, the proportions of each type varying from patient to patient, as does the degree of comprehension impairment. The precise balance between these factors combined with where the experimenter sets his boundary criterion will determine into which group a patient will fall. This inevitably means that within both groups there will be patients with a range of comprehension impairments and ratios of PRW/PRNW to URNW responses, and that the variation within groups may well be as great as that between groups. This serves to reiterate the fact that syndrome labels can be arbitrary and at times may be misleading. With this cautionary note in mind, much of interest has nevertheless emerged from studies of conduction aphasics (see Kohn, 1992, especially Buckingham's chapter reviewing the literature) and in particular from the analysis of the features characterising their phonological errors.

"Repetition" versus "reproduction" conduction aphasia

Following much debate in the literature regarding the nature of the deficit in conduction aphasia (e.g. Dubois et al., 1964; Lecours & Lhermitte, 1969; Saffran & Marin, 1975; Strub & Gardner, 1974; Warrington & Shallice, 1969), Shallice and Warrington (1977) suggested that conduction aphasia should be subdivided into two separate functional groups: "repetition" and "reproduction". The repetition group consists of patients whose repetition failure is due to a disturbance of auditory-verbal short-term memory. The patients show a variety of disturbances of recall and recognition of word and nonword lists but quite good single word production. Shallice and Warrington note that none of their patients (e.g. KF, Warrington & Shallice, 1969, 1972; Shallice & Warrington, 1970, 1974) made phonologically related (or unrelated nonword) errors in spontaneous speech. They suggest that these patients should be considered as patients with a deficit of short-term memory (STM) and the term "conduction aphasia" restricted to those patients with a disorder of reproduction (although these patients may have a co-occurring STM deficit).

Shallice and Warrington characterise the reproduction deficits as being an inability to reproduce on request individual words, which is exacerbated by using longer, less frequent words (e.g. LS, Strub & Gardner, 1974). In such cases, they suggest that the severity of the reproductive defect would be closely related to the severity of the phonological errors in their spontaneous speech, and probably also related to difficulty with object-naming and reading aloud. It is this deficit that is of interest here, and those patients who have primarily a short-term memory disorder and little or no spoken word output deficit will not be discussed.

Accounts of reproduction conduction aphasia

The literature on conduction aphasics contains reports on patients with, superficially, very similar patterns of deficits, yet very different accounts have been given for these deficits. Thus, excluding the STM analysis mentioned earlier, Caplan, Vanier, and Baker (1986) distinguish three different accounts: the "decoding" or multicomponential deficits theory of Strub and Gardner (1974); the "disconnection" account of Kinsbourne (1972); and Dubois et al.'s (1964) "encoding" or "output" account. Although these are offered as alternatives, Shallice and Warrington (1977) note that it is unclear how far they are actually substantively different rather than reformulations.

Caplan et al. (1986) describe the essential differences between these three accounts as being the extent to which the abnormal production of conduction aphasics is said to reflect "input" disturbances, the transmission of the products of input processing to motor planning mechanisms, or disturbances of motor planning mechanisms themselves. Strub and Gardner (1974) suggest that there is reduced efficiency in "decoding (words) for meaning" or in the ability to "synthesize ... phonemic components for eventual articulation". Kinsbourne (1972) argues that the defect in his patient, JT, is due to a pathologically limited channel from short-term memory to the speech response programme, which is very similar to the second part of Strub and Gardner's proposed deficit.

There are many different theories of the deficit in conduction aphasia, which might be termed "output" theories. For example, Dubois et al.

(1964) describe conduction aphasia as being a disorder of the "first articulation" (Martinet, 1949), resulting in difficulties of programming a word or a phrase, to be distinguished from deficits at the level of phonetic programming (the second articulation). This theory would appear to suggest that the lemma has been correctly accessed and that the deficit occurs either in accessing the phonological lexical representation or during the process of phonological encoding. These two possibilities may be distinguished, with some authors suggesting a locus for the deficit at the level of phonological encoding. Thus, Nespoulous, Joanette, Ska, Caplan, and Lecours (1987) argue that phonological errors in conduction aphasia are the result of "the disruption of different mechanisms whose objective is to compute linear phonological representations from deeper, more abstract and probably nonlinear lexico-phonological representations, retrieved from the lexicon" (pp.78–79), in other words, disruption of the slot-and-filler mechanism (Shattuck-Hufnagel, 1979, 1987). Similarly, Kohn (1988) suggests that "information about the phonological structure of the target is available, but there is difficulty constructing a string of phonemes from this information" (p.111; see also Butterworth, 1992; Caplan, 1987; Caplan et al., 1986; Kohn, 1984; Pate, Saffran, & Martin, 1987; Yamadori & Ikumura, 1975). In contrast, Kohn and Smith (1990; Kohn, 1989) argue that the deficit that causes their patient, CM, to produce phonologically related words and nonwords is an inability to clear information from a phonemic output buffer (cf. Kohn & Smith, 1994a). Béland, Caplan, and Nespoulous (1990) give yet another account, using a model where stored representations are abstract and highly underspecified. They account for the errors made by their conduction aphasic patient, RL, in terms of errors in applying the phonological rules that lead from underlying representations to surface representations.

The "post-lexical" accounts referred to earlier contrast with those "output" theories that locate the deficit in access to representations in the phonological output lexicon. For example, Valdois, Joanette, Nespoulous, and Poncet (1988) hypothesise "a difficulty in accessing complete segmental information" (p.87). Friedman and Kohn (1990) also describe their patient, HR, as having a deficit involving impaired access to the phonological output lexicon. They supported their interpretation using tests of homophony and rhyme to assess HR's ability to access phonological representations within the lexicon without the confounds of a possible output problem. They interpret HR's impaired performance on these tasks as evidence for impaired lexical phonological access (but see the earlier discussion of "silent phonology" tasks for difficulties interpreting this result).

Goodglass et al. (1976) asked patients whether they could identify the initial letter and the number of syllables of a target word they had been unable to produce in response to a picture (cf. tip-of-the-tongue studies, Chapter 1). They found a clear superiority on the part of their conduction aphasic group compared to Wernicke's and anomic groups. Thus, they argue that for the conduction aphasics "an inner auditory representation may be present but is prevented from setting into motion the final neural events which activate the articulatory system" (p.152).

In summary, we can see that the theories of the nature of the deficit in conduction aphasia are many and various. Once again we are drawn to the conclusion that the disagreement regarding the deficit is most likely a result of the fact that there is no one deficit that can characterise all the patients that are classified under the term conduction aphasia. Different patients may have different deficits that underlie very similar surface symptoms (principally phonological errors). We therefore return now to examining the characteristics of phonological errors and the factors affecting their production.

PHONOLOGICAL ERRORS AND COMPREHENSION

In Chapter 5 we discussed two patients, RD and EST, who showed different patterns of errors in spontaneous speech despite rather similar errors in picture-naming (PRW/PRNW). Ellis and Young (1988) suggested that part of the explanation of the difference between these patients might be due to a difference in auditory comprehension. They suggest that the "neologistic jargon aphasic", RD, had a severe auditory comprehension deficit, which led to impaired monitoring of his speech (and therefore no inhibition of errors), unlike the patient EST, who had good auditory comprehension and few phonological errors in spontaneous speech.

The patient JS, described by Caramazza, Berndt, and Basili (1983), showed a similar pattern to RD (Ellis et al., 1983), with severely impaired auditory comprehension in the context of good written comprehension, and produced literal paraphasias (PRNW) and neologisms (URNW) in spontaneous speech. Caramazza et al. account for JS's pattern of deficits in terms of a phonological processing deficit that affects performance in all tasks that require the generation of a phonological code. Miller and Ellis (1987) argue against this conclusion on a number of grounds, including that it is difficult to conceive of which aspects of information-processing models could be "the phonological processing system". There are a number of processing components that involve phonological codes; Miller and Ellis note that some of these components can be impaired but not others, which makes them loath to combine them into a "phonological super-module". Most importantly, patients with auditory comprehension deficits similar to those of JS, the so called "pure word deaf" (word-sound deaf) patients (e.g. Saffran, Marin, & Yemi-Komshian, 1976), do not necessarily exhibit the PRW, PRNW, and URNW in spontaneous speech shown by JS (and RD and KC). However, Best and Howard (1994a) argue that almost all reported cases of word-sound deaf patients do produce at least occasional phonological errors. They suggest that, rather than a direct causal relationship, a common factor may underlie both symptoms. They argue that one possibility is that these errors may arise because the impaired auditory processing system impedes (internal) monitoring of speech production (but see the discussion later in this section; they prefer another possibility to account for the deficits of their word-sound deaf patient—impaired operation of an "internal clock", which may be responsible for the timing necessary to both interpret auditory signals in reception and produce finely tuned motor movements in speech production).

Thus, a severe auditory comprehension deficit is not *sufficient* to produce neologistic speech. Butterworth (1985) argues that neither is an auditory comprehension disorder *necessary* for the production of neologistic jargon. He cites Lecours and Rouillon (1976), who distinguish three types of fluent aphasic speakers (excluding conduction aphasics) according to the incidence of neologisms, but no type could be distinguished on the basis of their receptive performance. Lecours, Osborn, Travis, Rouillon, and Lavallee-Huynh (1981) describe a patient, Mr. K, whose spontaneous speech exhibited large numbers of PRNW and URNW, but yet his "comprehension of oral and written language was nearly normal" (p.12). Similarly, Peuser and Temp's (1981) neologistic patient, Mr. W, scored nearly perfectly on single-word comprehension tasks and grammaticality judgements (although he was impaired on sentence comprehension).

Miceli, Gainotti, Caltagirone, and Masullo (1980) studied the relationships between expressive and receptive phonemic disorders in 69 aphasics. They found no correlation between degree of phonemic output disorder and the number of phonemic discrimination errors. When they examined the performance of individual patients, they found that some of their patients with severe phonemic output disorders did not show discrimination deficits (whereas other patients with similar or less severe output disorders were unable to make the phonemic discriminations required by their test). Thus, although it may be broadly true that neologistic jargon aphasics have disordered comprehension, there is no simple relationship between the two (see also Butterworth & Howard, 1987).

Nickels and Howard (1995b) also confirm these results, finding no significant correlation between proportion of phonological errors in naming and any measures of input processing (auditory synonym judgements, auditory lexical decision, and minimal pairs) for a group of 15 aphasics. By lesioning an implementation of Dell and O'Seaghdha's (1991; similar to Dell, 1989) computational model of speech production, Nickels and Howard found that the lesioned models demonstrated a strong correlation between proportion of phonological errors in naming and comprehension accuracy, unlike the group of aphasics. Thus, although their patient data are in accordance with models where there are distinct input and output processing systems, they are not consistent with Dell and O'Seaghdha's model, nor with other models where speech input and output share the same processing components (e.g. Allport, 1985) or with the position taken by Caramazza et al. (1983) of a "general" phonological processing deficit.

However, in Allport's model it is the lexicon containing phonological representations that is common to input and output. Therefore, although damage to the lexicon would result in a correlation between phonological errors in comprehension and production, deficits of access or retrieval from the lexicon can dissociate (input or output). As we discussed earlier, Butterworth (1992) argues that there was little evidence for any patient (at that point in time) having damage/loss of stored lexical representations and that the patients' deficits could be described in terms of impairments in the transmission of information from one subsystem to another. Nickels and Howard do not claim their patients were exceptions to this pattern. Thus, their data do not provide conclusive evidence against theories comprising a single phonological lexicon provided there are independent access routes for input and output phonology.

Nickels and Howard suggest that perhaps the issue is more complex. Speakers monitor and often self-correct almost any aspect of their speech, including phonological errors. In Chapter 3 it was suggested that one way this monitoring might be occurring is using the auditory processing system. However, having an intact auditory processing system, which would enable the patient to detect phonological errors, may not be enough. In order to detect and inhibit errors prior to articulation (pre-articulatory editing) the patient might also be thought to need intact "inner speech", whereby the output of the speech production system is passed to the auditory comprehension system for evaluation.

INNER SPEECH AND ERROR DETECTION

Goldstein (1948) suggested that the fundamental deficit in conduction aphasia (which he termed "central aphasia") was at the level of "inner speech". This was a central language process mediating between nonverbal thought and external speech: "Inner speech is the totality of processes and experiences which occur when we are going to express our thoughts, etc., in external speech and when we perceive heard sounds as language" (p.94).

Feinberg, Rothi, and Heilman (1986) tested Goldstein's hypothesis that conduction aphasia is a disturbance of inner speech, using homophone, rhyme, and syllable-length judgements from pictures. They tested five conduction aphasics who all had a severe disturbance in repetition and object-naming, but intact comprehension. Feinberg et al. argue that four of the patients successfully performed these judgements on words they could not produce, whereas one patient performed at chance (except on the syllable-length judgements, where Feinberg et al. suggest she may have been using orthographic information). Although the patients were mostly not performing at the levels of control subjects (and the absolute values differ little from those of Friedman and Kohn's patient, who was argued to be impaired), Feinberg et al. argue that they did show a significant dissociation between tests of spoken word production and inner speech. Thus, they propose that there are at least two types of conduction aphasia: Some patients only have a word-production deficit (the majority of their patients) and others have word-production and word-finding (lexical access) disturbances (cf. Kertesz & Phipps, 1977). It is also interesting to note that although three of their patients showed very similar levels of performance across all three tasks, one patient showed normal levels of performance on homophone and syllable-length judgements but was impaired relative to control subjects on rhyme judgements. This is in accordance with Howard and Franklin's (1987, 1990, 1993; Nickels, Howard, & Best, 1997) proposal that there are different loci for the performance of these tasks.

Howard and Franklin (1987, 1990, 1993) distinguish between homophone and rhyme judgements, arguing from normal subject data that an output phonological representation is sufficient for judging homophony, but that access to an auditory input code is required for rhyme judgements. They demonstrate that their patient, MK, is unimpaired on homophone judgements but performs at chance with written rhyme judgements (although he is able to perform auditory rhyme judgements accurately). MK is also unable to perform pseudohomophone detection (whether a written nonword sounds like a real word e.g. BROOZE vs. TROOZE). Howard and Franklin therefore argue that pseudohomophone detection also requires access to an auditory input code via an internal output-to-input feedback loop (Monsell's, 1987, "inner ear" loop). Thus, there is a distinction between the type of silent phonology tasks that can be performed at an output level (predominantly the type of "inner speech" abilities to which Feinberg et al. are referring) and those that can only be performed at input (via "inner ear" links). Inner speech in terms of the output-to-input link (inner ear) has been proposed as one method of monitoring in order to achieve pre-articulatory editing of errors (see Chapter 3).

Schlenck, Huber, and Willmes (1987) analysed the type and amount of linguistic repairs and prepairs produced by aphasic patients and nonaphasic controls. Prepairs seem to be viewed by the authors as similar to Levelt's (1983) "covert" repairs (self-correction or modification of errors in inner speech prior to the stage of articulation). Schlenck et al. found that repairs (overt attempts at self-correcting a word that has been articulated) were rare in their data. Although the patients produced significantly more errors, they did not differ from the controls in terms of number of repairs. Schlenck et al. suggest that the post-articulatory monitor cannot be functioning well in these patients. However, the pre-articulatory monitor seems to be unimpaired as large numbers of prepairs occurred.

Schlenck et al. argue that their data does not support a monitor that is exclusively based on language comprehension (like that of Levelt, 1983), as Wernicke's patients, despite their low auditory comprehension scores, did not show fewer prepairs than other aphasic groups (although overall, prepairs were positively correlated with comprehension). However, as prepairs are defined as pauses and filled pauses before production of an item, there is a possible confounding of the effects of failed lexical search (which might also result in pausing) and pre-articulatory editing mechanisms. Thus, the conclusions that can be drawn from Schlenk et al.'s data are limited.

Nickels and Howard (1995a) also examined the relationship between the inner ear, occurrence of behaviour indicative of self-monitoring (e.g. self-corrections), and auditory processing skills (auditory synonym judgements, auditory lexical decision, and minimal pairs) in their group of aphasic patients. First, they compared auditory processing skills and the proportion of phonological errors with (attempted) self-corrections, which imply successful detection of an error (patients did not tend to attempt to "correct" correct responses). However, no significant correlation was found, suggesting that there was no simple relationship between whether or not a patient had good comprehension (to enable detection of an error) and whether they attempted to correct an error.

Monitoring can occur via audition (listening to what you've just said). However, if pre-articulatory monitoring is to occur, then the internal feedback loop ("inner ear") needs to be intact to pass the potential output to the auditory input processes for evaluation (in accounts where the editor is equated with the auditory comprehension system). Nickels and Howard found no correlation between phonological errors in naming and auditory processing skills even when only those patients who had relatively "intact" feedback loops were included in the analysis (as measured by performance on silent rhyme judgements).

Nickels and Howard also performed a series of analyses to examine lexical bias in their patients' phonological errors. As discussed in Chapter 3, the presence of a lexical bias can be argued to reflect characteristics of the speech-editing mechanism (Baars et al., 1975; cf. Dell, 1986, 1989). This hypothesis predicts a correlation between the size of lexical bias (the proportion of phonologically related responses that are real words) and the degree of sparing of those processes involved in pre-articulatory editing (feedback loops and auditory input skills). However, no significant correlation was found between these factors. Moreover, none of the patients was found to have a significant lexical bias (i.e. they did not produce phonologically related word errors at greater than chance rates; see Chapter 5 for discussion of this issue).

Thus, Nickels and Howard argue that they provide a number of lines of evidence which suggest that in their group of patients monitoring is either not occurring, or not occurring in the hypothesised manner (see also Maher, Rothi, & Heilman, 1994). Even though they describe some patients who have all the components available for internal monitoring, including intact internal pre-articulatory feedback, this monitoring does not seem to occur (or at least does not result in a lexical bias). However, the presence of attempts at self-correction of phonological errors and false starts would seem to suggest that monitoring is occurring at least some of the time. Nickels and Howard note that every patient attempted to self-correct some of their phonological errors and some patients attempted to correct all of their errors.

Nickels and Howard suggest that the presence of a production-based pre-articulatory monitor could account for the occurrence of self-corrections and false starts in the absence of a correlation with comprehension. They draw comparisons with the checking mechanism suggested by Butterworth (1981), in which lexical selection occurs twice and the outputs are compared. They do, however, note that this checking mechanism must occur relatively late in the production process to detect errors arising due to deficits in phonological encoding processes subsequent to lexical selection. They also note that as a picture-naming task was used there is relatively little time for error detection prior to articulation. It is therefore possible that the observed self-corrections are also the result of this "pre-articulatory" production-based monitor, but due to the task demands an error is only detected subsequent to articulation.

However, although this does not preclude the presence of a comprehension-based monitor, Nickels and Howard suggest that this monitor is not reliably employed by some or all of the aphasic subjects studied here. This is supported in part by data from Boller, Vrtunski, Kim, and Mack (1978), who performed an experiment to examine the effects of delayed auditory feedback (DAF) on aphasic speech production. They found that although control subjects' speech was disturbed by DAF, some of the aphasic subjects showed significantly less disruption. Both Wernicke's aphasics, who had poor comprehension, and conduction aphasics, who had good comprehension, showed this pattern. (In contrast other, nonfluent, aphasics' speech was even more disrupted by DAF.) It could be argued that this pattern occurs because some aphasics "ignore" their own output and are therefore less disrupted by DAF. This could be strategic adaptation to their deficits; Panzeri, Semenza, and Butterworth (1987) argue for a dynamic relationship between functional deficit and strategic adaptation (for their patient, a strategic avoidance of attempting difficult lexical retrievals). Thus, for some patients attempts at monitoring via the comprehension system may be abandoned as even when errors are detected they cannot be corrected successfully.

CHARACTERISTICS OF PHONOLOGICAL ERRORS

The target-related phonological errors produced by aphasics have been analysed in detail by a number of authors, both in terms of their similarity to normal slips of the tongue and the characteristics of the errors themselves.

A number of authors have noted that the phonological errors patients produce usually obey the phonotactic rules of their language, as do normal speech errors (e.g. Blumstein, 1978; Buckingham & Kertesz, 1974).

Green (1969), Lecours and Lhermitte (1969), and Blumstein (1973) all note that, as with normal subjects, the target and the error phoneme that replaces it tend to be articulatorily and acoustically similar (see also Nespoulous et al., 1987; Valdois et al., 1988). Blumstein (1973) found that the distribution of errors was significantly different from that expected by chance, with errors that differed from the target by one distinctive feature being more frequent than those that differed by more than one. However, Miller and Ellis (1987) compared genuine consonant substitutions made by their patient, RD, with "pseudo-substitutions" created by randomly reassigning error phonemes to the error positions in the set of target words. They found that both genuine and pseudo-errors tended to differ from their targets by only one or two distinctive features. Moreover, the observed distribution of the genuine errors did not differ significantly from the distribution predicted by chance on the basis of the pseudo-errors. Similarly, Kohn and Smith (1990) note that many of the interacting consonants of their patient, CM, had little featural resemblance to one another.

CM was also unusual in that he showed more difficulty with vowels than consonants in sentence repetition, although not in single-word repetition. Burns and Canter (1977) found a significant increase in errors from vowels to single consonants to consonant clusters for both Wernicke's and conduction groups of aphasics on a picture-naming task. Vowels are involved in normal speech errors at a much lower rate than consonants (Laubstein, 1987, cited in Kohn & Smith, 1990).

Context and syllable position

Both normal and aphasic subjects have also been noted to show effects of context on errors, insofar as target and error phonemes involved in exchanges tend to share similar preceding and/or following phonemes. Lecours and Lhermitte (1969) note that phonemes appearing in contexts free of identical or similar units are not prone to aphasic transformations. They also argue that the creation (by addition of a phoneme) or destruction (by deletion of a phoneme) of a pair of identical or similar phonemes are basic phenomena in sequential errors. Similarly, target and substituting phonemes are argued to originate from similar positions in syllables (Blumstein, 1978).

Kohn and Smith (1990; Kohn, 1989) found that the majority of CM's anticipatory and perseverative errors shared syllabic position with their source segment (81%). Furthermore, 86% of the errors involved syllable rimes. (This might be considered unsurprising as CM showed more difficulty with vowels, which must occur in the rime, than consonants). Burns and Canter (1977) also found that groups of both Wernicke's and conduction aphasics made more errors in final than initial position. Kohn and Smith (1990) proposed that it was syllable-final and not word-final position that was important, as 61% of CM's coda errors involved word-medial consonants. This tendency for errors to occur on syllable rimes contrasts with the normal speech error data, where onset errors predominate (Shattuck-Hufnagel, 1987). In a single-word production task with aphasic patients, Martin, Wasserman, Gilden, Gerstman, and West (1975) found that errors occurred more frequently on the second (final) cluster than the first. However, Shattuck-Hufnagel (1987) no longer found a greater susceptibility to errors on initial phonemes for normal subjects in her tongue-twister task when phrasal structure was removed. Kohn (1989) argues that combining the normal tendency to produce consonant errors in word-onset position with CM's tendency to produce errors in rimes reinforces the notion that "onset + rime" is a functioning structure in word production.

Miller and Ellis (1987) tested the hypothesis that the phonological forms of words might be subject to an accelerated rate of decay in patients who make phonological errors. These errors reflect the patient's attempt to construct a pronunciation on the basis of a rapidly vanishing phonological trace. They suggest that the less time an item spends in storage the greater the likelihood that it will be produced correctly. Thus, in general, early phonemes in words will be less prone to decay than later ones, and so should be produced more accurately. They tested this prediction on RD's errors, and found that the observed and chance distributions did not differ significantly, although the accuracy of position one (word-initial) phonemes was higher than expected (as with CM). Miller and Ellis therefore rejected the decay hypothesis for RD.

Franklin (1989a) also performed this analysis on the PRW and PRNW errors of two patients, MK and EC, on a repetition task. MK showed no significant difference from the chance distribution. Although EC did show a significant difference and linear decay effect, Franklin argues that this cannot be the property of accelerated decay in the response buffer as EC does not show the same pattern of decay in oral reading. Instead, she argues that the linear decay for EC is a property of an impaired acoustic to phonological conversion system (used in repetition).

CM (Kohn, 1989; Kohn & Smith, 1990), like normal subjects, made mostly errors involving an interaction between two words. However, his errors were only anticipations and perseverations and never exchanges, which tend to predominate in normal speech errors. In contrast, for Pate et al.'s patient, NU, the domain within which phonemes interacted to induce errors seemed to be largely defined by the boundaries of individual words. They argue that the likelihood of error appeared to be dependent on characteristics of individual target words rather than on the contexts in which they were embedded. (It should be noted that although CM's data are primarily from analysis of sentence repetition, the data from NU were mostly obtained by recall of written material. This modality difference cannot be ruled out as a possible source of differences in the data).

Substitutions/omissions/additions

Burns and Canter (1977) analysed the phonological errors of Wernicke's and conduction aphasics and found that substitutions accounted for the majority (62%) of all errors made, with 30% additions and 9% omissions (Ardila, 1992, reports similar proportions for Spanish aphasics). There were, however, differences between the two groups, with conduction aphasics making twice the number of omissions, and additions being more prevalent in the responses of Wernicke's patients. In contrast, Pate et al. (1987) found that omissions were the most frequent type of segmental error for NU.

Miller and Ellis (1987) found that 82% of RD's picture-naming errors could be classified as substitutions by phonemes not found anywhere in the target, and 18% as transpositions of a phoneme from one position in the target word to another in the neologism. However, when all the error phonemes were extracted and randomly reassigned to the vacant slots in the neologisms, the number of "pseudotranspositions" was found to be the same as the number of apparent transpositions in the original corpus. They conclude that substitutions are the only type of error occurring in RD's neologisms, and that if a patient makes both apparent substitution and transposition errors, then the proportion of transpositions must be substantially over 20% before one can conclude with confidence that genuine phoneme movements are occurring.

Conduite d'approche

Aphasic patients frequently make more than one attempt at a target, which may or may not result in the eventual production of that target. This is commonly known as *conduite d'approche*. Joannette, Keller, and Lecours (1980) found that over sequences of phonemic approximations (SPAs) conduction aphasics as a group tended to show a continuous progression towards the target, both for vowels and for consonants. Broca's patients tended to show the same progression for vowels but not for consonants, and the Wernicke's patients did not show a progression towards the target for either consonants or vowels. Indeed, the consonants even tended to show a negative progression, that is, a progression away from the target.

Valdois, Joanette, and Nespoulous (1989) found a similar pattern, with their conduction aphasic, C1, showing a constant progression towards the target, whereas for two Wernicke's patients, W1 and W2, the longer the sequence of approximations, the further from the target was the last approximation. Valdois et al. suggest that the production of sequences in itself suggests that monitoring of speech production is relatively well preserved. However, they propose that C1's sequences support the existence of a comparitor mechanism (which tells the system an error has occurred) coupled with an error analyser, which provides a detailed analysis of the erroneous production. This possibly indicates which part of the production conforms to the target and what the exact nature and location of the error within the response is. Joanette et al. (1980) found that the only condition under which their conduction aphasics did not progress nearer the target was in the repetition of nonsense words. They suggest that this is due to the lack of a stored representation that can be called on (as a more long-standing comparator) as the temporary representation of the nonword is decaying over time.

Gandour, Akamanon, Dechongkit, Khunadorn, and Boonklam (1994) studied the SPAs made by a Thai conduction aphasic, PK. His sequences also showed a steady progression towards the target word (regardless of the eventual outcome of the final attempt or the length of the sequences). However, they point out that the SPAs are not especially effective in leading to the correct target word. On only 36% of occasions was PK's final response correct. They note that this is comparable to the rates of success reported by other authors (Kohn, 1984, 45%; Kohn, 1989, 30%; Valdois et al., 1989, 47%).

Kohn (1984) also looked at SPAs in Broca's, Wernicke's and conduction aphasics. She failed to find significant differences between the groups in terms of the number of correct targets produced at the end of each sequence. However, she did not compare overall proximity to the target for initial and final attempts, which might have given different results. Miller and Ellis (1987) did measure proximity for RD's sequences of errors and in fact found a significant bias towards the final response being further from the target than the initial attempt. They suggest that this is what would be predicted if the major determinant of a "correction" is in fact random variation.

Valdois et al. (1989) also found that despite the differences between C1 and W1-W2, all three subjects showed sensitivity to target word length, with errors tending to preserve the number of syllables present in the target. This same pattern was found to occur in RD's errors (Miller & Ellis, 1987), with 80% of errors sharing the same number of syllables as the target. This was significantly greater than the number of pseudo-errors sharing the correct number of syllables when errors were randomly reassigned to targets.

Thus, some authors have found evidence for sequences of errors to get closer to the targets (i.e. *conduite d'approche* does occur), but this is by no means the case for every patient who makes sequences of responses. It seems likely that there are a number of prerequisites for *conduite d'approche* to occur. First the patient must detect the error, then, as Valdois et al. (1989) suggest, there must be a mechanism by which the error is compared with the target and only correct phonemes "re-used" on a second attempt.

VARIABLES AFFECTING THE PRODUCTION OF PHONOLOGICAL ERRORS

Word length

Goodglass et al. (1976) noted that naming failure rates increase in each of their aphasic syndrome groups (e.g. Broca's, Wernicke's) with increasing syllable length but that the diagnostic groups were not affected equally by increasing word length. Their "anomic" group had only a minimal increase in failures with length, but all the other groups, and in particular the conduction aphasics, showed a marked relationship between word length and naming success. Although Howard et al. (1984) found a significant correlation between word length and naming success for their group as a whole, 6 of their 12 patients showed no significant correlation. They therefore stress that (as for word frequency) treating the data from the patients as a group leads to much higher estimations of the importance of word length than is justified from the effects on individual subjects.

Dubois et al. (1964) note that for the conduction aphasics they studied, monosyllabic words were more disturbed in repetition than bisyllabic words, which in turn were more disturbed than trisyllabic words. For nonwords they report the opposite effect, with monosyllabic nonwords producing fewer errors than bisyllabic and trisyllabic nonwords, although producing similar numbers of errors to monosyllabic *words*. Dubois et al. argue that the basis for this effect is not the length of each item but the quantity of information in each syllable. In a nonword, the quantity of information is equal for each of the syllables, as they are all equally improbable. In contrast, when a polysyllabic *word* is used, the later syllables carry less information and the recognition of the form is determined by the first syllables. Thus, they argue that for words, length is a facilitating factor. This explanation would seem to hinge on an input disorder; for instance, Howard and Franklin (1988) noted that their patient, MK, demonstrated better comprehension of trisyllabic than monosyllabic words (assessed by word definition). They argue that this effect is due to trisyllabic words having fewer phonologically similar word neighbours than monosyllabic words, resulting in trisyllabic words being less easily confused. For example, there are more words that are phonologically similar to cat (e.g. can, kit, bat, etc.) than crocodile.

Dubois et al.'s (1964) findings contrast with the vast majority of the cases reported in the literature (except Best, 1995; see Chapter 5). Goodglass et al. (1976) found that Broca's, Wernicke's and conduction aphasics all showed a significant deterioration in naming performance with an increase in the number of syllables in a word. Similarly, RD (Ellis et al., 1983, Miller & Ellis, 1987), RL (Caplan, 1987; Caplan et al., 1986), NU (Pate et al., 1987), CM (Kohn, 1989; Kohn & Smith, 1990), and HR (Friedman & Kohn, 1990) all make greater numbers of errors with increasing syllable length. In contrast to the majority of the studies, Caplan (1987) reports data (citing a personal communication with Béland) that disambiguate whether this syllable length effect is truly an effect of number of syllables or simply due to the increased number of phonemes. RL was tested on a set of words all of which contained four phonemes but varied between one and three syllables; testing confirmed that the length effect was due to the number of syllables rather than the number of phonemes (although no details are given on whether these stimuli are matched in any way).

Caplan locates the deficit for RL in an error-prone process between underlying and surface phonological representations. This would seem similar to Butterworth's (1992) account of information loss between the phonological lexical representations and the translation processes (with some kind of capacity limit to spelling out intact information in the phonological representations).

Nickels and Howard (in prep.) also attempted to dissociate effects of length in terms of number of phonemes and number of syllables. They studied 12 aphasics and found that 7 patients showed significant effects of number of phonemes on repetition performance (and 5 of these also showed effects in naming, Nickels and Howard, 1995b). That is, they were worse at repeating words with more phonemes, even when the syllable number was the same (i.e. in comparisons of one-syllable words with three, four, or five phonemes; two-syllable words with four, five, or six phonemes). In contrast, Martin et al. (1975) found that for ten aphasic subjects there was no difference in the frequency of errors for two- or five-phoneme monosyllabic words.

However, none of Nickels and Howard's patients showed effects of number of syllables, i.e. worse performance with words of more syllables when number of phonemes is controlled. In fact, three patients showed the reverse effect—they were worse at repeating one-syllable than two-syllable words when they were matched for number of phonemes. Nickels and Howard argue that this reverse syllable-length effect arises because of the confound with complexity of syllable structure— one-syllable words will inevitably contain more consonant clusters than two-syllable words with the same number of phonemes (compare the four phoneme words "paste" and "skill" with "tiger" and "urban"). This will be discussed further in the next section.

Nickels and Howard's data support any model that allows a dissociation between effects of number of syllables and number of phonemes, such as that of Levelt (1989, 1992). They also examined the relationship between targets and errors and found that only around 50% of all errors maintained the syllabic (CVC) structure of the target for any of the patients (nor was the onset-nucleus-coda structure maintained, except in the case of one patient). In other words, errors involved phoneme omission and addition as well as substitution. Nickels and Howard argue that it therefore seems unlikely that these patients' deficits involve errors when copying segments into fully specified slots (one for each segment) as described by, for example, Shattuck-Hufnagel (1979, 1987), which would predict maintenance of syllabic structure. However, although incompatible with a fully specified metrical frame (Butterworth, 1992; Shattuck-Hufnagel, 1979, 1987), these results are entirely consistent with Levelt's (1989, 1992) model, which associates segments with more global metrical frames that only specify syllable weight (and do not have slots for individual segments). In this model a deficit in associating segments with frames need not result in an error that maintains syllabic structure.

Pate et al. (1987) found that the length effect in their patient, NU, was not simply due to the increased number of opportunities to make errors when a word has a greater number of syllables. They compared the proportion of syllables correct in one-, two-, three- and four-syllable words and found that NU correctly pronounced over 90% of syllables correctly in one- and two-syllable words, compared with around 80% of syllables in three-syllable words and less than 60% in four-syllable words. In order to determine whether the syllable effect applied across as well as within words, Pate et al. also examined the effect of unit length in syllables across phrases and word blocks. Although NU was less successful at producing longer than shorter multiword units, the effect did not parallel the syllable constraint in words. Thus, NU's production even of eight-syllable or longer multiword units was more accurate than his production of single four-syllable words. Pate et al. conclude that NU's pattern of impairment reflects a constraint on the amount of phonological information that can be programmed within a unit and that this constraint applies primarily within and not across word boundaries.

Pate et al. find that their data does not fit easily with an explanation in terms of either the slot-and-filler model (Garrett, 1980;

Shattuck-Hufnagel, 1979) or interactive activation models (Dell, 1986; Stemberger, 1985). They suggest that accounts in terms of models that represent multiple independent levels of phonology (e.g. prosodic structure, syllable structure, segment structure), such as those subsequently developed by Butterworth (1992) and Levelt (1989), look promising and might ultimately provide an adequate account of their data.

Complexity of syllabic structure

It has often been noted that some aphasics have greater difficulty in accurately producing words containing consonant clusters than single consonants (e.g. Mackenzie, 1982; Trost & Canter, 1974). This may be explained in terms of "articulatory complexity", that is, a deficit in implementing the motor programmes.

Nickels and Howard (in prep.) examined effects of complexity of structure on aphasic repetition by contrasting repetition of pairs of words that differed only in whether a single consonant or a consonant cluster occurred in a particular position (e.g. tool–stool; wick–quick; fell–felt, fine–find). There is, of course, a problem when examining effects of complexity on performance as it is inevitably confounded with number of phonemes (within a syllable). The more phonemes a syllable has the more clusters it will have. Nickels and Howard attempted to distinguish these variables by using regressional statistics (logistic regression—similar to multiple regression but for use when there is a dichotomous dependent variable) to determine whether any unique effects of either number of phonemes or number of clusters could be found when the shared variance was accounted for. Five patients seemed to show effects of complexity of syllabic structure (clusters) on performance, with worse performance on words containing clusters than those containing only single consonants. Of these, two patients showed clear, independent effects of complexity (with two further patients showing possible effects) and one patient showed an independent effect of number of phonemes.

The two patients who showed effects of complexity showed very different error patterns: EMM's errors predominantly involved reduction of the consonant cluster to a single consonant (90% of errors); in contrast, LAC reduced less than a quarter of consonant clusters (errors were phoneme substitutions and omissions elsewhere in the word). It seems plausible that two rather different processes underlie their errors. It is interesting that EMM did not show an effect of phonemes on performance (whereas LAC showed effects of both complexity and phonemes), demonstrating that although highly confounded the effects of these variables are dissociable.

Nickels and Howard discuss Levelt's (1989) proposal that in the process of segmental spell-out clusters require an additional procedure. This takes the cluster as input and produces the component segments as output. They suggest that a deficit at this level would predict the complexity effect found. If this cluster spell-out procedure fails completely, then, they argue, one might expect a single consonant to be produced in place of the cluster (as was the case for EMM).

Nickels and Howard also discuss a number of other possibilities for the source of a complexity effect, including the process of associating segments with more general frames (specifying, for example, onset, nucleus, and coda, rather than slots for individual segments; Levelt, 1992). This rule-governed procedure could be error-prone, not only in terms of actually inserting the segments into the frames but also with respect to the rules that govern insertion. For example, consonants are, by default, attached to the onset of a syllable. However, as the frame does not specify whether the onset comprises a singleton or a cluster, if the process is prone to error but maintains the syllable structure as defined by the frame (in terms of syllable weight, as onset and rime, or morae) then cluster reduction is likely. The resulting syllable can be "well-formed" even with omission of a consonant within a cluster, which may not be the case for other phonemes. Nickels and Howard also speculate that this level of deficit might be thought to predict both an effect of syllabic complexity and number of phonemes (if there is a certain probability of an error occurring, then the more phonemes there are in a word the greater the likelihood of an error). This is, of course, the pattern shown by LAC. They suggest that the fact that she makes both cluster reduction and other types of error might also fit with this type of deficit. While cluster reduction might occur more frequently, other errors may occur. For instance, if a phoneme is omitted in part of the syllable where a segment is obligatory, then another (perhaps randomly generated) phoneme may be inserted in its place, resulting in a substitution error.

Nickels and Howard also note that a source of an effect of clusters on performance might be at the articulatory level. The articulatory "gestures" required for articulating consonant clusters will often involve more complex sequences of movements than those for single consonants. Thus, in those patients with articulatory difficulties clusters may cause more difficulties. This may lead to either errors in the successful completion of the articulatory gestures or even reduction of the cluster to the (easier to articulate) single consonant. Indeed, EMM, one of the patients that showed effects of complexity, had been classified as having apraxia of speech (see later) and so an explanation at this level could be appropriate for her.

Lexical stress

Stress errors have received relatively little attention in the aphasic word production literature, although Pate et al. (1987) did note that their conduction aphasic patient, NU, had a tendency to omit unstressed syllables (but not stressed syllables; see also Patterson, 1980). A similar finding is reported by Niemi, Koivuselka-Sallinen, and Hanninen (1985), where 84% of the phoneme omission errors for three Finnish Broca's aphasics were found in unstressed syllables. Goodglass, Fodor, and Schulhoff (1967) contrasted production of function words when stressed and unstressed in a sentence context and conclude that "Broca's aphasics depend on the stressed features of an intended utterance in order to initiate and then maintain the flow of speech". There are also reports in the dyslexia literature of a different type of stress error—usually misassignment of stress within an otherwise correct production (e.g. Coltheart, Masterson, Byng, Prior, & Riddoch, 1983; Miceli & Caramazza, 1993).

Few authors have attempted to manipulate stress experimentally, contrasting different lexical stress patterns. However, Black and Byng (1986) compared the ability of six deep dyslexic subjects to read aloud matched sets of two-syllable words that are stressed on either the first or second syllable. They found that those words with stress on the second syllable were more likely to result in errors (see also Black & Byng, 1989; Cutler, Howard, & Patterson, 1989). Cutler et al. (1989) also note that one of Black and Byng's patients (PW) made more errors on picture-naming for a small sample of words with unstressed first syllables than on a set of words (matched on frequency and length) with stressed initial syllables.

Nickels and Howard (submitted) examined this issue further by comparing repetition of matched sets of bisyllabic words that varied in whether primary stress was on the first or second syllable (e.g. 'tiger, 'habit; ca'noe, sa'lute). They found effects of lexical stress on word production for six of their twelve patients. All patients were significantly worse at repeating bisyllabic words with primary stress on the second syllable (second-stress words). Five of these patients showed significantly different distribution of error types across bisyllabic words with primary stress on the first or second syllable. Characteristic errors on second-stress words, for the five patients that showed differences, involved (1) syllable deletion of the initial (relatively "unstressed") syllable (e.g. reward → ward; erupt → rupt) and (2) phoneme reduplication (a kind of phoneme "harmony", e.g. romance → momance; obese → bobese).

No patient made errors in stress assignment where primary stress was placed on the initial rather than the final syllable. This is the kind of error that is characteristic of the stress errors reported in the normal speech error literature (Cutler, 1980) and the literature on "surface dyslexia" (e.g. Miceli & Caramazza, 1993). The fact that these errors are absent makes it unlikely that the deficit is that suggested by Butterworth (1992) where, when the stress pattern is not retrieved from the phonological representation, a default is generated. This default is the most common stress pattern for bisyllabic words in English (strong-weak). Although this level of deficit would indeed predict poorer performance on second-stress words as found here, the errors should be stress misassignment, not syllable deletion and/or phoneme reduplication.

Nickels and Howard discuss a number of possible accounts as to why unstressed syllables in word-initial position should be particularly vulnerable to syllable omission or phoneme reduplication. They argue that there is no immediately obvious account for this phenomenon within Levelt's (1989, 1992) and Butterworth's (1992) descriptions of phonological encoding. Nickels and Howard suggest that perhaps the most plausible account for this phenomenon is at the articulatory level (for some, as yet undefined, reason unstressed initial syllables are "difficult" to articulate and that to facilitate production, "simplification" occurs by means of deletion of initial syllable or reduplication of consonants). However, Nickels and Howard note that the problem with this account is that it largely amounts to a redescription of the data, and indeed it is not the case that all the patients who show this pattern are those who might be traditionally be thought of as having "articulatory" deficits (e.g. one patient has "fluent" speech).

Phoneme and syllable frequency
Blumstein (1973) found that the frequency distribution of phonemes in aphasic speech was significantly correlated with the distribution of phonemes found in the spontaneous speech of normal subjects. She also found that as the frequency of occurrence of a phoneme increased, the relative frequency of errors decreased. Currently no research appears to have been performed regarding effects of syllable frequency on aphasic errors. However, Levelt and Wheeldon (1994) found effects of this variable on normal naming latencies (independent of effects of word frequency) and it may therefore play a role in aphasic errors too.

Markedness
Blumstein (1973) examines phonological errors in terms of an aspect of phonological theory known as "markedness". This characterises the hierarchical relationship between phonemes based on the positive or negative value of the features used to describe them. The unmarked

member of a phonological opposition is argued to represent the more basic or "natural" value. For example, [+ voice] is considered the marked value, and [– voice] the unmarked value. Blumstein suggests that the prediction for aphasic data is for an overall simplification of the phonological system and that consequently performance on the marked structures will be impaired more than on the unmarked structures. Results were found to be significant in the predicted direction for the groups of Broca's and Wernicke's aphasics but not for the conduction aphasics, although they showed a tendency for marked phonemes to be substituted by unmarked more than vice versa. Nespoulous, Joanette, Béland, Caplan, and Lecours (1984; Nespoulous et al., 1987) also found that Broca's patients showed preferences for certain phonemes as substitutes, although they caution against assuming this is necessarily a markedness effect. Their conduction aphasics showed no preferential error patterns in their substitutions. Thus, they found that whereas Broca's patients were likely to reduce consonant clusters to single segments (marked to unmarked), their group of conduction aphasics were as likely to produce new clusters in errors as to reduce target clusters. They argue that this is consistent with the finding that the errors are "pre-motoric" and cite Shattuck-Hufnagel and Klatt's (1979) finding that consonant substitutions in normal subjects also do not show markedness effects.

Sonority
Clements (1988) describes a markedness hierarchy that is based on the sonority differentials of demisyllables (onset-vowel; vowel-coda). Sonority refers to the perceptual prominence of one phoneme relative to another. The sonority hierarchy is ordered from least to most sonorant: Obstruent (stops, fricatives, affricates)-Nasal-Liquid-Glide-Vowel (for initial demisyllables; for final demisyllables the order is reversed). This sequence of sonority orders onset and coda phonemes (together with language-specific phonotactic constraints). A number of studies have suggested that sonority may influence the mechanisms underlying phoneme substitutions, omissions, additions, and transpositions in aphasic phonological errors (Bastiaanse, Gilbers, & van der Linde, 1995; Blumstein, 1973; Buckingham, 1990b). However, Christman (1994) argues that these studies often fail to distinguish between constraints of sonority and those of phonotactics. She studied the "target-related neologisms" (PRNW) of three aphasics and concludes that they may be formed by processes constrained by sonority independent of phonotactics (although this also played a part). However, statistically significant effects were only found for dissociations between sonority and phonotactic constraints for substitution errors (not addition and

omission errors). Phonemic substitutions tended to replace nasals, liquids, and glides with obstruents, and obstruents tended to be replaced by other obstruents. She suggests that when processing failures occur, replacement segments are generated by default (cf. Butterworth, 1992), with sonority (and presumably phonotactics) being a constraint on this mechanism.

SUBTLE PHONETIC DEFICIT IN FLUENT APHASIA

The distinction has long been drawn between fluent aphasia (Wernicke's/conduction aphasics with, it is claimed, posterior lesions) and nonfluent aphasia (Broca's-type aphasics with, it is claimed, anterior lesions). As is clear from the discussions in this chapter, fluent aphasics' errors are generally considered to be phonological (or phonemic) in origin (from deficits in accessing phonological representations or encoding these representations for output). In contrast, the deficits of the "nonfluent" patients, and in particular Broca's aphasics and/or apraxics, have been considered more phonetic in nature (see later). However, Buckingham and Yule (1987) state that the "once cherished dichotomy between phonetic and phonemic disintegration ascribed to anterior and posterior patients, respectively, cannot be so easily drawn" (p.123). They argue that "there is likely to be a subtle articulatory disruption in the fluent aphasics that affects the acoustic picture, which leads to hearer inconsistency and to false evaluation of the phonemic intentions of the fluent aphasic speakers" (p.120).

Vijayan and Gandour (1995) review the acoustic, physiological, and perceptual studies that have examined this phenomenon. They argue that the acoustic evidence (e.g. Baum & Ryan, 1993; Blumstein, Cooper, Goodglass, Statlender, & Gottlieb, 1980; Ryalls, 1986; Tuller & Story, 1987) yields conflicting results and that what is most striking is the heterogeneity of the findings for fluent aphasics. They suggest that "given the inconsistency in findings, and the knowledge that variability in performance is characteristic of brain damage, one should exercise caution in interpreting increased variability as a defining feature of a subtle phonetic deficit" (p.113). They suggest that perceptual and physiological evidence points to a "speech motor deficit in anterior patients and in some conduction aphasic patients, but not in Wernicke's aphasic patients" (p.114). Vijayan and Gandour conclude that there is currently little convincing evidence for the notion of a "subtle phonetic deficit" in fluent aphasia. Of course, this is not to say that some individual patients may not present with a fluent aphasia and also a co-occurring deficit that results in phonetic errors—this issue will be discussed further in the next section with reference to apraxia of speech.

BROCA'S APHASIA AND APRAXIA OF SPEECH

Apraxia of speech has been defined as "an articulatory disorder resulting from impairment, as a result of brain damage, of the capacity to program the positioning of speech musculature and the sequencing of muscle movements for the volitional production of phonemes. The speech musculature does not show significant weakness, slowness, or inco-ordination when used for reflex and automatic acts. Prosodic alterations may be associated with the articulatory problem, perhaps in compensation for it" (Darley, 1969, cited in Rosenbek, Kent, & LaPointe, 1984).

One of the long-standing debates in the field of aphasiology is whether apraxia of speech as a disorder exists as a separate entity or whether patients given this label are in reality merely suffering from a type of aphasia or dysarthria. I shall not attempt a comprehensive review of the issue here (see, for example, Buckingham, 1981; Critchley, 1970; Lebrun, 1989; Poeck, 1988; Rosenbek et al., 1984; Wertz, Lapointe, & Rosenbek, 1984) but will instead merely give a glimpse of the complexities involved in the interpretation of the literature.

As is common in other areas, one of the major problems stems from differences in terminology, with different authors giving different names to what appear to be the same disorders. For example, the disorder Wertz et al. (1984) call apraxia of speech seems equivalent to Broca's (1861) "aphemia", and Marie's (1906) "anarthria". Buckingham (1981a) also lists frontal speech apraxia, Broca's aphasia, motor aphasia, verbal aphasia, phonetic disintegration of speech, apraxic dysarthria, cortical dysarthria, and oral verbal apraxia; see also Lebrun (1989) for further details of the historical debates. Similarly, some authors will use the same term to refer to different symptom complexes. For example, Broca's aphasia for some authors refers to a disorder distinct from apraxia of speech, which may itself co-occur with Broca's aphasia (e.g. Goldstein, 1948; Itoh et al., 1982), whereas for other authors a necessary part of the syndrome of Broca's aphasia is the presence of apraxia of speech (e.g. Shinn & Blumstein, 1983; Trost & Canter, 1974), or they consider the two disorders indistinguishable (e.g. Kohn, 1988). Kertesz (1979) notes that "the relationship of Broca's aphasia to apraxia of speech remains controversial" (p.3).

There has been a tendency none the less to consider together and compare the results of studies that examine patients in groups defined by different criteria (and which may or may not be given the same label).

For example, in her review of phonological production deficits in aphasia, Kohn (1988) compares as equivalent the findings of Blumstein and colleagues (e.g. Blumstein, Cooper, Zurif, & Caramazza, 1977; Blumstein et al., 1980; Shinn & Blumstein, 1983) and Itoh and colleagues (e.g. Itoh, Sasanuma, Hirose, Yoshioka, & Ushijima, 1980; Itoh et al., 1982). However, Blumstein et al. used patients classified as Broca's aphasics on the basis of "results of the Boston Diagnostic Aphasia Examination (Goodglass & Kaplan, 1972), neurological tests (including brain scans or CAT scans), and consensus at aphasia rounds" (Shinn & Blumstein, 1983, p.94). In contrast, Itoh et al. used patients defined as having apraxia of speech. For example, "all of the apraxic patients exhibited a conspicuous impairment in articulation, as well as in prosody, due to apraxia of speech. Two of these patients demonstrated a relatively 'pure' form of apraxia of speech without any symbolic disturbance due to aphasia, while the other two patients had mild aphasia in addition to apraxia of speech" (Itoh et al., 1982, p.194). Most probably the two populations of patients used by Itoh et al. and Blumstein et al. overlap to some extent but they are also likely to differ in nontrivial ways. How meaningful, then, is Kohn's (1988) resulting conclusion that "a deficit in phonetically recoding phonemic strings appears to best characterise the phonological production that distinguishes Broca's aphasics from members of the other two subgroups (Wernicke's and conduction aphasics)" (p.111)?

Munhall (1989) also criticises many of these studies on methodological grounds (see also Vijayan & Gandour, 1995). He argues that in examining the variability of patients with apraxia of speech—in terms of voice-onset time (VOT) or ability to reach specific articulatory targets—the methods of analysis are often unsophisticated and sometimes inappropriately used. People clearly speak at different rates, move their articulators different amounts, and speak with more or less precision, but comparisons of variability between clinical and normal populations are frequently made without the aid of good normative data. For example, Itoh and Sasanuma (1984) based their comparison on data from a single control subject. Munhall also points out that speaking rate and movement amplitude need to be controlled between control and apraxic groups. Itoh and Sasanuma (1984) report that the velar movements of their apraxic patient were more variable than normal. However, the patient had a much slower speaking rate than the control. It is impossible to determine what role the slower speaking rate played in the observed patterns in the data.

Given these cautionary notes regarding the interpretation of the literature, what are the features often associated with apraxia of speech? Darley (1982, pp.10–13) lists 13 characteristics:

1. Articulatory errors increase as the presumed complexity or difficulty of the speech motor task increases. Thus errors increase in the order: vowels, singleton consonants, consonant clusters (see e.g. Burns & Canter, 1977; Canter, Trost, & Burns, 1985; Johns & Darley, 1970; Monoi, Fukasako, Itoh, & Sasanuma, 1983; Shankweiler & Harris, 1966; Trost & Canter, 1974).

2. Errors may be made more often on initial consonants than consonants in other positions (e.g. Canter et al., 1985; Odell, McNeil, Rosenbek, & Hunter, 1991; Shankweiler & Harris, 1966; Trost & Canter, 1974; but see Johns & Darley, 1970; LaPointe & Johns, 1975).

3. Both a consistency effect and an adaptation effect are observed as an apraxic patient repeatedly reads the same material. That is, although errors tend to occur in the same places in the text, the overall number of errors declines on successive readings (Deal, 1974).

4. Phoneme frequency influences consonant production accuracy: Phonemes with relatively high frequency of occurrence tend to be more accurately articulated than those with relatively low frequency (Trost & Canter, 1974).

5. Feature analysis of errors showed that the majority of substitution errors were close approximations to their targets (one or two features different) but they varied in the nature of the feature change (Blumstein, 1973; Canter et al., 1985; Monoi et al., 1983; Trost & Canter, 1974).

6. Transposition (anticipation/perseveration/metathesis) errors account for a very small proportion of error types (7%; LaPointe & Johns, 1975). Monoi et al. (1983) and Canter et al. (1985) note that substitution errors are the most frequent error type.

7. Automatic and reactive speech production tends to be much better than volitional-purposive speech (Schuell, Jenkins, & Jiminez-Pabon, 1964).

8. Repetition tends to be characterised by more articulatory errors than spontaneous speech (Johns & Darley, 1970; Schuell et al., 1964; but see Canter et al., 1985; Monoi et al., 1983).

9. Errors increase with increased word length (Johns & Darley, 1970).

10. Errors in oral reading of text are more frequent on words that "carry linguistic or psychologic 'weight' and that are more essential to communication" (p.12). "Weight" is assigned taking into account grammatical class, difficulty of initial phoneme, position in sentence, and word length (Deal & Darley, 1972).

11. Mode of stimulus presentation can affect accuracy, with better results for live presentation by a visible examiner than for tape-recorded or written stimuli (Johns & Darley, 1970; Trost & Canter, 1974).

12. The likelihood of a correct response is greater following repeated attempts at production than it is with repeated stimulus presentation (Johns & Darley, 1970).

13. Accuracy is unaffected by a number of visual, auditory, and psychological variables (Deal & Darley, 1972): availability of visual monitoring in a mirror; masking noise to reduce or prevent perception of errors; an enforced delay between stimulus presentation and an attempted response; instructional set (expectation of task difficulty); availability of rhythmic auditory stimulation (metronome).

Subsequently, a number of other characteristics have been argued to be characteristic of apraxia of speech, including (in no particular order):

14. Vowels may have distorted articulation including prolongation and greater variability (Monoi et al., 1983; Odell et al., 1991).

15. Voice-onset time (VOT) distributions may be abnormal with overlap of the distributions for voiced and voiceless cognates (Blumstein et al., 1980; Freeman, Sands, & Harris, 1978; Itoh & Sasanuma, 1984; Itoh et al., 1982). Itoh and Sasanuma (1984) interpret this as indicating that dyspraxics' control over timing of laryngeal and supralaryngeal articulatory events is disturbed.

16. Studies of dyspraxics' lingual-palatal contacts using electropalatography (EPG) show variability between underspecification of target values and overshooting (Edwards & Miller, 1989; Hardcastle, Morgan-Barry, & Clark, 1985). Other instrumental investigations show a similar picture: Itoh et al. (1980) used X-ray microbeam tracking to observe simultaneously several articulators during speech. They found that the temporal organisation between different articulators (e.g. lip, velum, tongue) was sometimes disturbed in the production of a word and velocity slowed. Fibre-optic observation of velar movements in one apraxic patient showed greater variability than normal subjects, although the pattern did approximate to normal (Itoh & Sasanuma, 1984).

17. Ziegler and von Cramon (1985, 1986) argue that there is disturbed co-articulation in apraxia of speech, in particular, delayed onset of co-articulatory gestures.

It is of note that several of the features listed are also reported for aphasic subjects producing phonological errors (e.g. 1, 2, 4, 5, 6, and 9 have all be claimed to be true of at least some aphasic phonological errors). Indeed, Nickels and Howard (1995b) note that, when assessed using Dabul's (1979) Apraxia Battery for Adults, on the "inventory of articulation characteristics of apraxia" all of their patients who made "phonological" errors in speech production showed some of the characteristics on this inventory. Two "fluent" patients showed 7–8 (of 15) characteristics (compared to an "apraxic" patient who showed 11). Miller (1992) also found no difference between apraxic speech and phonological paraphasic speech in terms of consistency of errors on repeated attempts. These facts highlight the possibility that perhaps "pure" phonological and "pure" apraxic deficits represent two ends of a continuum, and that many patients may have less well-defined deficits that result in errors arising from many different levels of speech production (from phonological encoding to performance of articulatory gestures). It is certainly difficult to dissociate the deficits that would be predicted from different levels of breakdown as the models stand (for example, length effects are predicted from almost every level of post-lexical deficit).

Even if we assume that the patients reported in the literature have no co-occurring phonological encoding deficits, it may still be the case that the difficulty in defining the features of apraxia of speech could be a consequence of attempting to include in the same syndrome symptoms that are the result of different levels of deficit. If we consider Levelt's model of speech production, even after the retrieval of the stored syllable plans there are a number of possible levels of breakdown that could be interpreted as "disorders of motor programming". The syllable plans are motor plans for the execution of sequences of articulatory movements. Levelt (1989, p.421; see Chapter 3) suggests that these plans must be unpacked, making available a hierarchy of plans prior to their execution. Thus, it is possible that deficits could occur of either unpacking or execution. What might the consequences of such deficits be? Levelt suggests that more complex motor units will involve more unpacking. This would suggest that an unpacking deficit might result in more errors on articulatorily more complex phonemes and phoneme sequences (e.g. fricatives and consonant clusters). Difficulties executing the plans might result in articulatory distortions and slowed speech if targets are not reached or the sequence of commands is slow to be executed. It is also possible that execution of more complex commands will be more error-prone than execution of simple commands, leading to the same effect of articulatory complexity as a deficit in unpacking the commands.

A key feature of apraxia of speech is an effect of articulatory complexity, but we have suggested that both an unpacking and an execution deficit could result in an effect of articulatory complexity. Thus, patients could show this symptom but yet have different levels of breakdown, and therefore they may also have different co-occurring features (as yet undefined). Other patients may show this symptom but as a result of deficits prior to this level of processing (see the earlier discussion of articulatory complexity effects on phonological errors).

It is clear that the literature on features of apraxia of speech and/or Broca's aphasia must be interpreted with caution. However, it does seem likely that there are some patients for whom the source of their speech errors is a later stage of processing than phonological encoding. These patients may show difficulty in correctly reaching articulatory targets or achieving correct voice-onset times (VOT). In order to obtain a full picture of these disorders, detailed descriptions of single cases are needed, looking at all aspects of that patient's speech and language, not just VOT or articulatory variability. As some of the features associated with apraxia of speech are probably predicted from deficits at a number of levels in speech production, it is no wonder that there has been considerable controversy regarding the features of the disorder, and indeed whether it exists independently from aphasia. These seem to be the wrong questions to ask: Instead, what is needed is a way of distinguishing the possible levels of deficit that can lead to the different features of the disorder and how they co-occur.

SUMMARY

In this chapter we have discussed errors that are related in sound to the target—focusing primarily on phonological errors (as opposed to phonetic/articulatory errors). It seems there is no simple causative relationship between either comprehension deficits and the occurrence of phonological errors in speech or the ability to monitor one's speech. Patients show considerable variety in terms of how similar target and error phonemes are, where the majority of errors occur in a word or syllable, and the types of errors that predominate.

There is evidence for a number of variables affecting the likelihood of a phonological error occurring. Effects of word length are very widespread, indeed virtually all the patients in the literature that produce phonological errors show more difficulty with longer words in speech production (i.e. in naming or spontaneous speech but not necessarily in repetition tasks). Moreover, effects of length can be easily accommodated by most models of phonological encoding (indeed, deficits at a number of different levels can predict these effects). Less attention has been paid to whether models might predict effects of number of syllables independent of number of phonemes, although it appears that both these factors may have independent effects on patients. Other variables have also been found to influence performance, including consonant clusters, lexical stress, and markedness, although it remains unclear how some of these can be incorporated into models such as those of Levelt (1989, 1992).

In many ways this chapter has fallen short of the stated aim of this book to avoid discussions that centre on syndromes and groups of patients. We discussed two such syndromes in particular—conduction aphasia and apraxia of speech. This is a reflection of the relative paucity of detailed single-case studies or case series in the literature. This, in turn, is a reflection of the relative underspecification (at the level of phonological encoding) of the models used to evaluate neuropsychological data (e.g. logogen model). Even where single-case studies exist, they use very different models to evaluate their data, and report different analyses (compare, for example, Béland et al., 1990, and Pate et al., 1987), making cross-case comparison difficult.

Butterworth (1992) gives a list of methodological desiderata for data collection when looking at phonological errors, which future research would do well to heed. These include: Several observations of the production of each target (especially for dissociating impairments of storage from those of access); assessment of the probability of error for each target in relation to known lexical factors (e.g. word frequency) and in relation to the phonological features of the targets (e.g. length, structure); nonword repetition and reading are suggested in order to eliminate lexical deficits (in fact, the use of converging evidence from multimodality testing is to be encouraged); and tests of phonological judgement (e.g. homophony, rhyme), where the intactness of later, articulatory, processes are in doubt. This list will provide adequate (and consistent) data on which to base further detailed analyses of the features of phonological errors.

Cohesive models have now been described that specify the processes of phonological encoding in far more detail (e.g. Butterworth, 1992; Levelt, 1989, 1992). It is hoped that this will lead to further research evaluating levels of breakdown and dissociating patterns of errors, with patients being evaluated in terms of the same basic model (and the models, of course, evaluated by the patient data). However, even these models seem lacking in the necessary level of specification to be able to predict precisely what the results of damage will be.

Clinically it is premature to be able to hope for clear therapeutic goals as a result of these analyses of patients' production—we are still at the stage of trying to tease apart the different levels of breakdown and their features. However, we are beginning to get some idea of the factors that may be important in influencing the occurrence of phonological errors, and these at least may be manipulated in therapy (as indeed some have been in the past, e.g. word length or articulatory complexity).

Postscript

Having reached the end of this review of spoken word production and its breakdown in aphasia, what, if anything, can we conclude? First, it is clear that this is an area of immense complexity—despite having been rigorous in my attempt to restrict the scope of this book, a diverse range of literature remains. Part 1 of this book concentrated on the models of spoken word production and the motivation for their development (primarily) from experimental studies and observation of speech errors. The resulting models seemed detailed and specific. However, when we turned to the aphasic data (in Part 2), it became clear that the models were far from sufficiently specified. In order to be able to test the adequacy of these models we need to be able to predict the consequences of breakdown of different types (e.g. access/storage; noise/decay rate) and at different levels. At present any attempt to do this raises more questions than it answers.

What are we to do? Cognitive neuropsychologists should not consider themselves "at the mercy" of the "model builders" and sit back and wait until an adequate model is built. Nor should they abandon the models and use ones of their own (unrelated to the psycholinguistic data). I would argue that it is essential that the models used by cognitive neuropsychologists are those that have been shown to be able to account for "normal" data—and indeed that when discussing patient data each of the different models is considered and not just the one favoured by the experimenter. Thus, when attempting a theoretical account of patient data, the different possible specifications of the models should be considered, difficult as this might be. In addition, authors should not only account for the pattern shown by their particular patient but also consider whether their proposed model (or modifications to a model) will account for other patients in the literature (or indeed still account for the "normal" data).

We have come a long way from the early days of cognitive neuropsychology and a simple division between semantic and phonological anomia—deficits are becoming increasingly fractionated. Although models are also being fractionated, the two have yet to converge as a coherent whole. Clinically the day of convergence will be most welcome, with deficits being pinpointed within a model and the direction of therapy obvious. This, I fear, is a dream still some distance away. However, deficits are being defined in greater detail and therapy can be targeted more accurately—even in the absence of a full understanding of the theoretical import of a particular deficit (or a "theory of therapy").

My hope is that increasingly the "model builders" will come to realise the importance of neuropsychological data in specifying and testing their models, and that the cognitive neuropsychologists will use these carefully developed models in describing their data. A truly interdisciplinary approach is the way ahead.

References

Aitchison, J. (1994). *Words in the mind: An introduction to the mental lexicon.* (2nd edn.). Oxford: Blackwell

Allport, D.A. (1984). Auditory-verbal short-term memory and aphasia. In H. Bouma & D.G. Bouwhuis (Eds.), *Attention and performance X: Control of language processes.* London: Lawrence Erlbaum Associates Ltd.

Allport, D.A. (1985). Distributed memory, modular systems and dysphasia. In S.K. Newman & R. Epstein (Eds.), *Current perspectives in dysphasia.* Edinburgh: Churchill Livingstone.

Allport, D.A., & Funnell, E. (1981). Components of the mental lexicon. *Philosophical Transactions of the Royal Society of London, B295,* 397–410.

Ardila, A. (1992). Phonological transformations in conduction aphasia. *Journal of Psycholinguistic Research, 21,* 473–484.

Baars, B.J., Motley, M.T., & MacKay, D. (1975). Output editing for lexical status from artificially elicited slips of the tongue. *Journal of Verbal Learning and Verbal Behaviour, 14,* 382–391.

Baddeley, A.D. (1983). Working Memory. *Philosophical Transactions of the Royal Society of London, B302,* 311–324.

Balota, D.A., & Chumbley, J.I. (1985). The locus of word-frequency effects in the pronunciation task: Lexical access and/or production? *Journal of Memory and Language, 24,* 89–106.

Bastiaanse, R., Gilbers, D., & van der Linde, K. (1995). Sonority substitutions in Broca's and Conduction aphasia. *Journal of Neurolinguistics, 8,* 247–255.

Baum, S.R., & Ryan, L. (1993). Rate of speech effects in aphasia: voice onset time. *Brain and Language, 44,* 431–445.

Bayles, K.A., & Tomoeda, C.K. (1983). Confrontation naming impairment in dementia. *Brain and Language, 19,* 98–114.

Béland, R., Caplan, D., & Nespoulous, J.-L. (1990). The role of abstract phonological representations in word production: Evidence from phonemic paraphasias. *Journal of Neurolinguistics, 5*, 125–164.

Benson D.F. (1979) Neurologic correlates of anomia. In H. Whittaker & H.A. Whittaker (Eds.), *Studies in neurolinguistics* (Vol.4, pp.293–328). New York: Academic Press.

Best, W.M. (1994). From meaning to speech: Evidence from the investigation and treatment of anomia. Unpublished PhD thesis, University of London.

Best, W.M. (1995). A reverse length effect in dysphasic naming: When elephant is easier than ant. *Cortex, 31*, 637–652.

Best, W.M. (1996). When racquets are baskets but baskets are biscuits, where do the words come from? A single-case study of formal paraphasic errors in aphasia. *Cognitive Neuropsychology, 13*, 443–480.

Best, W.M., & Howard, D. (1994a). Word sound deafness resolved? *Aphasiology, 8*, 223–256.

Best, W.M., & Howard, D. (1994b). The reverse length effect in naming: data and simulations. Paper presented at the British Neuropsychological Society Autumn Meeting (Anomia), London.

Black, M., & Byng, S. (1986). Prosodic constraints on lexical access in reading. *Cognitive Neuropsychology, 3*, 369–409.

Black, M., & Byng, S. (1989). Re-stressing prosody: a reply to Cutler, Howard and Patterson. *Cognitive Neuropsychology, 6*, 85–92.

Blanken, G. (1990). Formal paraphasias: a single case study. *Brain and Language, 38*, 534–554.

Blumstein, S.E. (1973). *A phonological investigation of aphasic speech*. The Hague: Mouton.

Blumstein, S.E. (1978). Segment structure and the syllable in aphasia. In A. Bell & J.B. Hooper (Eds.), *Syllables and segments*. Amsterdam: North Holland.

Blumstein, S.E., Cooper, W.E., Goodglass, H., Statlender, S., & Gottlieb, J. (1980). Production deficits in aphasia: A voice-onset time analysis. *Brain and Language, 9*, 153–170.

Blumstein, S.E., Cooper, W.E., Zurif, E.B., & Caramazza, A. (1977). The perception and production of voice-onset time in aphasia. *Neuropsychologia, 15*, 371–383.

Boller, F., Vrtunski, P.B., Kim, Y., & Mack, J.L. (1978). Delayed auditory feedback and aphasia. *Cortex, 14*, 212–226.

Bramwell, B. (1897). Illustrative cases of aphasia. *Lancet, 1*, 1256–1259. Reprinted in 1984 as: A case of word meaning deafness. *Cognitive Neuropsychology, 1*, 249–258.

Breedin, S.D., Saffran, E.M., & Coslett, H.B. (1994). Reversal of the concreteness effect in a patient with semantic dementia. *Cognitive Neuropsychology, 11*, 617–660.

Broca, P. (1861). Remarques sur le siege de la faculté de langage suivies d'une observation d'aphemie. *Bulletin de la Société d'Anatomie, 6*, 330–57.

Browman, C., & Goldstein, L. (1991). Gestural structures: Distinctiveness, phonological processes and historical change. In I.G. Mattingly & M. Studdert-Kennedy (Eds.), *Modularity and the motor theory of speech perception*. Hillsdale, NJ: Lawrence Erlbaum Associates Inc.

Browman, C., & Goldstein, L. (1992). Articulatory phonology: an overview. *Phonetica, 49*, 155–180.

Brown, A.S. (1991). A review of the tip-of-the-tongue experience. *Psychological Bulletin, 109*, 204–223.

Brown, G.D.A., & Watson, F.L. (1987). First in, first out: Word learning age and spoken word frequency as predictors of word familiarity and word naming latency. *Memory and Cognition, 15*, 208–216.

Brown, J.W. (1972). *Aphasia, apraxia and agnosia: Clinical and theoretical aspects*. Springfield, IL: Thomas.

Brown, J.W. (1977). *Mind, brain and consciousness*. New York: Academic Press.

Brown, R., & McNeill, D. (1966). The "tip of the tongue" phenomenon. *Journal of Verbal Learning and Verbal Behaviour, 5*, 325–337.

Buckingham, H.W. (1977). The conduction theory and neologistic jargon. *Language and Speech, 20*, 174–184.

Buckingham, H.W. (1981a). Explanations for the concept of apraxia of speech. In M.T. Sarno (Ed.), *Acquired aphasia*. New York: Academic Press

Buckingham, H.W. (1981b). Where do neologisms come from? In J.W. Brown (Ed.), *Jargonaphasia* (pp.39–62). New York: Academic Press.

Buckingham, H.W. (1987). Phonemic paraphasias and psycholinguistic production models for neologistic jargon. *Aphasiology, 1*, 381–400.

Buckingham, H.W. (1990a). Abstruse neologisms, retrieval deficits and the random generator. *Journal of Neurolinguistics, 5*, 213–235.

Buckingham, H.W. (1990b). Principle of sonority, doublet creation and the checkoff monitor. In J.-L. Nespoulous & P. Villiard (Eds.), *Morphology, phonology and aphasia*. New York: Springer.

Buckingham, H., & Kertesz, A. (1974). A linguistic analysis of fluent aphasia. *Brain and Language, 1*, 43–61.

Buckingham, H.W., & Yule, G. (1987). Phonemic false evaluation: Theoretical and clinical aspects. *Clinical Linguistics and Phonetics, 1*, 113–125.

Burke, D., MacKay, D.G., Worthley, J.S., & Wade, E. (1991). On the tip of the tongue: What causes word finding failure in young and older adults? *Journal of Memory and Language, 30*, 237–246.

Burns, M.S., & Canter, G.J. (1977). Phonemic behaviour of aphasic patients with posterior cerebral lesions. *Brain and Language, 4*, 492–507.

Butterworth, B. (1975). Hesitation and semantic planning in speech. *Journal of Psycholinguistic Research, 4*, 75–87.

Butterworth, B. (1979). Hesitation and the production of verbal paraphasias and neologisms in jargon aphasia. *Brain and Language, 8*, 133–161.

Butterworth, B. (1980). Evidence from pauses. In B.L. Butterworth (Ed.), *Language production, Vol.1: Speech and talk*. London: Academic Press.

Butterworth, B. (1981). Speech errors: old data in search of new theories. *Linguistics, 19*, 627–662.

Butterworth, B. (1983). Lexical representation. In B.L. Butterworth (Ed.), *Language production, Vol. 2: Development, writing and other language processes*. London: Academic Press.

Butterworth, B. (1985). Jargon aphasia: Processes and strategies. In S.K. Newman & R. Epstein (Eds.), *Current perspectives in dysphasia*. Edinburgh: Churchill Livingstone.

Butterworth, B. (1989). Lexical access in speech production. In W. Marslen-Wilson (Ed.), *Lexical representation and process*. Cambridge, MA: MIT Press.

Butterworth, B. (1992). Disorders of phonological encoding. *Cognition, 42*, 261–286.

Butterworth, B., & Howard, D. (1987). Paragrammatisms. *Cognition, 26,* 1–37.

Butterworth, B.L., Howard, D., & McLoughlin, P.J. (1984). The semantic deficit in aphasia: The relationship between semantic errors in auditory comprehension and picture naming. *Neuropsychologia, 22,* 409–426.

Canter, G.J., Trost, J.E., & Burns, M.S. (1985). Contrasting speech patterns in apraxia of speech and phonemic paraphasia. *Brain and Language, 24,* 204–222.

Caplan, D. (1987). Phonological representations in word production. In E. Keller & M. Gopnik (Eds.), *Tutorials in motor behaviour.* Hillsdale, NJ: Lawrence Erlbaum Associates Inc.

Caplan, D., Vanier, M., & Baker, C. (1986). A case study of reproduction conduction aphasia. I: Word production. *Cognitive Neuropsychology, 3,* 99–128.

Caramazza, A., Berndt, R.S., & Basili, A.G. (1983). The selective impairment of phonological processing: a case study. *Brain and Language, 18,* 128–174.

Caramazza, A., & Hillis, A.E. (1990). Where do semantic errors come from? *Cortex, 26,* 95–122.

Caramazza, A., & Hillis, A.E. (1991). Lexical organisation of nouns and verbs in the brain. *Nature, 349,* 788–790.

Carney, R., & Temple, C.M. (1993). Prosopanomia? A possible category-specific anomia for faces. *Cognitive Neuropsychology, 10,* 185–195.

Carroll, J.B., & White, M.N. (1973). Word frequency and age of acquisition as determiners of picture-naming latency. *Quarterly Journal of Experimental Psychology, 25,* 85–95.

Christman, S.S. (1994). Target-related neologism formation in jargonaphasia. *Brain and Language, 46,* 109–128.

Cipolotti, L., McNeil, J.E., & Warrington, E.K. (1993). Spared written naming of proper nouns: A case report. *Memory, 1,* 289–311.

Clarke, R., & Morton, J. (1983). Cross-modality facilitation in tachistoscopic word recognition. *Quarterly Journal of Experimental Psychology, 35A,* 79–96.

Clements, G.N. (1988). The role of the sonority cycle in core syllabification. Working papers of the Cornell Phonetics Laboratory, No. 2, Ithaca, NY.

Collins, A.M., & Loftus, E.F. (1975). A spreading-activation theory of semantic processing. *Psychological Review, 82,* 407–428.

Collins, A.M., & Quillian, M.R. (1969). Retrieval time from semantic memory. *Journal of Verbal Learning and Verbal Behaviour, 8,* 240–247.

Coltheart, M. (1980). The semantic error: types and theories. In M. Coltheart, K. Patterson, & J. Marshall (Eds.), *Deep dyslexia.* London: Routledge & Kegan Paul.

Coltheart, M., Masterson, J., Byng, S., Prior, M., & Riddoch, J. (1983). Surface dyslexia. *Quarterly Journal of Experimental Psychology 35A,* 469–496.

Coltheart, M. Patterson, K., & Marshall, J. (Eds.). (1980). *Deep dyslexia.* London: Routledge & Kegan Paul.

Critchley, M. (1970). *Aphasiology and other aspects of language.* London: Edward Arnold.

Crowder, R.G. (1983). The purity of auditory memory. *Philosphical Transactions of the Royal Society of London, B302,* 251–265.

Cutler, A. (1980). Errors of stress and intonation. In V.A. Fromkin (Ed.), *Errors in linguistic performance.* New York: Academic Press.

Cutler, A., Howard, D., & Patterson, K.E. (1989). Misplaced stress on prosody: A reply to Black and Byng. *Cognitive Neuropsychology, 6,* 67–83.

Dabul, B.L. (1979). *Apraxia battery for adults.* Austin, TX: Pro-ed.

Darley, F.L. (1969). The classification of output disturbance in neurologic communication disorders. Paper presented at the American Speech and Hearing Association Convention, Chicago.

Darley, F.L. (1982). *Aphasia.* Philadelphia, PA: W.B. Saunders.

Davis, S. (1989). On a non-argument for the rhyme. *Journal of Linguistics, 25,* 211–217.

De Renzi, E., & Lucchelli, F. (1994). Are semantic systems separately represented in the brain? The case of living category impairment. *Cortex, 30,* 3–25.

Deal, J.L. (1974). Consistency and adaptation in apraxia of speech. *Journal of Communication Disorders, 7,* 135–140.

Deal, J.L., & Darley, F.L. (1972). The influence of linguistic and situational variables on phonemic accuracy in apraxia of speech. *Journal for Speech and Hearing Research, 15,* 639–653.

Dell, G.S. (1984). Representation of serial order in speech: Evidence from the repeated phoneme effect in speech errors. *Journal of Experimental Psychology: Learning, Memory and Cognition, 10,* 222–233.

Dell, G.S. (1986). A spreading activation theory of retrieval in sentence production. *Psychological Review, 93,* 283–321.

Dell, G.S. (1989). The retrieval of phonological forms in production: Tests of predictions from a connectionist model. In W. Marslen-Wilson (Ed.), *Lexical representation and process.* Cambridge, MA: MIT Press.

Dell, G.S., & O'Seaghdha, P.G. (1991). Mediated and convergent lexical priming in language production: A comment on Levelt et al. (1991). *Psychological Review, 98,* 604–614.

Dell, G.S., & O'Seaghdha, P.G. (1992). Stages of lexical access in language production. *Cognition, 42,* 287–314.

Dell, G.S., & Reich, P.A. (1981). Stages in sentence production: An analysis of speech error data. *Journal of Verbal Learning and Verbal Behaviour, 20,* 611–629.

Dubois, J., Hecaen, H., Angelergues, R., Maufras de Chatelier, A., & Marcie, P. (1964). Neurolinguistic study of conduction aphasia. *Neuropsychologia, 2,* 9–44.

Edwards, S., & Miller, N. (1989). Using EPG to investigate speech errors and motor agility in a dyspraxic patient. *Clinical Linguistics and Phonetics, 3,* 111–126.

Ellis, A.W. (1979). Speech production and short term memory. In J. Morton & J.C. Marshall (Eds.), *Psycholinguistics series* (Vol.2). *London: Elek.*

Ellis, A.W. (1985). The production of spoken words: A cognitive neuropsychological perspective. In A.W. Ellis (Ed.), *Progress in the psychology of language* (Vol.2). London: Lawrence Erlbaum Asssociates Ltd.

Ellis, A.W., Kay, J., & Franklin, S. (1992). Anomia: Differentiating between semantic and phonological deficits. In D. Margolin (Ed.), *Cognitive neuropsychology in clinical practice.* New York: Oxford University Press.

Ellis, A.W., Miller, D., & Sin, G. (1983). Wernicke's aphasia and normal language processing: A case study in cognitive neuropsychology. *Cognition, 15,* 111–144

Ellis, A.W., & Young, A.W. (1988). *Human cognitive neuropsychology*. London: Lawrence Erlbaum Associates Ltd.

Eriksen, C.W., Pollock, M.D., & Montague, W.E. (1970). Implicit speech: Mechanisms in perceptual encoding? *Journal of Experimental Psychology, 84*, 502–507.

Farah, M.J., McMullen, P.A., & Meyer, M.M. (1991). Can recognition of living things be selectively impaired? *Neuropsychologia, 29*, 185–193.

Farah, M.J., & Wallace, M.A. (1992). Semantically-bounded anomia: Implications for the neural implementation of naming. *Neuropsychologia, 30*, 609–621.

Fay, D., & Cutler, A. (1977). Malapropisms and the structure of the mental lexicon. *Linguistic Inquiry, 8*, 505–520.

Feinberg, T., Rothi, L., & Heilman, K. (1986). Inner speech in conduction aphasia. *Archives of Neurology, 43*, 591–593.

Feyereisen, P., van der Borght, F., & Seron, X. (1988). The operativity effect in naming: A re-analysis. *Neuropsychologia, 26*, 401–415.

Fodor, J.A., Garrett, M.F., Walker, E.C.T., & Parkes, C.H. (1980). Against definitions. *Cognition, 8*, 1–105.

Forster, K. (1976). Accessing the mental lexicon. In R.J. Wales & E.C.T. Walker (Eds.), *New approaches to language mechanisms*. Amsterdam: North-Holland.

Fowler, C.A., Rubin, P., Remez, R.E., & Turvey, M.T. (1980). Implications for speech production of a general theory of action. In B.L. Butterworth (Ed.), *Language production, Vol.1: Speech and talk*. London: Academic Press.

Fowler, C.A., Treiman, R., & Gross, J. (1993). The structure of English syllables and polysyllables. *Journal of Memory and Language, 32*, 115–140.

Francis, W.N., & Kucera, H. (1982). *Frequency analysis of English usage: Lexicon and grammar*. Boston, MA: Houghton Mifflin.

Franklin, S.E. (1989a). Understanding and repeating words: evidence from aphasia. Unpublished PhD thesis, City University, London.

Franklin, S. (1989b). Dissociations in auditory word comprehension: Evidence from nine "fluent" aphasic patients. *Aphasiology, 3*, 189–207.

Franklin, S.E., Howard, D., & Patterson, K.E. (1994). Abstract word meaning deafness. *Cognitive Neuropsychology, 11*, 1–34.

Franklin, S.E., Howard, D., & Patterson, K.E. (1995). Abstract word anomia. *Cognitive Neuropsychology, 12*, 549–566.

Freeman, F.J., Sands, E.S., & Harris, K.S. (1978). Temporal coordination of phonation and articulation in a case of verbal apraxia: A voice onset time study. *Brain and Language, 6*, 106–111.

Friedman, R.B., & Kohn, S.E. (1990). Impaired activation of the phonological lexicon: Effects upon oral reading. *Brain and Language, 38*, 278–297.

Fromkin, V. (1971). The nonanomalous nature of anomalous utterances. *Language, 47*, 27–52.

Fromkin, V. (Ed.) (1973a). *Speech errors as linguistic evidence*. The Hague: Mouton.

Fromkin, V. (1973b). Slips of the tongue. *Scientific American, 229*, 110–116.

Fry, D.B. (1959). Phonemic substitution in an aphasic patient. *Language and Speech, 2*, 52–61.

Funnell, E., & Allport, A. (1987). Non-linguistic cognition and word meanings: Neuropsychological exploration of common mechanisms. In A. Allport, D. Mackay, W. Prinz, & E. Scheerer (Eds.), *Language perception and production*. London: Academic Press

Funnell, E., & Sheridan, J. (1992). Categories of knowledge? Unfamiliar aspects of living and non-living things. *Cognitive Neuropsychology, 9*, 135–153.

Gainotti, G. (1976). The relationship between semantic impairment in comprehension and naming in aphasic patients. *British Journal of Disorders of Communication, 11*, 77–81.

Gainotti, G. (1982). Some aspects of semantic-lexical impairment in aphasia. *Applied Psycholinguistics, 3*, 279–294.

Gainotti, G., Miceli, G., Caltagirone, C., Silveri, M.C., & Masullo, C. (1981). The relationship between type of naming error and semantic-lexical discrimination in aphasia. *Cortex, 17*, 401–410.

Gainotti, G., Silveri, M.C., Villa, G., & Miceli, G. (1986). Anomia with and without lexical comprehension disorders. *Brain and Language, 29*, 18–23.

Gandour, J., Akamanon, C., Dechongkit, S., Khunadorn, F., & Boonklam, R. (1994). Sequences of phonemic approximations in a Thai conduction aphasic. *Brain and Language, 46*, 69–95.

Gardner, H. (1973). The contribution of operativity to naming capacity in aphasic patients. *Neuropsychologia, 11*, 213–220.

Gardner, H. (1974). The naming of objects and symbols by children and aphasic patients. *Journal of Psycholinguistic Research, 3*, 133–149.

Garrett, M. (1982). Production of speech: Observations from normal and pathological language use. In A. W. Ellis (Ed.), *Normality and pathology in cognitive functions*. London: Academic Press.

Garrett, M.F. (1975). The analysis of sentence production. In G.H. Bower (Ed.), *The psychology of learning and motivation*. New York: Academic Press.

Garrett, M.F. (1976). Syntactic processes in sentence production. In R.J. Wales & E. Walker (Eds.), *New approaches to language mechanisms*. Amsterdam: North-Holland.

Garrett, M.F. (1980). Levels of processing in sentence production. In B.L. Butterworth (Ed.), *Language production, Vol.1: Speech and talk*. London: Academic Press.

Garrett, M.F. (1984). The organisation of processing structure for language production: Applications to aphasic speech. In D. Caplan, A.R. Lecours, & A. Smith (Eds.), *Biological perspectives on language*. Cambridge, MA: MIT Press.

Gernsbacher, M.A. (1984). Resolving 20 years of inconsistent interactions between lexical familiarity and orthography, concreteness, and polysemy. *Journal of Experimental Psychology: General, 113*, 256–281.

Gilhooly, K.J., & Logie, R.H. (1980). Age-of-acquisition, imagery, concreteness, familiarity and ambiguity measures of 1944 words. *Behaviour Research Methods and Instrumentation, 12*, 395–427.

Gilhooly, K.J., & Logie, R.H. (1981a). Word age-of-acquisition, reading latencies and auditory recognition. *Current Psychological Research, 1*, 251–262.

Gilhooly, K.J., & Logie, R.H. (1981b). Word age-of-acquisition and visual recognition thresholds. *Current Psychological Research, 1*, 215–226.

Gilhooly, K.J., & Watson, F.L. (1981). Word age-of-acquisition effects: A review. *Current Psychological Reviews, 1*, 269–286.

Gipson, P. (1984). A study of the long-term priming of auditory word recognition. Unpublished PhD thesis, University of Cambridge.

Gipson, P. (1986). The production of phonology and auditory priming. *British Journal of Psychology, 77*, 359–375.

Glaser, W.R., & Dungelhoff, F.-J. (1984). The time course of picture-word interference. *Journal of Experimental Psychology: Human Perception and Performance, 10,* 640–654.

Goldstein, K. (1948). *Language and language disturbances.* New York: Grune & Stratton.

Goodglass, H., Fodor, I.G., & Schulhoff, C.L. (1967). Prosodic factors in grammar—evidence from aphasia. *Journal of Speech and Hearing Research, 10,* 5–20.

Goodglass, H., Hyde, M.R., & Blumstein, S. (1969). Frequency, picturability and availability of nouns in aphasia. *Cortex, 5,* 104–119.

Goodglass, H., & Kaplan, E. (1972). *The assessment of aphasia and related disorders.* Philadelphia, PA: Lea and Febiger.

Goodglass, H., & Kaplan, E. (1983). *The assessment of aphasia and related disorders* (2nd edn.). Philadelphia, PA: Lea and Febiger.

Goodglass, H., Kaplan, E., Weintraub, S., & Ackerman, N. (1976). The tip-of-the-tongue phenomenon in aphasia. *Cortex, 12,* 145–153.

Green, E. (1969). Phonological and grammatical aspects of jargon in an aphasic patient: A case study. *Language and Speech, 12,* 103–118.

Greene, R.L., & Crowder, R.G. (1984). Modality and suffix effects in the absence of auditory stimulation. *Journal of Verbal Learning and Verbal Behaviour, 23,* 371–382.

Hankamer, J. (1989). Morphological parsing and the lexicon. In W. Marslen-Wilson (Ed.), *Lexical representation and process.* Cambridge, MA: MIT Press.

Hardcastle, W., Morgan-Barry, R.A., & Clark, C. (1985). Articulatory and voicing characteristics of adult dysarthric and verbal dyspraxic speakers: An instrumental study. *British Journal of Disorders of Communication, 20,* 249–270.

Harley, T.A. (1993). Phonological activation of semantic competitors during lexical access in speech production. *Language and Cognitive Processes, 8,* 291–309.

Harley, T.A., & MacAndrew, S.B.G. (1992). Modelling paraphasias in normal and aphasic speech. *Proceedings of the 14th Annual Conference of the Cognitive Science Society* (pp.378–383). Bloomington, IN.

Hart J., Berndt, R.S., & Caramazza, A. (1985). Category specific naming deficit following cerebral infarction. *Nature, 316,* 439–440.

Henaff-Gonon, M.A., Bruckert, R., & Michel, F. (1989). Lexicalization in an anomic patient. *Neuropsychologia, 27,* 391–407.

Hillis, A.E., & Caramazza, A. (1991a). Category specific naming and comprehension impairment: A double dissociation. *Brain, 114,* 2081–2094.

Hillis, A.E., & Caramazza, A. (1991b). Mechanisms for accessing lexical representations for output: Evidence from a category-specific semantic deficit. *Brain and Language, 40,* 106–144.

Hillis, A.E., & Caramazza, A. (1995). Converging evidence for the interaction of semantic and sublexical phonological information in accessing lexical representations for spoken output. *Cognitive Neuropsychology, 12,* 187–227.

Hillis, A.E., Rapp, B.C., Romani, C., & Caramazza, A. (1990). Selective impairment of semantics in lexical processing. *Cognitive Neuropsychology, 7,* 191–243.

Hinton, G., & Shallice, T. (1991). Lesioning an attractor network: investigations of acquired dyslexia. *Psychological Review, 98,* 74–95.

Hirsh, C. & Ellis, A.W. (1994). Age of acquisition and lexical processing in aphasia; A case study. *Cognitive Neuropsychology, 6*, 435–458.

Hittmair-Delazer, M., Denes, G., Semenza, C., & Mantovan, M.C. (1994). Anomia for people's names. *Neuropsychologia, 32*, 465–476.

Hodges, J.R., Patterson, K.E., Oxbury, S., & Funnell, E. (1992). Semantic dementia. *Brain, 115*, 1783–1806.

Hodges, J.R., Salmon, D.P., & Butters, N. (1990). Differential impairment of semantic and episodic memory in Alzheimer's and Huntington's diseases: A controlled prospective study. *Journal of Neurology, Neurosurgery and Psychiatry, 53*, 1089–1095.

Hodges, J.R., Salmon, D.P., & Butters, N. (1991). The nature of the naming deficit in Alzheimer's and Huntington's disease. *Brain, 114*, 1547–1558.

Hodges, J.R., Salmon, D.P., & Butters, N. (1992). Semantic memory impairment in Alzheimer's disease: failure of access or degraded knowledge? *Neuropsychologia, 30*, 301–314.

Howard, D. (1985). The semantic organisation of the lexicon: Evidence from aphasia. Unpublished PhD thesis, University of London.

Howard, D. (1995). Lexical anomia (or the case of the missing entries). *Quarterly Journal of Experimental Psychology, 48A*, 999–1023.

Howard, D., Best, W.M., Bruce, C., & Gatehouse, C.E.P. (1995). Operativity and animacy effects in aphasic naming. *European Journal of Disorders of Communication, 30*, 286–302.

Howard, D., & Franklin, S. (1987). Three ways for understanding written words, and their use in two contrasting cases of surface dyslexia. In A. Allport, D. MacKay, W. Prinz, & E. Scheerer (Eds.), *Language perception and production: relationships between listening, speaking, reading and writing*. London: Academic Press.

Howard, D., & Franklin, S. (1988). *Missing the meaning?* Cambridge, MA: MIT Press.

Howard, D., & Franklin, S. (1990). Memory without rehearsal. In T. Shallice & G. Vallar (Eds.), *Neuropsychological impairments of short-term memory*. Cambridge: Cambridge University Press.

Howard, D., & Franklin, S. (1993). Dissociations between component mechanisms in short-term memory: Evidence from brain-damaged patients. In D.E. Meyer & S. Kornblum (Eds.), *Attention and Performance XIV: Synergies in experimental psychology, artificial intelligence, and cognitive neuroscience*. Cambridge, MA: MIT Press.

Howard, D., & Orchard-Lisle, V.M. (1984). On the origin of semantic errors in naming: evidence from the case of a global dysphasic. *Cognitive Neuropsychology, 1*, 163–190.

Howard, D., & Patterson, K.E. (1992). *Pyramids and palm trees*. Bury St. Edmunds, UK: Thames Valley Test Company.

Howard, D., Patterson, K.E., Franklin, S., Morton, J., & Orchard-Lisle, V.M. (1984). Variability and consistency in picture naming by aphasic patients. In F.C. Rose (Ed.), *Advances in neurology, 42: Progress in aphasiology*. New York: Raven Press.

Howes, D. (1964). Application of the word frequency concept to aphasia. In A.V.S. de Rueck & M. O'Connor (Eds.), *Disorders of language: Proceedings of a Conference held 21–23 May 1963*. London: Churchill.

Huber, W. (1981). Semantic confusions in aphasia. In B.B. Reiger (Ed.), *Empirical semantics*. Bochum: Brockmeyer.

Humphreys, G.W., & Riddoch, M.J. (1987). To see but not to see: A case study of visual agnosia. London: Lawrence Erlbaum Associates Ltd.

Humphreys, G.W., Riddoch, M.J., & Quinlan, P.T. (1988). Cascade processes in picture identification. *Cognitive Neuropsychology, 5,* 67–103.

Itoh, M., & Sasanuma, S. (1984). Articulatory movements in apraxia of speech. In J.C. Rosenbek, M.R. McNeil, & A.E. Aronson (Eds.), *Apraxia of speech: Physiology, acoustics, linguistics and management.* San Diego, CA: College Hill Press.

Itoh, M., Sasanuma, S., Hirose, H., Yoshioka, H., & Ushijima, T. (1980). Abnormal articulatory dynamics in a patient with apraxia of speech: X-ray microbeam observation. *Brain and Language, 11,* 66–75.

Itoh, M., Sasanuma, S., Tatsumi, I.F., Murakami, S., Fukusako, Y., & Suzuki, T. (1982). Voice onset time characteristics in apraxia of speech. *Brain and Language, 17,* 193–210.

Joanette, Y., Keller, E., & Lecours, A.R. (1980). Sequences of phonemic approximations in aphasia. *Brain and Language, 11,* 30–44.

Johns, D.F. & Darley, F.L. (1970). Phonemic variability in apraxia of speech. *Journal for Speech and Hearing Research, 13,* 556–583.

Jones, G.V. (1985). Deep dyslexia, imageability and ease of predication. *Brain and Language, 24,* 1–19.

Jones, G.V. (1989). Back to Woodworth: The role of interlopers in the tip of the tongue phenomenon. *Memory and Cognition, 17,* 69–76.

Jones, G.V., & Langford, S. (1987). Phonological blocking in the tip of the tongue state. *Cognition, 26,* 115–122.

Katz, J.J., & Fodor, J.A. (1963). The structure of a semantic theory. *Language, 39,* 170–210.

Kay, J., & Ellis, A.W. (1987). A cognitive neuropsychological case study of anomia: Implications for psychological models of word retrieval. *Brain, 110,* 613–629

Kay, J., & Patterson, K. (1985). Routes to meaning in surface dyslexia. In K.E. Patterson, J.C. Marshall, & M. Coltheart (Eds.), *Surface dyslexia: Neuropsychological and cognitive analyses of phonological reading.* London: Lawrence Erlbaum Associates Ltd.

Keele, S.W. (1981). Behavioural analysis of movement. In V. Brooks (Ed.), *Handbook of physiology. The nervous system: Vol.2. Motor control.* Bethesda, MD: American Physiology Society.

Kempen, G., & Huijbers, P. (1983). The lexicalisation process in sentence production and naming: Indirect election of words. *Cognition, 14,* 185–209.

Kertesz, A. (1979). *Aphasia and associated disorders: Taxonomy, localisation and recovery.* New York: Grune & Stratton.

Kertesz, A., & Benson, D.F. (1970). Neologistic jargon: A clinicopathological study. *Cortex, 6,* 362–386.

Kertesz, A., & Phipps, J.B. (1977). Numerical taxonomy of aphasia. *Brain and Language, 4,* 1–10.

Kertesz, A., & Poole, E. (1974). The aphasia quotient: The taxonomic approach to the measurement of aphasic disability. *Canadian Journal of Neurological Science, 1,* 7–16.

Kinsbourne, M. (1972). Behavioural analysis of the repetition deficit in conduction aphasia. *Neurology, 22,* 1126–1132.

Klapp, S.T., Anderson, W.G., & Berrian, R.W. (1973). Implicit speech in reading reconsidered. *Journal of Experimental Psychology, 100,* 368–374.

Klapp, S.T., & Erwin, C.I. (1976). Relation between programming time and duration of the response being programmed. *Journal of Experimental Psychology: Human Perception and Performance, 2*, 591–598.

Kohn, S.E. (1984). The nature of the phonological disorder in conduction aphasia. *Brain and Language, 23*, 97–115.

Kohn, S.E. (1988). Phonological production deficits in aphasia. In H.A. Whitaker (Ed.), *Phonological processes and brain mechanisms*. New York: Springer.

Kohn, S.E. (1989). The nature of the phonemic string deficit in conduction aphasia. *Aphasiology, 3*, 209–239.

Kohn, S.E. (Ed.) (1992). *Conduction aphasia*. Hillsdale, NJ: Lawrence Erlbaum Associates Inc.

Kohn, S., & Smith, K.L. (1990). Between-word speech errors in conduction aphasia. *Cognitive Neuropsychology, 7*, 133–156.

Kohn, S., & Smith, K.L. (1994a). Distinctions between two phonological output deficits. *Applied Psycholinguistics, 15*, 75–95.

Kohn, S., & Smith, K.L. (1994b). Evolution of impaired access to the phonological lexicon. *Journal of Neurolinguistics, 8*, 267–288.

Kohn, S., Wingfield, A., Menn, L., Goodglass, H., Gleason, J.B., & Hyde, M. (1987). Lexical retrieval: The tip-of-the-tongue phenomenon. *Applied Psycholinguistics, 8*, 245–266.

Koriat, A., & Lieblich, I. (1974). What does a person in a TOT state know that a person in the don't know state doesn't know? *Memory and Cognition, 2*, 647–655.

Kremin, H. (1986). Spared naming without comprehension. *Journal of Neurolinguistics, 2*, 131–150.

Kremin, H. (1988). Naming and its disorders. In F. Boller & J. Grafman (Eds.), *Handbook of neuropsychology* (Vol.1). Amsterdam: Elsevier.

Kremin, H., Beauchamp, D., & Perrier, D. (1994). Naming without picture comprehension? Apropos the oral naming and semantic comprehension of pictures by patients with Alzheimer's disease. *Aphasiology, 8*, 291–294.

Kucera, H., & Francis, W.N. (1967). *A computational analysis of present-day American English*. Providence, RI: Brown University Press.

Lachman, R., Schaffer, J.P., & Hennrikus, D. (1974). Language and cognition: Effects of stimulus codability, name-word frequency, and age of acquisition on lexical reaction time. *Journal of Verbal Learning and Verbal Behaviour, 13*, 613–625.

Laiacona, M., Barbarotto, R., & Capitani, E. (1993). Perceptual and associative knowledge in category specific impairment of semantic memory: A study of two cases. *Cortex, 29*, 727–740.

LaPointe, L., & Johns, D.F. (1975). Some phonemic characteristics in apraxia of speech. *Journal of Communication Disorders, 8*, 259–269.

Lashley, K.S. (1951). The problem of serial order in behaviour. In L.A. Jefress (Ed.), *Cerebral mechanisms in behaviour*. New York: Wiley.

Laubstein, A.S. (1987). Syllable structure: The speech error evidence. *Canadian Journal of Linguistics, 32*, 339–363.

Lebrun, Y. (1989). Apraxia of speech: The history of a concept. In P. Square-Storer (Ed.), *Acquired apraxia of speech in aphasic adults*. London: Taylor & Francis Ltd.

Lecours, A.R., & Lhermitte, F. (1969). Phonemic paraphasias: Linguistic structures and tentative hypotheses. *Cortex, 5*, 193–228.

Lecours, A.R., & Lhermitte, F. (1972). Recherches sur le langage des aphasiques: 4. Analyse d'un corpus de neologismes; notion de paraphasie monémique. *Encephale, 61*, 295–315.

Lecours, A.R., Osborn, E., Travis, L., Rouillon, F., & Lavallee-Huynh, G. (1981). Jargons. In J.W. Brown (Ed.), *Jargonaphasia*. New York: Academic Press.

Lecours, A.R., & Rouillon, F. (1976). Neurolinguistic analysis of jargonaphasia and jargonagraphia. In H. Whitaker & H.A. Whitaker (Eds.), *Studies in neurolinguistics* (Vol.2). New York: Academic Press.

Le Dorze, G., & Nespoulous, J.-L. (1989). Anomia in moderate aphasia: Problems in accessing the lexical representation. *Brain and Language, 37*, 381–400.

Levelt, W.J.M. (1983). Monitoring and self-repair in speech. *Cognition, 14*, 41–104.

Levelt, W.J.M. (1989). *Speaking: From intention to articulation*. Cambridge, MA: MIT Press.

Levelt, W.J.M. (1992). Accessing words in speech production: Stages, processes and representations. *Cognition, 42*, 1–22.

Levelt, W.J.M., Schriefers, H., Vorberg, D., Meyer, A.S., Pechmann, T., & Havinga, J. (1991a). The time course of lexical access in speech production: A study of picture naming. *Psychological Review, 98*, 122–142.

Levelt, W.J.M., Schriefers, H., Vorberg, D., Meyer, A.S., Pechmann, T., & Havinga, J. (1991b). Normal and deviant lexical processing: Reply to Dell and O'Seaghdha (1991). *Psychological Review, 98*, 615–618.

Levelt, W.J.M., & Wheeldon, L. (1994). Do speakers have access to a mental syllabary? *Cognition, 50*, 239–269.

Li, E.C., & Canter, G. (1987). An investigation of Luria's hypothesis on prompting in aphasic naming disturbances. *Journal of Communication Disorders, 20*, 469–475.

Li, E.C., & Williams, S.E. (1991). An investigation of naming errors following semantic and phonemic cueing. *Neuropsychologia, 29*, 1083–1093.

Liberman, A.M., Cooper, F.S., Shankweiler, D.P., & Studdert-Kennedy, M. (1967). Perception of the speech code. *Psychological Review, 74*, 431–461.

Lindblom, B.E.F. (1963). Spectographic study of vowel reduction. *Journal of the Acoustical Society of America, 35*, 1773–1781.

Lindblom, B., Lubker, J., & Gay, T. (1979). Formant frequencies of some fixed-mandible vowels and a model of speech motor programming by predictive simulation. *Journal of Phonetics, 7*, 147–161.

Lindsley, J.R. (1976). Producing simple utterances: Details of the planning process. *Journal of Psycholinguistic Research, 5*, 331–354.

Lucchelli, F., & De Renzi, E. (1992). Proper name anomia. *Cortex, 28*, 221–230.

Lupker, S.J. (1979). The semantic nature of response competition in the picture-word interference task. *Memory and Cognition, 7*, 485–495.

Lupker, S.J., & Katz, A.N. (1981). Input, decision and response factors in picture-word interference. *Journal of Experimental Psychology: Human Learning and Memory, 7*, 269–282.

Luria, A. R. (1970). *Traumatic aphasia*. The Hague: Mouton.

Mackenzie, C. (1982). Aphasic articulatory defect and aphasic phonological defect. *British Journal of Disorders of Communication, 17*, 27–46.

Maher, L.M., Rothi, L.J.G., & Heilman, K.M. (1994). Lack of error awareness in an aphasic patient with relatively preserved auditory comprehension. *Brain and Language, 46*, 402–418.

Marcel, A.J., & Patterson, K.E. (1978). Word recognition and production: Reciprocity in clinical and normal studies. In J. Requin (Ed.), *Attention and performance VII*. Hillsdale, NJ: Lawrence Erlbaum Associates Inc.

Marie, P. (1906). La troisième circonvolution ne joue aucun rôle special dans la fonction du langage. *Semaine Médicale, 26*, 241–247.

Markman, E.M. (1989). *Categorisation and naming in children: Problems of induction.* Cambridge, MA: MIT Press.

Markman, E.M., & Wachtel, G.F. (1988). Children's use of mutual exclusivity to constrain the meanings of words. *Cognitive Psychology, 20*, 121–157.

Marshall, J.C., & Newcombe, F. (1966). Syntactic and semantic errors in paralexia. *Neuropsychologia, 4*, 169–176.

Marslen-Wilson, W.D., Tyler, L.K., Waksler, R., & Older, L. (1994). Morphology and meaning in the English mental lexicon. *Psychological Review*, 101, 3–33.

Martin, A.D., Wasserman, N.H., Gilden, L., Gerstman, L., & West, J.A. (1975). A process model of repetition in aphasia: An investigation of phonological and morphological interactions in aphasic error performance. *Brain and Language, 2*, 434–450.

Martin, N., Dell, G.S., Saffran, E.M., & Schwartz, M.F. (1994). Origins of paraphasias in deep dysphasia: Testing the consequences of a decay impairment to an interactive spreading activation model of lexical retrieval. *Brain and Language, 47*, 609–660.

Martin, N., & Saffran, E.M. (1992). A computational account of deep dysphasia: Evidence from a single case study. *Brain and Language, 43*, 240–274.

Martin, N., Weisberg, R.W., & Saffran, E.M. (1989). Variables influencing the occurrence of naming errors: implications for models of lexical retrieval. *Journal of Memory and Language, 28*, 462–485.

Martinet, A. (1949). La double articulation linguistique. *Travaux du Cercle Linguistique de Copenhague, 5*, 30–37.

McCann, R.S., & Besner, D. (1987). Reading pseudohomophones: Implications for models of pronunciation assembly and the locus of word-frequency effects in naming. *Journal of Experimental Psychology: Human Perception and Performance, 13*, 14–24.

McClelland, J.L. (1979). On the time relations of mental processes: An examination of systems of processes in cascade. *Psychological Review, 86*, 287–330.

McKenna, P., & Warrington, E.K. (1980). Testing for nominal dysphasia. *Journal of Neurology, Neurosurgery and Psychiatry, 43*, 781–788.

McNeil, J.E., Cipolotti, L., & Warrington, E.K. (1994). The accessibility of proper names. *Neuropsychologia, 32*, 717–728.

McRae, K., Jared, D., & Seidenberg, M.S. (1990). On the roles of frequency and lexical access in word naming. *Journal of Memory and Language, 29*, 43–65.

Mesulam, M.M. (1982). Slowly progressive aphasia without generalized dementia. *Annals of Neurology, 11*, 592–598.

Meyer, A.S. (1990). The time course of phonological encoding in language production: The encoding of successive syllables of a word. *Journal of Memory and Language, 29*, 524–545.

Meyer, A.S. (1991). The time course of phonological encoding in language production: Phonological encoding inside a syllable. *Journal of Memory and Language, 30*, 69–89.

Meyer, A.S. (1992). Investigation of phonological encoding through speech error analyses: Achievements, limitations and alternatives. *Cognition, 42*, 181–212.

Meyer, A.S., & Bock, K. (1992). The tip-of-the-tongue phenomenon: Blocking or partial activation? *Memory and Cognition, 20*, 715–726.

Meyer, A.S., & Schriefers, H. (1991). Phonological facilitation in picture-word interference experiments: Effects of stimulus onset asynchrony and types of interfering stimuli. *Journal of Experimental Psychology: Human Perception and Performance, 17*, 1146–1160.

Miceli, G., & Caramazza, A. (1993). The assignment of word stress in oral reading: Evidence from a case of acquired dyslexia. *Cognitive Neuropsychology, 10*, 273–296.

Miceli, G., Gainotti, G., Caltagirone, C., & Masullo, C. (1980). Some aspects of phonological impairment in aphasia. *Brain and Language, 11*, 159–169.

Miceli, G., Giustolisi, L., & Caramazza, A. (1991). The interaction of lexical and non-lexical processing mechanisms: Evidence from anomia. *Cortex, 27*, 57–80.

Miceli, G., Silveri, M.C., Nocentini, U., & Caramazza, A. (1988). Patterns of dissociation in comprehension and production of nouns and verbs. *Aphasiology, 2*, 351–358.

Miller, D., & Ellis, A.W. (1987). Speech and writing errors in "Neologistic jargonaphasia: A lexical activation hypothesis". In M. Coltheart, R. Job, & G. Sartori (Eds.), *The cognitive neuropsychology of language*. Hillsdale, NJ: Lawrence Erlbaum Associates Inc.

Miller, G.A. (1969). A psychological method to investigate verbal concepts. *Journal of Mathematical Psychology, 6*, 169–191.

Miller, N. (1992). Variability in dyspraxia. *Clinical Linguistics and Phonetics, 6*, 77–85.

Miozzo, A., Soardi, M., & Cappa, S.F. (1994). Pure anomia with spared action naming due to a left temporal lesion. *Neuropsychologia, 32*, 1101–1109.

Monoi, H., Fukusako, Y., Itoh, M., & Sasanuma, S. (1983). Speech sound errors in patients with conduction and Broca's aphasia. *Brain and Language, 20*, 175–194.

Monsell, S. (1987). On the relation between lexical input and output pathways for speech. In A. Allport, D. MacKay, W. Prinz, & E. Scheerer (Eds.), *Language perception and production: Relationships between listening, speaking, reading and writing*. London: Academic Press.

Monsell, S. (1991). The nature and locus of word frequency effects in reading. In D. Besner & G.W. Humphreys (Eds.), *Basic processes in reading: Visual word recognition*. Hillsdale, NJ: Lawrence Erlbaum Associates Inc.

Monsell, S., & Banich, M.T. (unpublished manuscript). Repetition priming across input and output modalities: Implications for the functional anatomy of the lexicon.

Monsell, S., Doyle, M.C., & Haggard, P.N. (1989). The effects of frequency on visual word recognition tasks: Where are they? *Journal of Experimental Psychology: General, 118*, 43–71.

Morrison, C.M., Ellis, A.W., & Chappell, T.D. (in press). Age of acquisition norms for a large set of object names and their relation to adult estimates and other variables. *Quarterly Journal of Experimental Psychology*.

Morrison, C.M., Ellis, A.W., & Quinlan, P.T. (1992). Age of acquisition, not word frequency, affects object naming, not object recognition. *Memory and Cognition, 20*, 705–714.

Morton, J. (1969). The interaction of information in word recognition. *Psychological Review, 76,* 165–178.

Morton, J. (1970). A functional model for memory. In D.A. Norman (Ed.), *Models of human memory.* New York: Academic Press.

Morton, J. (1979). Word recognition. In J. Morton & J.C. Marshall (Eds.), *Psycholinguistics series* (Vol.2). London: Elek.

Morton, J. (1985). Naming. In S.K. Newman & R. Epstein (Eds.), *Current perspectives in dysphasia.* Edinburgh: Churchill-Livingstone.

Morton, J., & Patterson, K. (1980). A new attempt at an interpretation, or, an attempt at a new interpretation. In M. Coltheart, K. Patterson, & J. Marshall (Eds.), *Deep dyslexia.* London: Routledge & Kegan Paul.

Morton, J., & Smith, N.V. (1974). Some ideas concerning the acquisition of phonology. In *Proceedings of the Symposium on Current Problems in Psycholinguistics.* Paris: CNRS.

Motley, M.T., & Baars, B.J. (1976). Laboratory induction of verbal slips: A new method for psycholinguistic research. *Communication Quarterly, 24,* 28–34.

Motley, M.T., Camden, C.T., & Baars, B.J. (1982). Covert formulation and editing of anomalies in speech production: Evidence from experimentally elicited slips of the tongue. *Journal of Verbal Learning and Verbal Behaviour, 21,* 578–594.

Munhall, K.G. (1989). Articulatory variability. In P. Square-Storer (Ed.), *Acquired apraxia of speech in aphasic adults.* London: Taylor & Francis.

Nairne, J.S., & Pusen, C. (1984). Serial recall of imagined voices. *Journal of Verbal Learning and Verbal Behaviour, 23,* 331–342.

Nairne, J.S., & Walters, V.L. (1983). Silent mouthing produces modality—and suffix-like effects. *Journal of Verbal Learning and Verbal Behaviour, 22,* 475–483.

Nebes, R.D. (1989). Semantic memory in Alzheimer's disease. *Psychological Bulletin, 106,* 377–394.

Neely, J.H. (1991). Semantic priming effects in visual word recognition: A selective review of current findings and theories. In D. Besner & G.W. Humphreys (Eds.), *Basic processes in reading: Visual word recognition.* Hillsdale, NJ: Lawrence Erlbaum Associates Inc.

Nespoulous, J.-L., Joanette, Y., Béland, R., Caplan, D., & Lecours, A.R. (1984). Phonologic disturbances in aphasia: Is there a "markedness effect" in aphasic phonetic errors? In F.C. Rose (Ed.), *Advances in neurology, 42: Progress in aphasiology.* New York: Raven Press.

Nespoulous, J.-L., Joanette, Y., Ska, B., Caplan, D., & Lecours, A.R. (1987). Production deficits in Broca's and Conduction Aphasia: Repetition versus reading. In E. Keller & M. Gopnik (Eds.), *Motor and sensory processes of language.* Hillsdale, NJ: Lawrence Erlbaum Associates Inc.

Newcombe, F., Oldfield, R.C. & Wingfield, A.R. (1965). Object naming by dysphasic patients. *Nature, 207,* 1217.

Nickels, L.A. (1992a). Spoken word production and its breakdown in aphasia. Unpublished PhD thesis, University of London.

Nickels, L.A. (1992b). The Autocue? Self-generated phonemic cues in the treatment of a disorder of reading and naming. *Cognitive Neuropsychology, 9,* 155–182.

Nickels, L.A. (1995). Getting it right? Using aphasic naming errors to evaluate theoretical models of spoken word production. *Language and Cognitive Processes, 10,* 13–45.

Nickels, L.A., & Best, W.M. (1996a). Therapy for naming deficits (Part I): Principles, puzzles and progress. *Aphasiology, 10*, 21–47.

Nickels, L.A., & Best, W.M. (1996b). Therapy for naming disorders (Part II): Specifics, surprises and suggestions. *Aphasiology, 10*, 109–136.

Nickels, L.A., Byng, S., & Black, M. (1991). Sentence processing deficits: A replication of therapy. *British Journal of Disorders of Communication, 26*, 175–199.

Nickels, L.A., & Howard, D. (1994). A frequent occurrence? Factors affecting the production of semantic errors in aphasic naming. *Cognitive Neuropsychology, 11*, 289–320.

Nickels, L.A., & Howard, D. (1995a). Aphasic naming: What matters? *Neuropsychologia, 33*, 1281–1303.

Nickels, L.A., & Howard, D. (1995b). Phonological errors in aphasic naming: Comprehension, monitoring and lexicality. *Cortex, 31*, 209–237.

Nickels, L.A., & Howard, D. (in prep.). Effects of phonemes, syllables and syllabic complexity on aphasic word production.

Nickels, L.A., & Howard, D. (submitted). Effects of lexical stress on aphasic word production.

Nickels, L.A., Howard, D., & Best, W.M. (1997). Fractionating the articulatory loop: Dissociations and associations in phonological recoding in aphasia. *Brain and Language, 56*, 161–182.

Niemi, J., Koivuselka-Sallinen, P., & Hanninen, R. (1985). Phoneme errors in Broca's aphasia: Three Finnish cases. *Brain and Language, 26*, 28–48.

Nooteboom, S.G. (1972). A survey of some investigations into the temporal organisation of speech. *Institut voor Perceptie Onderzoek, Annual Progress Report, 7*, 17–29.

Odell, K.H., McNeil, M.R., Rosenbek, J.C., & Hunter, L. (1991). Perceptual characteristics of vowel and prosody production in apraxic, aphasic and dysarthric speakers. *Journal of Speech and Hearing Research, 34*, 67–80.

Oldfield, R.C., & Wingfield, A. (1965). Response latencies in naming objects. *Quarterly Journal of Experimental Psychology, 17*, 273–281.

Panzeri, M., Semenza, C., & Butterworth, B. (1987). Compensatory processes in the evolution of severe jargon aphasia. *Neuropsychologia, 23*, 913–933.

Pate, D.S., Saffran, E.M., & Martin, N. (1987). Specifying the nature of the production deficit in conduction aphasia: A case study. *Language and Cognitive Processes, 2*, 43–84.

Patterson, K.E. (1980). Reading errors of PW and DE. In M. Coltheart, K.E. Patterson, & J.C. Marshall (Eds.), *Deep dyslexia*. London: Routledge & Kegan Paul.

Patterson, K.E., Purell, C., & Morton, J. (1983). Facilitation of word retrieval in aphasia. In C. Code & D.J. Muller (Eds.), *Aphasia therapy*. London: Edward Arnold.

Patterson, K.E., & Shewell, C. (1987). Speak and spell: Dissociations and word-class effects. In M. Coltheart, R. Job, & G. Sartori (Eds.), *The cognitive neuropsychology of language*. Hillsdale, NJ: Lawrence Erlbaum Associates Inc.

Pavio, A. (1971). *Imagery and verbal processes*. New York: Holt, Rinehart & Winston.

Pavio, A. (1991). Dual coding theory: Retrospect and current status. *Canadian Journal of Psychology, 45*, 255–287.

Pease, D. M., & Goodglass, H. (1978). The effects of cueing on picture naming in aphasia. *Cortex, 14*, 178–189.

Perkell, J.S. (1980). Phonetic features and the physiology of speech production. In B. Butterworth (Ed.), *Language production: Vol.1. Speech and talk*. London: Academic Press.

Peuser, G., & Temp, K. (1981). The evolution of jargon aphasia. In J.W. Brown (Ed.), *Jargonaphasia*. New York: Academic Press.

Pick, A. (1931). *Aphasie*. [English translation by J.W. Brown, 1973. *Aphasia*. Springfield, IL: C.C. Thomas.]

Plaut, D., & Shallice, T. (1991). Effects of word abstractness in a connectionist model of deep dyslexia. *Proceedings of the Cognitive Science Society, 1991*.

Plaut, D., & Shallice, T. (1993). Deep Dyslexia: A case study of connectionist neuropsychology. *Cognitive Neuropsychology, 10*, 377–500.

Poeck, K. (1988). The relationship between aphasia and motor apraxia. In F.C. Rose, R. Whurr, & M.A. Wyke (Eds.), *Aphasia*. London: Whurr.

Poeck, K., & Luzzatti, C. (1988). Slowly progressive aphasia in three patients: The problem of accompanying neuropsychological deficit. *Brain, 111*, 151–168.

Postman, L., & Keppel, G. (1970). *Norms of word association*. New York: Academic Press.

Richardson, J.T.E. (1975). The effect of word imageability in acquired dyslexia. *Neuropsychologia, 13*, 281–288.

Rinnert, C., & Whitaker, H.A. (1973). Semantic confusions by aphasic patients. *Cortex, 9*, 56–81.

Riddoch, M.J., & Humphreys, G.W. (1987). A case of integrative visual agnosia. *Brain, 110*, 1431–1462.

Riddoch, M.J., Humphreys, G.W., Coltheart, M., & Funnell, E. (1988). Semantic systems or system: Neuropsychological evidence re-examined. *Cognitive Neuropsychology, 5*, 1, 3–25.

Rochford, G., & Williams, M. (1962). Studies in the development and breakdown of the use of names I & II: The relationship between nominal dysphasia and the acquisition of vocabulary in childhood. *Journal of Neurology, Neurosurgery and Psychiatry, 25*, 222–233.

Rochford, G., & Williams, M. (1965). Studies in the development and breakdown of the use of names IV: The effects of word frequency. *Journal of Neurology, Neurosurgery and Psychiatry, 28*, 407–413.

Roelofs, A. (1992). A spreading-activation theory of lemma retrieval. *Cognition, 42*, 107–142.

Rosch, E., Mervis, C.B., Gray, W.D., Johnson, D.H., & Boyes-Braem, P. (1976). Basic objects in natural categories. *Cognitive Psychology, 8*, 382–439.

Rosenbek, J.C., Kent, R., & LaPointe, L. (1984). Apraxia of speech and overview and some perspectives. In J.C. Rosenbek, M. McNeil, & A. Aronson (Eds.), *Apraxia of speech: Physiology, acoustics, linguistics and management*. San Diego, CA: College Hill Press.

Rumelhart, D.E., & McClelland, J.L. (1986). PDP models and general issues in cognitive science. In D.E. Rumelhart & J.L. McClelland (Eds.). *Parallel distributed processing: Explorations in the microstructure of cognition: Vol.1: Foundations*. Cambridge, MA: MIT Press.

Ryalls, J.H. (1986). An acoustic study of vowel production in aphasia. *Brain and Language, 29*, 48–67.

Sacchett, C., & Humphreys, G. W. (1992). Calling a squirrel a squirrel but a canoe a wigwam: A category specific deficit for artefactual objects and body parts. *Cognitive Neuropsychology, 9,* 73–86.

Saffran, E.M. (1982). Neuropsychological approaches to the study of language. *British Journal of Psychology, 73,* 317–338.

Saffran, E.M., & Marin, O.S.M. (1975). Immediate memory for word lists and sentences in a patient with a deficient auditory short-term memory. *Brain and Language, 2,* 420–433.

Saffran, E., Marin, O., & Yemi-Komshian, G. (1976). An analysis of speech perception in word deafness. *Brain and Language, 3,* 209–228.

Saltzman, E., & Kelso, J.A.S. (1987). Skilled actions: A task-dynamic approach. *Psychological Review, 94,* 84–106.

Sartori, G., & Job, R. (1988). The Oyster with four legs: A neuropsychological study on the interaction of visual and semantic information. *Cognitive Neuropsychology, 5,* 105–132.

Savage, G.R., Bradley, D.C., & Forster, K.I. (1990). Word frequency and the contribution of articulatory fluency. *Language and Cognitive Processes, 5,* 203–236.

Schlenck, K.-J., Huber, W., & Willmes, K. (1987). "Prepairs" and repairs: Different monitoring functions in aphasic language production. *Brain and Language, 30,* 226–244.

Schriefers, H., Meyer, A.S., & Levelt, W.J.M. (1990). Exploring the time course of lexical access in language production: Picture-word interference studies. *Journal of Memory and Language, 29,* 86–102.

Schuell, H.M., Jenkins, J.J. & Jimenez-Pabon, E. (1964). *Aphasia in adults: Diagnosis, prognosis and treatment.* New York: Harper & Row.

Schwartz, R.J., & Leonard, L.B. (1982). Do children pick and choose? An examination of phonological selection and avoidance in early lexical acquisition. *Journal of Child Language, 9,* 319–336.

Selkirk, E. (1984). *Phonology and syntax: The relation between sound and structure.* Cambridge, MA: MIT Press.

Semenza, C., & Sgaramella, T.M. (1993). Production of proper names: A clinical case study of the effects of phonemic cueing. *Memory, 1,* 248–263.

Semenza, C., & Zettin, M. (1988). Generating proper names: A case of selective inability. *Cognitive Neuropsychology, 5,* 711–721.

Semenza, C., & Zettin, M. (1989). Evidence from aphasia for the role of proper names as pure referring expressions. *Nature, 342,* 678–679.

Sevald, C.A., & Dell, G.S. (1994). The sequential cueing effect in speech production. *Cognition, 53,* 91–127.

Shallice, T. (1987). Impairments of semantic processing: multiple dissociations. In M. Coltheart, R. Job, & G. Sartori (Eds.), *The cognitive neuropsychology of language.* Hillsdale, NJ: Lawrence Erlbaum Associates Inc.

Shallice, T. (1988). *From neuropsychology to mental structure.* Cambridge: Cambridge University Press.

Shallice, T., & Kartsounis, L.D. (1993). Selective impairment of retrieving people's names: A category specific disorder? *Cortex, 29,* 281–291.

Shallice, T., McLeod, P., & Lewis, K. (1985). Isolating cognitive modules with the dual-task paradigm: Are speech perception and production separate processes? *Quarterly Journal of Experimental Psychology, 37A,* 507–532.

Shallice, T., & Warrington, E.K. (1970). Independent functioning of the verbal memory stores: A neuropsychological study. *Quarterly Journal of Experimental Psychology, 22*, 261–273.

Shallice, T., & Warrington, E.K. (1974). The dissociation between short-term retention of meaningful sounds and verbal material. *Neuropsychologia, 12*, 553–555.

Shallice, T., & Warrington, E.K. (1977). Auditory-verbal short-term memory impairment and conduction aphasia. *Brain and Language, 4*, 479–491.

Shankweiler, D.P., & Harris, K.S. (1966). An experimental approach to the problem of articulation in aphasia. *Cortex, 2*, 277–292.

Shattuck, S.R. (1975). Speech errors and sentence production. Unpublished doctoral dissertation, Massachusetts Institute of Technology.

Shattuck-Hufnagel, S. (1979). Speech errors as evidence for a serial order mechanism in sentence production. In W.E. Cooper & E.C.T. Walker (Eds.), *Sentence processing: Psycholinguistic studies presented to Merrill Garrett*. Hillsdale, NJ: Lawrence Erlbaum Associates Inc.

Shattuck-Hufnagel, S. (1987). The role of word-onset consonants in speech production planning: New evidence from speech error patterns. In E. Keller & M. Gopnik (Eds.), *Motor and sensory processes of language*. Hillsdale, NJ: Lawrence Erlbaum Associates Inc.

Shattuck-Hufnagel, S. (1992). The role of word structure in segmental serial ordering. *Cognition, 42*, 213–259.

Shattuck-Hufnagel, S., & Klatt, D.H. (1979). Minimal use of features and markedness in speech production. *Journal of Verbal Learning and Verbal Behaviour, 18*, 41–55.

Shinn, P., & Blumstein, S.E. (1983). Phonetic disintigration in aphasia: Acoustic analysis of spectral characteristics for place of articulation. *Brain and Language, 20*, 90–114.

Silveri, M. C., & Gainotti, G. (1988). Interaction between vision and language in category specific semantic impairment. *Cognitive Neuropsychology, 5*, 677–709.

Smith, A. (1988). A cognitive neuropsychological investigation of the origin of phonological errors in two aphasic individuals. Unpublished undergraduate dissertation, University of Newcastle-upon-Tyne.

Snodgrass, J.G., & Vanderwart, M. (1980). A standardized set of 260 pictures: norms for name agreement, image agreement, familiarity and visual complexity. *Journal of Experimental Psychology: Human Learning and Memory, 6*, 174–215.

Snowden. J.S., Goulding, P.J., & Neary, D. (1989). Semantic dementia: A form of circumscribed cerebral atrophy. *Behavioural Neurology, 2*, 167–182.

Stemberger, J.P. (1982). The nature of segments in the lexicon: Evidence from speech errors. *Lingua, 56*, 253–259.

Stemberger, J.P. (1984). Lexical bias in errors in language production: Interactive components, editors, and perceptual biases. Unpublished manuscript, Indiana University.

Stemberger, J.P. (1985). An interactive activation model of language production. In A.W. Ellis (Ed.), *Progress in the psychology of language* (Vol.1). London: Lawrence Erlbaum Associates Ltd.

Stemberger, J.P., & MacWhinney, B. (1986). Form-oriented inflectional errors in language processing. *Cognitive Psychology, 18*, 329–354.

Sternberg, S., Monsell, S., Knoll, R.L., & Wright, C.E. (1978). The latency and duration of rapid movement sequences: Comparisons of speech and typewriting. In G.E. Stelmach (Ed.), *Information processing in motor control and learning*. New York: Academic Press.

Stevens, K.N. (1983). Design features of speech sound systems. In P.F. MacNeilage (Ed.), *The production of speech*. New York: Springer.

Stewart, F., Parkin, A. & Hunkin, N.M. (1992). Naming impairments following recovery from Herpes Simplex Encephalitis; Category specific? *Journal of Experimental Psychology, 44A*, 2, 261–284.

Stimley, M.A., & Knoll, J.D. (1991). The effects of semantic and phonemic pre-stimulation cues on picture naming in aphasia. *Brain and Language, 41*, 496–509.

Strub, R.L., & Gardner, H. (1974). The repetition deficit in conduction aphasia: Mnestic or linguistic? *Brain and Language, 1*, 241–255.

Treiman, R., Fowler, C.A., Gross, J., Berch, D., & Weatherston, S. (1995). Syllable structure or word structure? Evidence for onset and rime units in disyllabic and trisyllabic stimuli. *Journal of Memory and Language, 34*, 132–155.

Trost, J.E., & Canter, G.J. (1974). Apraxia of speech in patients with Broca's aphasia: A study of phoneme production accuracy and error patterns. *Brain and Language, 1*, 63–79.

Tuller, B., & Story, R.S. (1987). Anticipatory coarticulation in aphasia. In J. Ryalls (Ed.), *Phonetic approaches to speech production in aphasia and related disorders*. Boston, MA: College Hill Press.

Tulving, E. (1972). Episodic and semantic memory. In E. Tulving & W. Donaldson (Eds.), *Organization of memory*. New York and London: Academic Press.

Valdois, S., Joanette, Y., Nespoulous, J.-L., & Poncet, M. (1988). Afferent motor aphasia and conduction aphasia. In H.A. Whitaker (Ed.), *Phonological processes and brain mechanisms*. New York: Springer.

Valdois, S., Joanette, Y., & Nespoulous, J.-L. (1989). Intrinsic organization of sequences of phonemic approximations: A preliminary study. *Aphasiology, 3*, 55–73.

Vijayan, A., & Gandour, J. (1995). On the notion of a "subtle phonetic deficit" in fluent/posterior aphasia. *Brain and Language, 47*, 106–119.

Vitkovitch, M., & Humphreys, G.W. (1991). Perseverant responding in speeded naming to pictures: Its in the links. *Journal of Experimental Psychology: Learning, Memory and Cognition, 17*, 664–680.

Warrington, E.K. (1975). The selective impairment of semantic memory. *Quarterly Journal of Experimental Psychology, 27*, 635–657.

Warrington, E.K. (1981). Concrete word dyslexia. *Brain, 103*, 99–112.

Warrington, E.K., & McCarthy, R. (1983). Category-specific access dysphasia. *Brain, 106*, 859–878.

Warrington, E.K., & McCarthy, R. (1987). Categories of knowledge: Further fractionation and an attempted integration. *Brain, 110*, 1273–1296.

Warrington, E.K., & Shallice, T. (1969). The selective impairment of auditory verbal short-term memory. *Brain, 92*, 885–896.

Warrington, E.K., & Shallice, T. (1972). Neuropsychological evidence of visual storage in short-term memory tasks. *Quarterly Journal of Experimental Psychology, 24*, 30–40.

Warrington, E.K., & Shallice, T. (1984). Category specific semantic impairment. *Brain, 107*, 829–854.

Weigl, E., & Bierwisch, M. (1970). Neuropsychology and linguistics; Topics of common research. *Foundations of Language, 6*, 1–18.

Wertz, R.T., LaPointe, L.L., & Rosenbek, J.C. (1984). *Apraxia of speech in adults: The disorder and its management.* New York: Grune & Stratton.

Wickelgren, W.A. (1969). Context-sensitive coding, associative memory, and serial order in (speech) behaviour. *Psychological Review, 76*, 1–15.

Widlof, I. (1983). Lexical access: Evidence from the TOT phenomenon. Undergraduate project, University of Lancaster.

Wingfield, A., Goodglass, H., & Smith, K.L. (1990). Effects of word-onset cueing on picture naming in aphasia; a reconsideration. *Brain and Language, 39*, 373–390.

Winnick, W.A., & Daniel, S.A. (1970). Two kinds of response priming in tachistoscopic recognition. *Journal of Experimental Psychology, 84*, 74–81.

Wydell, T. (1991). Processing in the reading of Japanese: comparative studies between English and Japanese orthographies. Unpublished PhD thesis, University of London.

Yamadori, A., & Ikumura, G. (1975). Central (or conduction) aphasia in a Japanese patient. *Cortex, 11*, 73–82.

Ziegler, W., & von Cramon, D. (1985). Anticipatory coarticulation in a patient with apraxia of speech. *Brain and Language, 26*, 117–130.

Ziegler, W., & von Cramon, D. (1986). Disturbed coarticulation in apraxia of speech: Acoustic evidence. *Brain and Language, 29*, 34–47.

Zingeser, L.B., & Berndt, R. (1988). Grammatical class and context effects in a case of pure anomia: Implications for models of language production. *Cognitive Neuropsychology 5*, 473–516.

Author index

Subject index

Learning and Information Services

Division - Llandaff

City of Wales Institute, Cardiff

Avenue

CARDIFF
CF5 2YB   UWIC